"I love this book! Whether you call it gossip, dishing the dirt, or being connected to the grapevine, failure to exchange a wide-range of information is detrimental to your career. Dominique Darmon has done a terrific job of illuminating why you must be in the know at work and how you can do it respectfully and with integrity."
— Dr. Lois Frankel, author of the *New York Times* bestselling book *Nice Girls Still Don't Get the Corner Office*

"You haven't got this from me – but this is a scandalously good book! Ok, she cuts corners, but with a quick wit, a sharp pen, and a strong base in both literature and anecdote, who cares?"
— Gert Jan Hofstede, Prof. Dr. Ir. Artificial Sociality at Wageningen University and extraordinary professor at North-West University, Potchefstroom, South Africa, and co-author of the international bestsellers *Cultures and Organizations and Exploring Culture*

"*Have I Got Dirt For You* offers valuable insights in an inevitable and valuable aspect of human interaction: gossip. There are great lessons for both the office and Zoom sessions."
— Jonah Berger, Wharton professor and author of the bestselling books *Contagious, Invisible Influence*, and *The Catalyst*

"In this highly readable book, Dominique Darmon has made very clear that there are human behaviors that transcend cultures. Gossiping is a good example of this. While various cultures gossip in different ways, it will remain an important and meaningful activity for humankind. Recommended!"
— Fons Trompenaars, speaker, consultant, researcher, author of *Riding the Waves of Culture*, and co-author of *End of Discussion*

T0317742

"This is a must-read for everybody who thinks that gossiping is just for evil people. The author makes clear that gossiping can play a positive role, provided that you do it according to the rules of the game. Dominique Darmon explicitly and clearly describes these rules. Who wouldn't want to know more about that?"
— Len Middelbeek, former editor-in-chief at the NOS Journaal and RTL Nieuws, spokesperson at the Dutch Ministry of Economic Affairs and co-author of the book *Public Communication*

"An excellent approach to the concept of gossip and rumor. The science in Darmon's book is solid and will open your mind to a broader view of these fascinating human qualities. May it stand on equal footing with the art of complaining!"
— Bart Flos, bestselling author of *The Anti-Complain Book*

Have I Got Dirt For You

Using Office Gossip to Your Advantage

Dominique J. Darmon

Amsterdam University Press

Frontispiece drawing: Shirley Warlich, Ede

Author's photograph: Solography Studios, Montreal
Cover design: Robbie Smits
Lay-out: Crius Group, Hulshout

ISBN   978 94 6372 489 0
e-ISBN   978 90 4855 761 5 (ePub)
DOI   10.5117/ 9789463724890
NUR   801

Every effort has been made to obtain permission to use all copyrighted illustrations reproduced in this book. Nonetheless, whosoever believes to have rights to this material is advised to contact the publisher.

Printed and bound by CPI Group (UK) Ltd, Croydon CR0 4YY

To my parents, René and Nicole

Table of Contents

Introduction

Talk about gossip, and the first thing that usually comes to people's mind is bullying, a toxic workplace, and the violation of privacy. Many articles on the topic urge employees to refrain from gossiping, and for managers to implement a no-gossip policy at work.

Even though office gossip is generally frowned upon, many studies show that gossip in organizations is not only inevitable, but can even be a positive communication tool.

Research shows that people who claim to never gossip tend to be considered as socially inept, but those who are constantly gabbing at the coffee machine are quickly seen as untrustworthy.

There is an optimal amount of time one should gossip, which we call the *sweet spot of gossip*. Finding this optimal amount is a fine balancing act. However, it's not only the amount of time one spends gossiping that will make or break an employee or manager.

Francis McAndrew (2014) observes that most of the studies that have been conducted so far tend to mainly look at how often an individual does or does not participate in gossip. Very little has been done to study the actual content of gossip, and the way in which employees conduct themselves in gossip situations. The author insists that it is quality, not quantity, that counts, and that people who know how to gossip in a skillful way will be more appreciated by their peers and exert more social power. "Gossip is a social skill rather than a flaw," he writes. Another researcher, Brian Robinson (2016), even claims that gossiping well is a virtue.

With this book, I examine academic perspectives as well as observations from employees and managers from all over the world, when searching for this sweet spot of gossip. I will show that it is not just the amount that determines whether one gossips successfully.

Other factors such as reasons for gossiping (Chapter 1), credibility (Chapter 2), mechanisms (Chapter 3), with whom do we gossip (Chapter 4), culture (Chapter 5), and place (Chapter 6) all

play an equally crucial role in the art of gossiping successfully at work. Understanding these factors and knowing how to navigate each of them is of the essence. By gossiping in the wrong way, employees can easily lose the trust of their colleagues and very quickly be perceived negatively. And it's often a fine line that divides acceptable from unacceptable gossip.

After reading this book, readers will understand how and why people gossip, which codes and rules of conduct they should follow, and, by doing so, learn how to gossip more effectively.

The claims made in this book are backed by evidence-based studies on gossip and are illustrated by anecdotes and experiences coming from employees working at a variety of organizations from all over the world, as well as from movies, Netflix and television series, art, and literature. At the end of each chapter, concrete tips are given to managers and employees on how to avoid some of the common pitfalls.

Not only is the definition of gossip extremely subjective, so is the perception of various gossip scenarios. Different people will perceive the same situation and the same gossiper very differently. It is therefore important to keep in mind that there are no hard truths or tried-and-true formulas. The goal is to get readers to reflect on a variety of situations and, potentially, on their own behavior.

While it is tempting to focus solely on the effects gossip has on an absent third party—take studies on workplace bullying (Rayner et al., 2002; Riggio, 2010)—it is of equal importance to consider its effects on the gossiper and listener as well, according to Giardini & Wittek (2019a). This book will examine all three roles, with a strong emphasis on the gossiper, as our goal is to learn how to gossip well.

During the course of this research, I have worked on several research projects, given quite a few lectures and seminars on this topic, and had many of my students participate in my research. Students at ICM (International Communication Management), students taking my Journalism and Media minor, as well as students from other departments at The Hague University of Applied Sciences have conducted a wide range of interviews with people working in various types of organizations from all over the world.

This book also illustrates how people from different countries gossip differently, and how easy it is for foreigners to cross the line or fall prey to misunderstandings. As more and more organizations today work in a diverse environment, with multicultural teams, reading this book will help employees and managers build trust with each other.

While I have found that some reactions and experiences varied greatly across cultures, others didn't so much. As I always tell my students in my Intercultural Communications classes, one must take cross-cultural theories with a grain of salt. For one, it is impossible to make sweeping generalizations about one country (as a culture is made up of a variety of subcultures dictated by factors like region, socioeconomic factors, age, and personal characteristics, to name a few). Nonetheless, as interculturalists (such as Meyer, 2014) note, many cultural differences do hold true. For instance, we can easily claim that the Dutch are more direct than the Chinese. Although some Dutch people may be less direct than some of their countrymen, they will still always be a lot more direct than the most direct Chinese person. The goal here is, not to create stereotypes, but to make readers aware of potential differences in order to encourage reflection.

Many people have also asked me how the Covid pandemic has affected gossip, since the office has changed dramatically. Did this revolution not eliminate gossip altogether? Is gossip research not obsolete, now that we tend to work more remotely, behind our computer screens? My answer is a definite 'Absolutely not!' Gossip will always fulfill a strong human need, and will never go away. As we will discuss in Chapter 6, while screens may have kicked out the watercooler and coffee machines, they have also morphed into new gossip online environments, which are just as conducive to juicy banter. As many offices adopt hybrid working models, many of our observations about traditional offices, flex offices and online environments will definitely continue to apply to the current and future workplace.

Moreover, since gossiping is considered a sensitive topic, I have changed the names of our interviewees as well as the details of their organizations to maintain anonymity.

What is gossip?

Most academic researchers (Grosser et al., 2010; McAndrew, 2014) define gossip as "positive or negative information exchanged about an absent third party." So, saying something nice about a person, like: "Did you see Joe's presentation? It was really great!" would also be considered as gossip. Using this definition, we can also claim, as Truman Capote did, that "all literature is gossip." Journalism is also gossip.

However, the neutral, academic definition does not come to most people's minds when they hear the word 'gossip.' When the word 'gossip' comes up, people tend to think of something closer to Joseph Epstein's definition: "Telling things about other people that they would rather not have known." In his book *Gossip*, Epstein (2011) describes it as having a sense of secrecy and betrayal.

The fact that gossip is about an absent third party often (falsely) gives the impression that it is unkind and nasty. Yet, Levin & Arluke, cited in Capps (2012), conducted a study where a student sat in the student lounge and eavesdropped on the conversations of other students. They found that 27% of all student gossip was clearly positive, 27% clearly negative, and the rest was mixed. This shows that there is probably a lot less negative gossip than most people would assume, since gossip is generally thought of as being nasty talk only.

One of the challenges of this research is that many academics and people in general often have different understandings and definitions of the word 'gossip.' De Gouveia et al. (2005) for example, find the neutral, academic definition too vague, and offer a more detailed one: "Gossip in the workplace is the spreading of information between two or more people about a situation or person they may or may not know, behind their back, regarding information that is of no relevance to them. The content of the message is not for public consumption and the disclosure of the information leads to undesirable circumstances such as fueled speculation, false impressions and breakdown of trust."

While this could be an interesting definition, it certainly is a narrow one, and it provides a limited view of the functions of gossip.

The understanding of the word 'gossip' also tends to be quite tainted by culture and language. In Afrikaans, *skinder* means to gossip, but also to slander. 'Gossip' in Hebrew translates as *lashon harah*, which means 'the evil tongue.' In Arabic, *namima* (النميمه) refers to "sharing someone's words with others in order to ruin their friendly relationships" and is also considered a sin.

During a guest lecture in Paris, I asked the students how they translated the word 'gossip' into French. *Potins*, *ragots*, *commérages*, *cancans*, *racontars* they said. Indeed, all of these words do translate as 'gossip.' Yet, I was not completely satisfied, as somehow, these terms bring extra nuances with them. The act of gossiping in French seems more trivial and pejorative. *Cancan* initially meant to make a lot of noise about not much.

Racontar comes from the verb *raconter*, which means to tell, but the suffix '-ar' gives the word a negative connotation. The other terms are very female-oriented. *Potin* historically comes from *potine*, a small heater that women brought with them in the winter, when they met up to chat. *Commérage* refers to *commère*, a nosy woman (like a concierge), who talks a lot about others behind their backs. *Ragot* used to mean a small and chubby person. As the word evolved, its definition also included talk from such a person (typically a woman) that was usually malicious. In Quebec, the verb used for gossiping, *mémérer*, stems from *mémère*, an older, rather plump grandmother, who tends to be chatty and indiscreet. (As we will see in Chapter 4, gossip tends to be strongly associated with women.)

Origins of the word 'gossip'

Looking at the word 'gossip' itself, one can see that there is a strong gender bias from the very beginning. At its origins, the word 'gossip' is derived from the Old English *godsibb*, which means "God's sibling," referring to the spiritual bond between godparents and godchildren. The term refers to the female friends of a child's mother who were present at the child's birth. As they spent hours waiting for the baby to be born, they chatted, provided moral support, and, undoubtedly, bonded with each other. McAndrew (2014) notes that these friends were generally always women.

While the concepts of 'gossip' and 'gossiping' described a phenomenon strictly reserved to women, they were not considered as particularly negative. By the 1500s, the word had taken on a much more negative connotation. 'Gossip' first took on a negative ring in Shakespeare's *A Midsummer Night's Dream*, and described a woman "of light and trifling character" who is "a newsmonger" and a "tattler." After that, the word took on an even more pejorative meaning, and is still, today, strongly linked to women, according to McAndrew.

An important distinction that we make is that between gossip and rumors. DiFonzo & Bordia (2007) observe that the terms 'rumor' and 'gossip' are very often used interchangeably by both "naïve laypersons" and "professional scholars." They "are both referred to as 'informal communication,' 'unofficial communication' and 'hearsay.'" But there is a big difference between the two (see Chapter 2).

Many researchers (Foster, 2004; Noon & Delbridge, 1993) define rumors as generally speculative and unsubstantiated talk. Gossip, on the other hand, is considered to be more accurate, as the core message usually remains intact as it is being transmitted.

In this book, we will stick to the academic definition of gossip: positive or negative information about an absent third party, as much as possible, bearing in mind that the definition can fluctuate slightly along the way. During many of our interviews, we noticed how gossip was understood and used in different ways.

Attitudes towards gossip

While definitions may vary, societal attitudes towards gossip and gossipers tend to be very negative.

In *Friends*, Rachel (Jennifer Aniston) cries out with indignation: "I don't gossip! Well, maybe sometimes I find out things or I hear something, and I pass that information on, you know, kind of like a public service. It doesn't mean I'm a gossip!" Her friends, as well as the audience, laugh. The word 'gossip' is very loaded here. Its definition, far less.

Researching gossip: How transparent can you be?

During an ethics class, I ask my students what would be the best way to research a sensitive topic such as gossip. Most people certainly wouldn't openly share what their true intentions for gossiping are, nor what they actually gossip about.

Alex: I would choose a couple of colleagues who I think gossip really well. I'd get to know them, gossip with them, and take notes.

Me: So, you wouldn't tell them about your research?

Alex: No, otherwise they wouldn't talk to me. [The class laughs.]

Me: What you're describing here is a type of ethnographic research. Or participatory research since you'd be playing a role in the gossiping. And yes, this would be a good way of getting information. But is it ethical?

Alex: No, but how else can you get accurate information? As soon as you mention the word 'gossip'....

Anne: I wouldn't mention the word 'gossip,' but its definition.

Because gossip has such a bad reputation, and most people do not think of the more neutral, academic definition, that is what many of the academic researchers have done: they avoided using the word when conducting their studies. Martinescu et al. (2014) told their participants that they were doing a study about "informal group communication." Cole & Scrivener (2013) asked their subjects to take part in a study about "sharing information about others," while Farley, Timme, & Hart (2010) said that their survey was about "informal communication in the workplace." Beersma & Van Kleef (2012) used the definition rather than the word 'gossip' itself to avoid having interviewees censor their responses to appear more honorable. After conducting interviews and/or surveys, all researchers debriefed their subjects and revealed the purpose of their study.

One study by Peters & Kashima (2015) looked at how gossip is portrayed in popular culture and noted that 60% of quotes about gossip condemned gossipers as "immoral individuals who do harm to those that they talk about."

De Gouveia et al. (2005) from the University of Johannesburg also claim that gossip in the workplace is harmful and toxic. "Organizations could experience increased staff turnover, premature job resignations, as well as the loss of efficient and effective employees. [...] Gossip could also undermine an individual, a group or organization, break down trust between employees, and strain ethical values such as openness, transparency and honesty. Consequences such as these could decrease staff morale, motivation and interpersonal respect between employees."

When googling 'office gossip,' a large number of articles appear: 'How to address office gossip as a manager,' 'Managing: How to stop employees from gossiping,' 'Negative effects of office gossip on the work environment,' and 'How to stop office gossip once and for all.' In these articles, gossip clearly has a negative ring! Many, such as De Gouveia et al. (2005), recommend creating a "gossip-free working environment with high moral values" by implementing an anti-gossip policy.

Many organizations have tried. Even politicians. For example, the mayor of a small town in the Philippines instituted a law that made gossiping illegal, according to an article in *The Guardian*. Citizens swapping stories about their neighbors' affairs, divorces, or bankruptcies received a fine and were forced to do community service. The mayor's goal was to show that his town had "good people" and that it was "a good and safe place to stay" (Ellis-Petersen, 2019).

However, trying to get people to stop gossiping is far from a realistic goal, but certainly an understandable one. While we do not believe that it is possible, or even desirable, to eliminate gossip, there are ways to minimize it and to channel it in positive ways.

To add an extra layer of complexity, we noticed that people's attitudes to gossiping tend to differ significantly. When we asked several employees from different countries if they gossip at work (before giving them the more neutral definition of gossip), their responses were quite varied. Leonie (63), who works as a receptionist for a municipality in the Netherlands, claims: "I don't like to gossip myself. I really don't like it. And if I hear something, I keep it to myself."

Asha (27), who comes from Trinidad and now works in a large educational institution in the Netherlands, also explains: "I just really don't like gossip. I prefer a person who talks about ideas, situations, things, concepts, rather than people. In the office setting where I was, there was a lot of gossip going on, but whenever any gossip would start, I would just walk out. I just don't want to hear it. I just want to remain neutral. That's me."

Similarly, several of the Dutch employees that we interviewed initially claimed that they do not gossip and try to avoid it as much possible. With a little probing though, they did admit to indulging in it as well, but stayed well within the limits of what is considered acceptable.

Nevertheless, certain employees coming from Latin countries responded proudly, with some glee, that they love to gossip. Spanish marketing consultant Pietro (21) exclaimed: "Of course I gossip. It is part of the work. It is an entertaining thing to do and it helps you get away from work for a little while."

"I usually gossip a lot with my colleagues," Jean-Paul (24), a veterinary doctor from Brittany, France, admitted proudly. "We gossip about all sorts of things: peoples' family life, love life, problems at work, or anything else."

During my communications classes, when I ask my students whether they gossip, most laugh and admit that they sometimes do, with the same tone of voice that they would confess to cheating on tests from time to time. Some say they would never gossip about someone if it could seriously harm them. I agree. "But what would you do in this case?" I ask my third-year, international communications students during a class called Internship Prep. "You discover that two of your direct colleagues are having an affair. You are working as an intern for an international organization and have been there for a few months. Would you gossip about that? Should you?"

They laugh, joke a bit, and all agree that this bit of information is juicy indeed, but most answer that no, they would take the moral high ground and keep the information to themselves. "It would reflect badly on me if I gossip," one student explains.

I insist. "Would you want to hear the gossip about the affair from your colleagues? What could you gain from this knowledge?"

Figure 1 The informal organizational chart
(Braun & Kramer based on Brian Robertson)

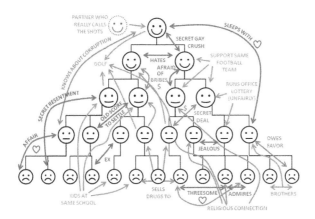

The majority of the students perceive this type of gossip as negative. "Actually, it's none of my business," one says. "If someone gossips about someone else, like this to me, I will think that they'll also be gossiping about me."

"But let's say that the CEO is having an affair with the secretary. Even though she is at the bottom of the pyramid in the organization, she will have a lot more power and influence than your line manager. Also, if you go out drinking with your colleagues, and she is there, you would probably avoid dissing your boss if you know she is intimate with him."

I remind the students about their internal communications classes, and how they often have to map an organization's structure to understand how communication flows internally. Who is at the top and who is at the bottom, in which departments? Which employees are the decision makers? If the secretary is friends with the manager, she may wield a lot more power than indicated on the flow chart. As Danielle Braun and Jitske Kramer state in *The Corporate Tribe* (2018), informal networks may be just as important to understand as the formal ones (see figure 1).

The students agree. In this case, gossip means survival.

In the television series *Emily in Paris*, Emily Cooper (Lily Collins), a young American from Chicago, moves to Paris to work in a French marketing firm. Emily meets Antoine (William Abadie), one of the firm's clients, at a party. Being the typical cliché of the womanizing Frenchman, Antoine openly flirts with Emily, even though he is married. The next day, Sylvie (Philippine Leroy-Beaulieu), Emily's manager (who is already quite hostile towards her), comments that she had quite the effect on Antoine. "Do you fancy him?" she asks. A bit later, Julien (Samuel Arnold), one of Emily's colleagues, tells her that Antoine is actually Sylvie's lover. Definitely important information to have before even thinking of taking such a flirtation any further!

Not only do people have different attitudes to gossiping in general, but they also differ on their perceptions towards various gossip situations.

There is an interesting study by De Gouveia et al. (2005), where several gossip case studies were presented to respondents who had to determine whether these scenarios were light gossip, quite a bit of gossip or not gossip at all.

One case was: "While sipping on their coffee, Jessica remarks to Brett that the boss is very late for work as it is already 10:00 am and there is no sign of him anywhere. Brett tells Jessica that their boss probably wouldn't be at work due to the loss of his mother the previous evening. One week later, while Brett is at his table doing some work, the boss calls him into his office and says, 'Brett, I would appreciate it if in the future you keep quiet about my personal life instead of sharing it with the entire office.'"

In this case, even if it is clear that the boss took offence, half the respondents considered that Bret did not gossip. The other half considered it to be either light gossip, and a few to be quite a bit of gossip.

People can easily interpret a gossip situation very differently. For each scenario in the study, opinions varied greatly. Some people found that certain types of gossip were inappropriate, whereas others found them to be totally acceptable. A person who particularly values privacy will judge someone harshly just for sharing information that someone else would not consider particularly private. That the study was conducted in South Africa already skews the results, as people from different cultures will likely interpret various situations even more differently (see Chapter 5).

It is important to realize that many people have a different understanding and interpretation of the same gossip situation. Everyone operates using different codes and values, especially if they come from a different country or work in a different corporate culture.

Why we can't we keep our mouths shut

While it is clear that gossiping is a minefield fraught with danger, we can hardly refrain from flapping our lips. Why is that?

Several studies (Elmer, 1994) state that gossip can be a valuable form of social communication and is actually inevitable. Apparently, up to two-thirds of all conversations include some references to third-party doings, and gossip makes up approximately 65% of the content of everyday conversation. So why is it suddenly big news when at a NATO convention, Canadian prime minister Justin Trudeau is caught on camera, huddled closely with colleagues French president Emmanuel Macron, British prime minister Boris Johnson, and Dutch prime minister Mark Rutte, gossiping about US president Donald Trump, during a reception at Buckingham Palace? According to *The Washington Post*, Trudeau could be heard saying incredulously: "He takes a 40-minute press conference off the top." Trudeau confirmed that was a reference to Trump's long and unscheduled question-and-answer session with journalists a few days earlier. Trudeau also said: "You just watched his team's jaws drop to the floor."

The footage was posted online by Canadian broadcaster CBC and has been viewed more than 5 million times. This incident was covered by major news outlets and broadcasters all over the world with headlines like: "Trudeau, Macron caught gossiping like 'mean girls.'" (Trump's reaction, when he found out, was to call Trudeau "two-faced"). Audiences all over the world seemed fascinated that something like this could happen. But why should it come as such a surprise that even world leaders could indulge in gossip from time to time?

In his bestselling book *Sapiens: A Brief History of Humankind*, Yuval Noah Harari (2014) asks: "Do you think that history professors chat about the reasons for World War One when they meet for lunch, or that nuclear physicists spend their coffee breaks at scientific conferences talking about quarks? Sometimes. But more often, they gossip about the professor who caught her husband cheating, or the quarrel between the head of the department and the dean, or the rumors that a colleague used his research funds to buy a Lexus."

Why? McAndrew (2014) claims that gossip is central to the social life of humans. Historical records and cross-cultural studies show that gossip has been shared by people of all ages and cultures. Gossip goes as far back as our prehistoric past, and it became a part of our evolutionary adaptation. People who were interested in other peoples' lives were more successful than those who were not. It is the genes of those individuals that have been transmitted from one generation to the next.

Harari (2014) notes that it is because of gossip that we, as a species, actually began to rule the planet. Before we began gossiping with other Homo sapiens, we were merely just like other mammals in the food chain. By learning to gossip, we were able to create friendships and alliances, which allowed us to cooperate with each other. Doing so gave us an edge over other animals. "Social cooperation is our key for survival and reproduction," the author claims. "It is not enough for individual men and women to know the whereabouts of lions and bison. It's much more important for them to know who in their band hates whom, who is sleeping with whom, who is honest and who is a cheat."

Although the nature of the gossip has evolved over time (we're no longer talking about which caveman to avoid or which tribe is hostile), and our channels of communication have become more sophisticated (as we also use emails, phone calls, and WhatsApp), we still gossip. Harari (2014) states: "It comes so naturally to us that it seems as if our language evolved for this very purpose."

Even in religious scripture gossip plays a central role. Capps (2012) maintains that the Gospels are very much the product of gossip. "Without gossip, no Gospels," he says. "We can open any Gospel at any page and begin reading, and what we find ourselves reading is a series of happenings. [...] And happenings are far more important than ideas." The author explains that such stories make a deeper impression than abstract concepts. Although the Bible is generally very critical of gossip (as we will see in Chapter 5), Capps argues that gossip actually gives the readers the impression of gaining mastery by taking possession of someone else's experience. In this case, readers of the Gospels can more easily "take possession of the very experience of Jesus, to make oneself an intimate of his."

"In short, the line between gossip and Gospel is a very fine one," Capps explains. "To say this is not to disparage the Gospel, but to elevate gossip."

This fine line applies to a variety of fields, such as literature, journalism, and marketing. As Barbara Walters, a well-known American journalist, said: "Show me someone who never gossips, and I'll show you someone who isn't interested in people."

In the fields of advertising and marketing, gossip (or, in this case, word of mouth) happens to be one of the most powerful marketing tools. In his book *Contagious*, Jonah Berger (2013) observes that word of mouth is the primary factor behind 20% to 50% of all purchasing decisions, and its impact largely surpasses that of traditional advertising. Similarly, *McKinsey Quarterly* claims that word of mouth generates more than twice the sales of paid advertising. And it's a lot cheaper.

People sharing their experiences about products, services, and salesmen can easily make or break someone's reputation. It's not a surprise that many salesmen have the motto: "If you hate our service, tell us. If you love it, tell others" (Rooks et al.,

2011). Gossip, according to Giardini & Wittek (2019a), is "key to sustaining or breaking cooperation in human societies."

Gossip, cooperation, and reputation are very much intertwined. But not only the reputation of the third party is affected: the gossiper's and listener's reputations are also very much at stake. The first question we may ask ourselves is, what is the optimal amount of time we should spend gossiping in front of the coffee machine?

How much is too much?

At which point does too much gossip become counterproductive? There are indeed moments where we should refrain from gossiping altogether, and moments where we are actually obligated to gossip.

Pim (28), a manager at an engineering firm in the Netherlands, says: "I think gossip is always something that will happen. You cannot avoid it. Gossip does show that the workplace can be fun, and we are all human, and we give people the space to be human. But when people gossip too much, it becomes a toxic environment and some employees might not feel safe at their workplace, and that is something that needs to be avoided at all costs."

Gossiping is healthy. Yet too much can easily become harmful. Studies show that people who either gossip too much or too little will be perceived negatively. Therefore, it is important for employees to be aware of just how much they should gossip.

If you are at the low end of the gossiping spectrum, and proudly claim that you never gossip at all, chances are high that you will be seen as not socially attuned, or that you have been excluded from your social network. Not to gossip (or not to show a minimum of interest for gossip) is to be "quickly marginalized from the local social fabric" (Foster, 2004).

Surprisingly, many managers encourage their employees to stay clear of gossip altogether, citing a loss of productivity. In an article called 'The next time you want to complain at work, do this instead' in the *Harvard Business Review*, Peter Bregman (2018) claims that in a study of 200 employees, the majority spent 10 or more hours per month complaining (i.e., gossiping)—or listening to others complain—about their bosses or upper management. "Even more amazing, almost a third spent 20 hours a month doing so." And that doesn't take into account the gossip that goes around about peers and employees. This time could be spent a lot more constructively, according to the author. He therefore recommends confronting the third party directly rather than gossip behind their back. In this way, there would be no need to gossip.

During the course of my research, interviewees often assured us that they don't gossip. If they have a problem with someone, they will tell them honestly. However, expecting employees to be direct may greatly conflict with one's culture (see Chapter 5).

Other studies (see Baumeister et al., 2004) confirm that never gossiping is indeed a bad strategy, and it often leads to negative consequences. An employee who does not pass along some gossip that could have been beneficial to a colleague, for example, could be poorly evaluated. Let's say that you know that your boss is a sleazebag and has a reputation for hitting on a record number of employees. If a new, young colleague comes to work for your department, and soon enough, you notice the sleazebag flirting with her but choose to say nothing, you will eventually be judged quite poorly.

On the other end of the spectrum, people who gossip too much may also be quickly perceived as "indiscriminate, unselective and untrustworthy." Despite the impression that gossipers may have a lot of friends, this is often just an illusion. "Perhaps high gossipers are individuals who are welcome into our social networks for fear of losing the opportunity to learn information, but we tend to keep them at arm's length," Farley (2011) writes. Moreover, high gossipers are often perceived as less "emotionally warm" and tend to be less likeable than low gossipers. Robinson (2016) also cautions that too much gossip becomes ineffective and counterproductive, as people stop listening and stop taking you seriously after a while.

Finding the *sweet spot of gossip*: Tips for employees and managers

So, you may wonder, at what point are gossipers perceived negatively? When is it that we cross the line? The curve representing what is the right amount to gossip is curvilinear. Kurland & Pelled (2000) note that gossipers will be well perceived and become more likeable until they reach a certain high point, and then, once they pass that point, their likeability will drop down again (see figure 2). Therefore, socially successful people know how to use gossip selectively. Gossiping in the right way is a fine balancing act.

Tips for employees

1. Be open to gossip.
Keeping your eyes and ears open and staying attuned to gossip at work are very important. Employees can certainly learn a lot about the culture of their organization by doing this and can avoid making the mistakes of their predecessors.

2. Don't say you never gossip.
For those employees who claim not to gossip, it's a mistake! They're missing out a lot and, most likely, chances are they are not very well perceived by their colleagues. I would even go as far as saying that staying clear of gossip is career suicide!

3. Brush up on your conversational skills.
During the course of my research, several people have told me that they hate engaging in small talk, and that's why they would never be caught dead gossiping in the hallway. According to Liz Luyben and Iris Posthouwer and their book *Small Talk Survival* (2019), many people admit that they have an aversion to small talk. They see it as a drag to chitchat with people they don't know well at the office party. Having superficial conversations is a waste of time. (I am certain that attitude towards small talk is

Figure 2   Gossiping the right amount

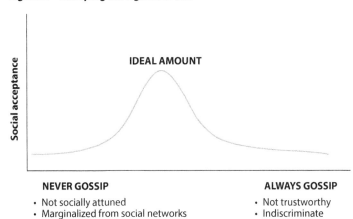

NEVER GOSSIP
- Not socially attuned
- Marginalized from social networks

ALWAYS GOSSIP
- Not trustworthy
- Indiscriminate

very much influenced by culture, as we will see in Chapter 5.) But the authors insist that just the opposite is true. "Without small talk, no big talk." By starting off with light talk about what you did over the weekend or where you will go on holiday, you are paving the way to more interesting talk. It's certainly worth the investment! The authors don't mention it, but by mastering this skill and gaining the trust of your colleagues, you will eventually be let in on some juicy office gossip.

Tips for managers

1.   Just accept that your employees will gossip (about you).
If managers just accept and understand that their employees will gossip, why they gossip, and realize that it is not necessarily a personal attack against them, a lot of stress and bad feelings will go away.

Claudia (52) is the head of human resources at a German logistics company. "I am a superior, so there will always be gossip about me," she says. "But that is only natural. Over the years I have gotten used to it and learned not to take it personally. Employees sometimes simply need to vent, and their superiors are the perfect target for blowing off some steam. So, while I have been the target of gossip, it has never really affected me in a serious way."

Jamie (55) works in financial services in a large, international bank in the UK. "In the past, I used to have people working for me," he recalls. "For sure, they would talk about me, because that is the position you put yourself in as a manager, as a leader, and as a boss. But you can't let that affect you. Hopefully, you do such a good job, that people have nothing bad to say about you."

2.   Reduce the amount of gossip. Be as open and transparent as possible.

Gorden (2007) shows that even though gossip is pretty much inevitable, managers can play a huge role in determining how much gossip will take place or not in their organization. If managers are insecure, and do not communicate effectively with their teams, employees will revert to gossip. Managers who give negative feedback rather than constructive criticism and encouragement create an atmosphere of jealousy and rivalry in their teams. If they hole themselves up in their offices to avoid their employees, they will also create a work culture that lets gossip thrive. Therefore "the presence of gossip should be seen by management as a reflection of their performance and organizational effectiveness" (Gorden, 2007).

De Gouveia et al. (2005) and numerous articles on LinkedIn also claim that top management can significantly reduce gossip by having "an open-door policy." Employees should be able to raise issues and potential concerns so that these can be quickly addressed. Organizations that instill values such as fairness, transparency, open communication, and trust will reduce the effects of office politics and destructive gossip or rumors.

Gossiping is indeed an inherent part of human nature. But since it is such a delicate act, one that could easily lead us to make faux pas or be perceived negatively, what are the reasons that keep pushing us, time and time again, to spill the beans (even if we feel bad afterwards)?

1.   Reasons for Gossiping

Three may keep a secret if two of them are dead.
—Benjamin Franklin

I was once at a dinner party. Two of my friends (who worked together for a health organization in Quebec, and were in a relationship) said that no one at work knows they are together, as they are very discreet. One person started to laugh. "Did you tell anyone about your relationship?"

"Well, actually just one person knows about us," one of my friends replied.

"Well then you can be sure that everybody knows!"

I had to agree with this.

Berger wrote in his book *Contagious* (2013): "Think about the last time someone shared a secret with you. Remember how earnestly she begged you not to tell a soul? And remember what you did next? Well, if you're like most people, you probably went and told somebody else."

Why is that? Berger maintains that if something is supposed to be a secret, people will probably talk about it even if they are not supposed to. That's because people talk about things that make them look good. People love to share: their thoughts, their experiences, stories about others. They want to come across as smart, hip, and entertaining. They want to show that they are in the know.

People want to be liked and admired. "The desire for social approval is a fundamental human motivation." And being in the know definitely gives you a lot of status (Berger, 2013).

We have many reasons to gossip. Not only do we want to look good and to gain status, but we also gossip to gather information, to maintain group norms, to learn about the corporate culture, to bond, to reciprocate, to vent and let out steam, to confirm our views, to make sense of confusing situations, to entertain, to compete, and to influence.

To gather information

An important motive for gossiping is to gather information. By gossiping, one can find out new information about a target person or check whether others share our opinion about a certain person. According to Foster (2004), gossip is often the only way of gathering accurate information. Julian (55), a Dutch lecturer working for a large educational institution in the Netherlands, explains:

> We were looking for a new team leader. One day, our manager announced that he had the perfect candidate: a team leader from another department that would be a great fit for our team. Of course, quite a few of us knew some colleagues from that department, so we asked about this potential team leader. Soon, all kinds of stories emerged: he was a bully and intimidated his employees if they refused to take on ridiculous amounts of work. He also had conflicts with a lot of people. Naturally, we gossiped about him. So, when our manager asked us whether we should invite him for an interview, we all vehemently refused. He was bewildered: "But you don't even know him! You can't just write off someone like that based on gossip!" Well, actually, you can. Although our manager would have liked to hire him, he did back off eventually, and we hired somebody else.

Throughout the history of mankind, we have always been drawn to stories—they're an important source of cultural learning and help us make sense of the world. By listening to gossip, we can learn a lot about what it is to be a good employee. As Jonah Berger notes, much information is gained by listening to stories or, in this case, gossip. "Think about other ways people could acquire this information," the author urges. "Trial and error might work, but it could be extremely costly and time consuming." If a friend tells you that they know a good car mechanic, that could save you a lot of time. "Imagine if finding an honest car mechanic required taking your car to two dozen places around town and getting work done at each one. It would be exhausting (and expensive)." Experiencing and observing things in this way would certainly not be very practical. And relying on ads is also not a sure proof way of getting information. As we know, ads tend not to be very trustworthy. Berger explains that powerful stories have important information or messages imbedded in them. And such information often travels "under the guise of what seems like idle chatter."

Some may even use gossip as a way to get references about a future or new employee. It's not that different from calling someone's references on a CV.

Daniel (45), an IT architect at a Hungarian bank, says: "In the last year, quite a few colleagues have been replaced within the company. And about the new ones coming, my boss asked around if anyone knows them. It is often said that 'the city is big, but the profession is small.' So, somewhere, someone surely knows something about them."

To maintain group norms

During a sermon he gave in September of 2020, Pope Francis proclaimed: "Gossip is a plague worse than Covid-19. Worse" (Associated Press, 2020). The devil is the "biggest gossiper" who is "seeking to divide the church with his lies. Let's make a big effort: no gossiping!" he urged his followers. When people do something wrong, he believes, it is best to discuss it with them privately. The article notes that the Catholic hierarchy has long relied on this type of "fraternal correction" to handle problems without airing them in public. But for survivors of sexual abuse, "this form of private reprimand has allowed abuse to fester in the church and let both predator priests and superiors who covered up for them escape punishment." Maybe gossip would have acted as a stronger deterrent and form of punishment for offenders? Maybe gossip is not the devil after all? If priests and bishops had gossiped more, maybe the multitude of scandals, and a lot of pain, could have been avoided.

An important function of gossip is to maintain group norms. Several researchers (Baumeister et al., 2004) describe gossip as "observational learning of a cultural kind." Gossip can be a powerful means of transmitting information about rules, norms, and unwritten codes of a given culture. And gossip usually focuses on wrongdoings. Harari (2014) considers gossipmongers to be "the original fourth estate, journalists who inform society about and thus protect it from cheats and freeloaders."

Not only does gossip educate the listener about these rules, but it also consolidates them. As a child, when you heard your mother talking to a friend about how rude Paul was because he didn't shake her hand when he ran into her at the corner store, you learned that you must greet people politely by shaking their hand. In France (depending on which region you come from), your mother would have gossiped about someone's lack of manners if she didn't kiss her four times on the cheeks. Similarly, people living in religious communities will hear more gossip about those who do not properly abide by the rules of their faith.

Rooks et al. (2011) describes how gossip can be a powerful tool to force businessmen to maintain certain professional norms. If a salesman has a negative experience with a supplier, he will certainly gossip about it, preferably with colleagues who know the supplier. The more things go wrong, the more likely it is that business people will get the impression that the norm "you should deliver as promised" is violated. Not only does gossiping about it make an "attractive war story during social talk," but it also provides a mechanism that sanctions such problems.

Ana (69) used to work in the accounting department of an insurance company in Latvia. "We used to have a manager who was shouting at us almost every week," she recalls. "He used to yell when one of us made a mistake in a document or when we came late to work. It seemed like screaming was just the way he preferred to communicate with us. None of us liked it, so we were discussing this a lot with each other. Finally, we decided to inform the labor union and in just a couple of days, our manager had been changed. No more screaming!"

By gossiping about this manager, Ana and her colleagues were able to take collective action and solve the problem. I don't know what happened to the screaming manager, but the odds are that he probably changed his ways in his next job. And the new manager—who will certainly hear about this story—will think twice about yelling at her employees.

Giardini & Wittek (2019a) explain that gossip provides two steps to the social control mechanism and provides learning to all three members of the triad (i.e., the gossiper, the listener, and the absent third party). To begin with, "it mainly affects the relation between sender and receiver because it leads to some joint deliberation about the kind of norm violation committed by the absent third party. In order to change the future behavior of the third party, the second step would be to sanction the third party, or to apply some other compliance-gaining strategy."

To learn about the corporate culture

Affirming certain rules and norms of behavior not only applies to culture as a whole, but also to corporate culture. With gossip, the company 'war stories' and the stories that communicate the firm's values can be told (Ivancevich et al., 2008).

In this way, employees can learn about their organizations' policies and rules without experiencing them firsthand. Whereas in one American multinational, having an affair with a colleague could lead to immediate dismissal, in a similar organization from another country, the same affair would hardly have any consequences. Rather than learning the hard way, most employees would probably prefer to find out over a drink at the bar, what happened to others in a similar situation.

Take this hilarious scene in *Seinfeld*. George Constanza's boss calls him in and says: "It's come to my attention that you and the cleaning woman engaged in sexual intercourse on the desk in your room. Is that correct?" To which George (Jason Alexander) replies: "Was that wrong? Should I not have done that? I tell you, I gotta plead ignorance on this. If someone had said anything at all about this when I started working here, that that sort of thing was frowned upon.... I worked in a lot of offices and ... ha ha ... people do that all the time." To no avail. George is fired on the spot. If he had the opportunity to gossip a little, this may not have happened!

Daniel Kahneman, the author of *Thinking, Fast and Slow* (2011), claims in a speech about the power of gossip that gossip may actually help you discover the mistakes that other people make, which in turn, can help you avoid making these same mistakes yourself.

"And it can be very useful," Kahneman explains. "Because if you have a group, say within an organization, of people watching each other make decisions and make judgements, and they're intelligent in watching the others, then you will have an educated community. And individuals are going to end up making better decisions. I call that the power of gossip. So, if you educate gossip, if you educate the way people discuss each other's judgements and decisions, you are going indirectly to achieve an improvement in the quality of decisions."

Research (Martinescu et al., 2014) also shows that gossip can play an important role in self-evaluation, as it gives us feedback as to how we function within a group. David (22) works for a green energy supplier in the Netherlands: "Obviously, we've got some house rules at work. We have ways to address the customers. We have ways to handle certain situations. And so, you really don't want to break those rules. Of course, when employees do break the rules, their colleagues will gossip about them."

Jean-Paul (24), a veterinary doctor in Brittany, France, says: "In our line of business, the way you dress is very important to our clients. Gossip is an excellent way to put pressure on our employees. So, out with shorts, skirts, and sandals!"

The same research shows that gossip recipients tend to use positive and negative gossip to improve, promote, and protect themselves. On one hand, positive gossip provides success stories which encourage people to compare themselves to their peers, which then may lead to self-improvement. Negative gossip, on the other hand, is used as a mechanism to keep people's behavior in check by pressuring them to adhere to prevailing social norms.

Anita (48), a French lecturer working in a large Dutch educational institution, confides: "One day, I was having lunch with two of my colleagues. They started talking about an ex-colleague that used to have really bad body odor. Nobody dared to confront him, they tell me, but one day, his manager offered him deodorant as a present. The ex-colleague was really embarrassed, but got the message, and after that, came to work smelling like a rose. When I thought back to that story a bit later, I couldn't help wonder whether my colleagues were also trying to tell me something? Maybe not, but I can tell you that I certainly used a lot more deodorant the next morning!"

Negative gossip used in this way could certainly help pass on a message that could be uncomfortable and embarrassing. This type of technique is typically used by people coming from high-context cultures, such as Asian countries (see Chapter 5), where feedback is given in a very indirect manner.

Contrarily to the general perception, gossip is not necessarily intended to hurt the target, but to help the gossiper and the listener learn. Negative gossip can also bring out feelings of self-protection as listeners may feel anxious and slightly threatened that they too may become the subject of gossip and criticism (Beersma & Van Kleef, 2012).

Gossip is often used to protect the group and warn group members against others that violate group norms and serves as a mechanism to control freeloading and cheating. If certain colleagues are not pulling their weight, and you hear about this through the grapevine, you may choose to work with other people on that new project and avoid problems down the road. At the same time, the freeloading colleague may also eventually adjust their behavior if they notice that they are not being considered for interesting projects. Let's say Joe is being sloppy at work. When Stella gossips about that with John, she's not only ostracizing (and punishing Joe to some extent), but she is also warning John that being sloppy at work is not acceptable. Chances are, John will be more careful to follow the work norms.

Therefore, spreading negative gossip can allow employees and businesspeople to "mutually agree and confirm which kinds of behavior are considered acceptable, and which are not," Rooks et al. (2011) observe. Gossip is used as a way of testing and reconfirming the industry's norms with peers.

We see this in *The Devil Wears Prada* (2006), when Andy (Anne Hathaway) comes to work as a personal assistant to Miranda Priestly (Meryl Streep), the powerful editor of a fictional fashion magazine called *Runway*. Andy is exploited by her tyrannical boss, but also has trouble fitting in at the magazine. She's rather frumpy and doesn't seem to have the right weight (she is a size 6 instead of a size 2 or 4), nor does she have much flair for fashion. In one scene, two of Andy's co-workers are gossiping about her. "I have no idea why Miranda hired her," Emily snickers. "Me neither," Serena agrees. "The other day we were in the beauty department, and she held the eyelash curler and said: 'What is this?'"

Both laugh in a condescending way.

"I just knew from the moment they hired her that she would be a complete and utter disas...."

Andy enters the room, after having had a complete makeover. The phone rings and with an elegant toss of her hair, she picks up and answers confidently, while the two gossipers stare at her in bewilderment.

"Are you wearing the...," Emily asks.

"The Chanel boots?" Andy says. "Yeah, I am."

This scene illustrates how the two gossipers are suddenly undermined when Andy proves that she actually can fit well into their corporate culture.

To bond and to belong

Often, people gossip in order to establish and confirm their belonging to a group or a subgroup, Giardini (2012) observes.

In the novel *The Last Flight* (2020) by Julie Clark, one of the main characters, Eva, becomes friends with her neighbor Liz, who is a visiting professor at Berkeley. One day, Liz invites Eva to a baseball game with her colleagues from the faculty. Eva sits next to them and quietly listens to them gossip about who would receive, or not receive, money for research; who got their articles published and who did not. She listens to them complain about the one who always let popcorn burn in the office microwave. For Eva, this was a glimpse into a life she was not a part of, but had always dreamed of. She would have loved to belong to this group: also complain about the fact that women didn't have the same opportunities as men when it came to receiving research funding. The excitement of publishing in an academic journal. Even being the one that let the popcorn burn in the office microwave.

Exchanging information about others can build trust within a group and bring people together. Stefanie (53) is from Indonesia and works at a large retail furniture e-commerce company in Jakarta. "We all talk about our bosses and how to deal with them, like Filip, who we call 'the public enemy.' We talk about what he wants, what he does, and how to deal with him," she explains. "If he WhatsApps, and there's no response in 10 to 15 minutes, then he will yell at you. So, we're all helping each other. When we have a boss like that who likes to contact us after hours, we give our colleagues advice on what to do. We talk about our experiences with him, like our struggles, and we end up brainstorming." Having this 'public enemy' certainly brought Stefanie and her colleagues closer together. Because of this, they felt the urge to meet up after work, eat out, and do fun things together.

Kim (29), who is employed at a large food corporation in the Netherlands, recalls: "A while back, there was a lot of conflict and division between colleagues. The atmosphere was very bad: colleagues would steal each other's clients in order to meet their sales targets. Then, one day, a new sales manager was hired to steer our team. This new manager was so annoying that everyone started talking about her behind her back. Suddenly, the atmosphere in our team became a lot better. We started to bond over this irritation that we all shared."

By sharing such gossip, social bonds and group membership are deepened. People realize that they think the same way about certain people, and this brings them closer together.

Moreover, gossip is used to create alliances and in-groups at work. If colleagues from the in-group gossip with you, it may feel like they are inviting you to become a member of their group. This is something most people want, and even need, in order to survive.

In *Psychology Today*, Nicholas DiFonzo (2011) describes just how important it is for many to be a part of an in-group and how such a need can easily be manipulated:

> In the final installment of C. S. Lewis's classic science-fiction trilogy, *That Hideous Strength* (1945), the central characters are a young professor of sociology named Mark Studdock and his wife, Jane. Mark is emotionally insecure and perennially pines to be included in the 'inner circle' of whatever social environment he finds himself part of. This occurs at (both fictitious) Bracton College and at the (secretly malevolent) National Institute of Coordinated Experiments (N.I.C.E.). The inner circles at the college and the N.I.C.E. don't actually like Mark, but woo him in order to capture Jane.

When Mark Studdock is included in the inner circle gossip, and realizes that he is now part of the collective 'we,' he feels intense pleasure. "So very recently he had been an outsider, watching the proceedings of what he then called 'Curry and his gang' with awe and with little understanding. [...] Now he was inside and 'Curry and his gang' had become 'we.' [...] It had all happened quite suddenly and was still sweet in the mouth." DiFonzo (2011) notes that "Mark continues to feel that his status rises as each new round of 'confidential' negative gossip about colleagues and coworkers is used to inflate his ego as being a member of the Important People Group. [...] This nicely illustrates the use of gossip both to include the hearer into one's clique and to exclude the person not present from the clique." This scene, according to the author, illustrates the political (and often negative) function of gossip, as it has the function of weakening and strengthening alliances, and it can be used for ulterior motives. But the urge to gossip in order to belong is overwhelming.

Psychologist Andreas Wismeijer (2020), from Tilburg University, suggests that the prospect of being excluded from the group, or of losing our social status or position within the group, can even cause physical pain. When people find out that others are gossiping about them and are excluding them, the section of the brain that signals pain is activated. So, we'll do anything to belong to the group, and gossiping is a way to do this.

To reciprocate

Another reason that causes us to gossip, is the phenomenon of reciprocity. When someone gives us something, we feel the instant urge to give back.

In her classic book *Nice Girls Still Don't Get the Corner Office*, Lois Frankel (2014) explains that in all relationships, whether we like it or not, quid pro quo plays an important role: quid pro quo being defined as "something that's exchanged in return for something else." It can be as obvious as "I give you a salary and in return I expect you to do a good job" or, as the author explains, if I speak at your event for free, and later down the road I ask you for a favor, you will remember what I have done for you. "It's an unspoken system of bartering that goes on in relationships." Trading grapevine information also follows these rules. (And as she mentions later on in her book, the grapevine is an important source of information, and being excluded from it would be harmful to your work.)

Foster (2004) also describes gossip as a "type of currency, traded like any other, and assessed for its value by the taker on the basis of timeliness, usefulness, and especially, rarity." If someone gives you a juicy bit of information, they probably expect something in return at some point. It's like going out for coffee with a friend who's always picking up the bill. If you never reciprocate, at some point, they will stop inviting you.

To vent and let out steam

Sharing your frustrations and negative experiences not only helps you bond with a colleague, but can also provide catharsis. If you come across a rude waiter or nasty service representative at an airport, talking with others about these experiences can be very helpful. Jonah Berger claims that for 90% of people sharing such negative experiences provides them with significant relief. Likewise, employees find solace in venting with others about negative experiences with colleagues at work.

Bilyana (26), an employee at an international soft drink company in Bulgaria, remembers when she felt the need to vent. "I was once very disappointed with my manager. I was told that if I met certain criteria, I would get a promotion. Well, I did what I had been told, but apparently, it wasn't enough for the promotion, which my manager had promised to give me. I also understood that someone else got promoted, so I called my manager. We had a very complicated talk. After that, I was extremely angry, so I just called my colleagues in a Teams meeting to tell them what happened and, yeah, just to share my disappointment and hear their opinions about this matter. So, yeah, I really felt the need to share what happened, and I did."

In the *Harvard Business Review*, Peter Bregman (2018) explains that this feeling of venting and letting out steam feels very good and can be addictive indeed. "Here's what happens: someone annoys us. We're dissatisfied with how they're behaving. Maybe we're angry, frustrated, or threatened. Those feelings build up energy in our bodies, literally creating physical discomfort. [...] When we complain about someone else, the uncomfortable feelings begin to dissipate because complaining releases the pent-up energy. That's why we say things like 'I'm venting' or 'I'm blowing off steam.'"

To confirm our views

You should only gossip with people who think the same as you.
Otherwise, you are a bad gossip.
—Jitske Kramer, Dutch author and corporate anthropologist

According to Riegel (2018), "we use gossip as a way to collect evidence that confirms our beliefs, satisfying our confirmation bias—the tendency to look for information that confirms what we already believe to be true." Heleen (18), Dutch, works for a cosmetics shop in The Hague. "We got a new assistant manager," she confides. "One of my colleagues, Sophie, entered our cafeteria when I was having lunch. She asked me what I thought of the new assistant manager. I was a bit nervous that someone would overhear us, but I was relieved to share my thoughts and hear hers. We both agreed that we had our doubts about the new assistant manager." Realizing that they both felt the same way gave them both a feeling of reassurance.

Several researchers (Gambetta, cited in Rooks et al., 2011) observe that employees often revert to gossip to test their opinions about an absent third party. The aim is to be able to gain or renew information about someone in cases where such information would normally be difficult to get.

By hearing that a co-worker had a similar negative experience with the same colleague, our existing beliefs are confirmed. And we get the satisfaction that comes from being right. As Judith Glaser (2013) explains in her article 'Your brain is hooked on being right' in the *Harvard Business Review*, when you feel that you are right, your brain gets a hit of adrenaline and dopamine, which makes you feel great. "We get addicted to being right."

To make sense of confusing situations

Several researchers consider gossip to be a form of sensemaking, which Weick (2001) defines as "the process of making experiences sensible." The idea is that people try to make sense of events that take place around them. They try to give meaning and order to these situations—especially those that tend to surprise or confuse us (Mills, 2010).

Anna (41), Russian, is a professor at a university in South Africa. She remembers how she and her colleagues gossiped to make sense of a situation they couldn't understand, and which seemed completely unfair to them. "I am a member of the project management team, and I have to decide about staff costs and how much money the project members will receive. My colleagues and I agreed on how to distribute the money, and then sent the proposal to the dean. We were waiting and waiting, for weeks, for months, for the dean to sign it. And then he sent me a message: 'Could you justify why one of your colleagues, Leah, is receiving money for the project?' And I told him Leah was helping me and assisting me while I was doing this and that, and therefore I had decided to pay her for her input. And he said: 'You know, that's part of her regular job, we can't give money to Leah.'"

Anna explained that every time she wanted to involve Leah in a project or a trip, the dean would refuse. She couldn't understand why the dean was treating Leah in such an unfair way. Of course, it soon became a topic of gossip. "We figured out that the dean was having an affair with his secretary. Afterwards, we realized that Leah is the first cousin of this secretary. And we know that she is jealous of Leah because they are cousins, you know. For sure, this secretary influenced the dean's decisions." How does Anna know all of this for sure? "Leah told me that she met that secretary at some family gathering," Anna laughs. "This secretary was showing photos of the dean all the time to everybody: 'This is my boss and blah blah blah.' It's not normal you know, that someone is showing photos of their boss at a family gathering. So, we assumed that she and the dean were in some sort of emotional relationship that is more than only professional."

Even if Anna admits that they could not really be sure about the veracity of this gossip, it helped them make sense of the situation. At least, being able to somewhat understand an incomprehensible situation provided a bit of logic and some relief.

To entertain

Another reason to gossip is to have fun (Foster, 2004). Many people gossip at work because they are bored. Don't we all welcome a break from writing a tedious report when a colleague comes into our office, closes the door, and, in a hushed tone, recounts the manager's latest blunder? Or tells us how the financial advisor grossly misbehaved at the Christmas party? And from the point of view of the gossiper, as Michael Scott (Steve Carell) in the television series *The Office* (US) observes: "When you have somebody's attention and their eyes are lighting up because they are very interested in what you have to say, that is a great feeling. It is wonderful to be the center of attention." You rarely get this type of attention when you give a lecture or a presentation to your team about the company's annual report.

Hakim (36), a Moroccan-Dutch employee at a large appliance store in the Netherlands, tells this story: "I remember one time that a colleague started dating one of our bosses. The whole work team knew about the relationship from the very beginning, but we were not told officially until six months later. We used to gossip about it almost every day and every time we saw them together. It sometimes seemed as we were watching a love reality show!"

Certain researchers (Morreal, cited in Capps, 2012) claim that gossiping is very much like joke telling. When the goal is to entertain, gossip very often uses humor.

And gossip and humor have a lot in common, according to Capps. Both provide a great deal of pleasure, both make use of narratives and storytelling, and both have as the ultimate goal to make people laugh. "Even as people have reputations as good or poor tellers of funny stories and jokes, people can be known as good or poor gossips."

But as we will see in Chapter 2, a big challenge for 'humorous gossip' and 'gossipy humor' is to remain truthful. And humor can become quite complicated when gossiping with colleagues from different cultures (see Chapter 5).

To compete

Gossip is often used in order to compete. Karin (21), a professional basketball player for the Dutch national team, confides: "In my basketball team, people gossip quite a bit about each other, coaches, and opponents. Probably because in our team, the ten of us are fighting for the four spots at the Olympic Games." And not only in professional sport. Having information on one's competitors can give us an edge.

Pietro (21), Spanish, describes how gossiping helped him win a competition at work. "I work in the marketing and fashion sectors and it is true that these are two very competitive areas where you always have to try to be the best. This type of environment tends to invite us to gossip about the person you are next to. For example, one of the clients we were trying to gain already had a community manager, so we were just doing a trial period. Whenever our potential client asked us our opinion about her team, we told her that her community manager was not efficient. So, she eventually fired her and hired us. We didn't do it on purpose, really, but there is a lot of rivalry in our area, so we took the chance."

Bilyana (26) works for an international soft drink company in Bulgaria. "By gossiping you keep an eye on your competition," she says. "You can check if someone's salary has increased and by how much it has increased. That can give you a sense of whether your salary is going to increase too." And if it doesn't, you will be more inclined to fight for a raise.

Being in the know also means having power, which can give you an edge over your competition. In some cases, people even compete over gossip.

Elena Ferrante describes this competition beautifully in the second volume of her Neapolitan Novels series, *The Story of a New Name* (2012). Lenu, the narrator, recognizes the power her friend is trying to exert over her: "She showed that she knew everything about those women [of her village], down to the tiniest details, in order to prove that no one told me anything but told her everything, or worse, in order to make me feel that I was wrapped in a fog, unable to see the suffering of the people around me."

Therefore, you may gossip about what your manager told you, not just because what he said was actually that interesting, but to show that the manager is talking to you and respects and trust you enough to share rather confidential information with you, which gives you an edge over your colleagues.

Gossip can also be used as a discreet way of bragging, Berger claims. He describes a man who gossips about the waitress flirting at the exclusive airline lounge he is a member of. He's not really that interested in the waitress herself, but really wants to show that he *was* at the exclusive lounge, and that he is a member of that exclusive club.

Having information about the people in your surroundings certainly gives you power. But it doesn't always make you very popular.

To influence

Another (and even less noble) reason for certain employees to gossip is to influence others and to manipulate their colleagues' opinions. Beersma & Van Kleef (2012) explain: "Person A tries to get some kind of advantage over person C, by trying to convince person B to revise his or her opinion about person C."

Nguyen (26), a sales executive at a large hotel in Vietnam, describes how two of her managers competed with each other and tried to rally the other employees to their side. "In my Sales office, there are six people working together: one manager, two senior executives, and three junior executives, including me. Those two senior executives, Hanh and Truc, don't get along well with one another. I would say there has been 'invisible hatred' between them. Hanh and Truc are rivals and usually compete against each other in terms of working performance. I remember there was one time when Truc made some minor mistakes and Hanh took a screenshot and sent it to me privately and started to say bad things about Truc: 'Nguyen, I couldn't count how many mistakes she made so far. Do you think this is acceptable?'" Hanh's gossiping started to backfire as Nguyen started to feel more sympathy for Truc. "Several people started to gossip about Hanh's personality and attitudes. After every weekly meeting, we would talk about how Hanh acted and behaved as if she was superior to everybody else." As there were employees on Hanh's side as well, this type of rivalry ended up dividing her team. "I really think this is an unhealthy competition within our department," Nguyen admits. "I think gossip can sometimes create some sort of entertainment and release stress. But gossip can also be toxic if someone makes use of it to say bad things about someone else in order to make themselves look better than others."

Kurland & Pelled (2000) claim that gossip plays a fundamental role in influencing others, in order to gain power at work. The authors define power as "the ability to exert one's will, influencing others to do things that they would not otherwise do." They distinguish between four types of power and influence a gossiper may have: coercive, reward, expert, and referent power.

Coercive power is when person A believes that person B has the power to punish him or her. So, in a work setting, negative gossip will enhance the gossiper's coercive power over his/her listeners. When listening to a colleague (person B) bad-mouthing Paul, we (person A) may, deep down, feel that the gossiper may punish us, too, at some point. We respect the gossiper for having this information about Paul but fear her at the same time.

Reward power is when person B perceives that person A has control over "valued outcomes." Hence, person A has a reward power over person B, and when a gossiper (person A) shares something positive about Paul, the listener (person B) may believe that the gossiper will also eventually spread positive information about him, too. The gossiper here has reward power.

With expert power, a gossiper has relevant knowledge about persons in the organization and a good position within their network, which gives them some authority and power over their listeners. Referent power refers to person's B desire to be associated with person A.

As we see here, gossip may be used to influence in a variety of ways. When gossip seeks to influence by destroying the reputation of an absent third party, it is usually for selfish or self-serving reasons. Needless to say, this can quickly backfire.

Researching gossip: Quantitative studies

In my article 'Researching the mechanisms of gossip in organizations: From fly on the wall to fly in the soup' (Darmon, 2018), I explore what would be the best research method to use when dealing with a sensitive topic such as gossip. What are the ethical issues that come up?

Many of the academic studies on gossip are quantitative, where researchers break down the notion of gossip into finite variables or categories. One study (Kurland & Pelled, 2000) distinguishes between three types of gossip: sign, credibility, or work relatedness. Other researchers (Martinescu et al., 2014) broke down topics of gossip into several categories: appearance, personality, peculiarities, or competence. Who we gossip with (Wittek & Wielers, 1998), why we gossip (Martinescu et al., 2014), the functions of gossip (Baumeister et al., 2004; Beersma & Van Kleef, 2012) were all broken down into measurable and operationalizable variables.

Moreover, the majority of these quantitative studies use questionnaires in which participants are anonymous. One study (Peters & Kashima, 2015), for instance, asked 206 university students to fill in an anonymous online questionnaire, responding to gossip scenarios using a seven-point Likert scale. Another (Dijkstra et al., 2014) sent a survey to 97 Dutch policemen to study how they gossip about their managers. Yet another (Martinescu et al., 2014) had 183 undergraduate students complete an online survey. Similarly, others (Farley, 2011; Cole & Scrivener, 2013) asked (mainly) university students to fill out a questionnaire. In all of these cases, participation was kept anonymous and/or confidential. Therefore, the researchers did not have to worry about potentially harming their participants. They could stay in the background and not risk influencing the research process. Data were more easily collected and correlations were neatly drawn. Because quantitative studies avoid many ethical pitfalls, I found them particularly tempting to use.

But, while these variables give some insight as to people's general attitudes towards gossip, I find that they do not offer much depth as to what really goes on in an organization. By taking such a distanced view, these studies often do not provide enough insight into the dynamics, the details, and the context of the gossiping process. As Alvesson (2003) noted, in many quantitative studies, "acts, practices, relations, feelings and cognitions are totally lost to the correlation of variables." Whereas a study can conclude that negative gossipers are perceived less favorably than positive gossipers, it does not give much nuance as to the type of negative gossip they are engaging in. Saying that someone is bad at her job, for example, is quite different than saying that she is ugly and smells, yet they are both lumped under the category of negative gossip. Context, nuances, and emotions are lost.

After examining some of the quantitative studies done on gossip in organizations, Van Iterson et al. (2011) also observed that when taken out of context and scrutinized, "the uniqueness and authenticity" of gossip easily gets lost, and in the end, becomes "rather meaningless."

Specific triggers

I often wondered: is there a specific moment, a sudden itch, that makes it irresistible for us to spill the tea? Are there also reasons that make people decide *not* to gossip? By understanding these triggers, we can then become more effective at limiting it or, at least, controlling it.

When you walk into a room where you do not know anybody, it is likely you will not be very interested in gossip about anyone specifically. But if you stay there long enough, you probably will. I have often wondered when exactly that turning point would be. I had a great opportunity to find out when I started doing research on gossip at my university. As a first step, I wanted to study how people talk about their colleagues and managers when undergoing a change. Thanks to my research group, I was invited to observe such a process taking place at another department at my university, where they were trying to implement a new curriculum. The only people I knew in this department were a couple of colleagues from my research group (who were also on the steering committee of the curriculum project).

Since I didn't know the other colleagues at all, I was oblivious to their internal politics and didn't feel the need to gossip about anyone. Honestly, I didn't really care enough to want to find out the gossip on anyone there. I started interviewing a few people and they quite openly told me what they thought of the change process. Some expressed criticism towards the managers, while the managers criticized some of the colleagues who were resisting the change. I very quickly felt that I was gaining power as I became one of those in the know. The more I heard stories, the more I became interested in the various colleagues, purely out of curiosity. But it didn't take too long for things to change. I suddenly had the feeling that some of the colleagues from my research group were becoming a bit hostile towards me. And indeed, a few days later, I received an email from one of the managers asking me to put my research on hold, claiming that my research design was not helping their process move forward.

I had no idea how they came to hold that idea. Were they talking to my colleagues from the research group? I suddenly felt like I (and my research) had become the object of gossip. I was also disappointed to have been put on hold. Despite the fact that I had vowed not to gossip about the managers or any of the participants, I could hardly resist the urge, and I discussed some of my experiences with a colleague from the research group. I wanted to find out whether he had heard anything from our colleagues. Did he think that one of them could have been causing my setbacks? What did he think of some of the participants of the project? The more insecure I felt, the greater my urge to gossip (Darmon, 2018).

I also felt angry and let down, and, later on, when I reflected on the situation, I realized that these emotions most certainly triggered me to gossip.

According to Berger (2014), some of the triggers that particularly help loosen our lips (other than the common reasons for us to gossip that we just discussed) are emotion and arousing situations.

Emotion

Emotion is a key factor that will determine whether we will spill the beans or not. Berger (2014) shows that especially those emotions that trigger activation or physiological arousal will also trigger the urge to share certain stories. "Arousal is a state of activation and readiness for action. [...] Physiological arousal motivates a fight-or-flight response that helps organisms catch food or flee from predators." Certain positive emotions, like awe, excitement, and humor, provoke high arousal, whereas contentment induces low arousal. Therefore, if you share a story about people who are happy and have no worries, it will likely not be considered extremely interesting to share. "When people are content, they relax. Their heart rates slow, and their blood pressure decreases. They're happy but they don't particularly feel like *doing* anything." However, if one of your colleagues does something awe inspiring or gets a promotion against all odds, you will most likely want to share the story of it with others.

Certain negative emotions like sadness are low arousal and decrease sharing. Others, like anger and anxiety, have the opposite effect. I still remember sitting in a restaurant with a group of friends. The food took two hours to come, and when my turn to be served finally came, just as all my friends were finishing their meals, without apologizing, the waiter said: "We don't have your fish and chips anymore. We ran out." I was furious and had a strong urge to write a scathing review online. (I didn't, but certainly gossiped about the horrible waiter with quite a few friends.)

Another study (Rooks et al., 2011) found that the first reason that people spread negative gossip is when they feel they are treated badly or unfairly—it's an emotional response. Employees' or suppliers' fear of negative gossip can be a powerful tool, as it "is a way of maintaining the sanctioning system and to harm the reputation of the cheating partner."

When you have a bad experience with your manager, or a management decision frustrates you or causes anxiety, you will most certainly be tempted to gossip.

Arousing situations

Berger observes that when people find themselves in arousing situations, they are prone to overshare, and to disclose more than they should. In the Hollywood romantic comedy *Can You Keep a Secret?* (2019), based on the Sophie Kinsella novel with the same title, Emma Corrigan (Alexandra Daddario) is a New York junior marketing representative who works for an organic food company. After botching a sales deal in Chicago, she gets drunk on the flight back to New York. The plane suddenly hits turbulent patches, and Emma thinks they are going to crash. She turns to the handsome man sitting next to her, and she starts talking about her work and personal problems and even spills some of her secrets to him.

One arousing situation that is particularly conducive to oversharing is pillow talk. In the Spanish series *Money Heist* (*La Casa de Papel*), a group of thieves led by 'the Professor' (Álvaro Morte) are orchestrating a massive heist at the Bank of Spain. At one point, things go awry, and the Professor wonders how the information leaked. Maybe there was a mole among them? To which Lisbon (his lover, played by Itziar Ituño) points out that the leak probably happened because of pillow talk. "People talk in bed," she sighs. "Including you. That's what people do. They open up in bed and reveal secrets that put people's lives in danger. Your brother did that, you did that, and so did I." Another reason to think twice before starting an affair at work!

How gossiping affects you

When we are just about to share a very juicy piece of gossip, our brains receive a hit of dopamine, a substance that gives us a high and makes us feel good. Dopamine is also extremely addictive. This, according to Andreas Wismeijer (2020) from Tilburg University, explains why we love to gossip and can't help ourselves from joining in.

But have you ever had the feeling that you spoke too much? That you said the wrong thing? That if you could take everything back that you've blurted out over those after work drinks, you certainly would?

Cole & Scrivener (2013) have studied how people felt right after a gossip session. They found that gossipers suffered from a lower self-esteem right after giving negative gossip about a target person they did not know well. When they gave positive gossip, their self-esteem did not change. In a second study, the authors asked their subjects to gossip positively and negatively about someone they knew, and they found that regardless of the nature of the gossip, the subjects felt less good about themselves right after the session. So why do we do it if it tends to make us feel bad? The researchers believe that despite the negative consequences, people still can't keep themselves from gossiping; the initial bonding opportunity they share with their listeners at that moment is much greater than any thoughts about potential negative feelings.

Similarly, other researchers (Spacks, cited in Foster, 2004) observe that few people gossip without guilt. "It seems that at times gossip generates as much guilt as its production simultaneously relieves."

Jessica (42), a manager at a large German food chain, explains that the initial high she feels right after having gossiped quickly turns into a darker emotion. "There was once this new guy who worked insanely slowly. I explained some stuff already three times, but he still didn't get it. Every time I explained something to him, he would just hit me with a 'WOW.' A colleague and I liked to laugh about it. In the beginning, it felt good, but then I realized that it's also not good. To gossip with ease is not right and my colleague learned that, too. Of course, you have to get rid of some of the negative thoughts, but it can get damaging."

Sometimes the negative and guilt feelings come up later, when we find out more about the object of gossip. Sofia (49), who works in the human resources department at a German pharmaceutical company, recalls:

> I once had a colleague that nobody really liked and everyone always talked badly about him, because he was always in such a bad mood every day. He was often rude and disrespectful towards his co-workers and just nobody could really deal with his attitude. I did understand that some employees were really annoyed with him, because he wasn't very cooperative with anyone.
>
> Several times, people came up to me and just started bad-mouthing him and how they cannot deal with him and his way of working and I did understand. I myself even got to a point where I couldn't stand it anymore and couldn't help but let my frustration out by talking to others about it. So, one time I came up to him and we had a conversation about some things he was in charge of and suddenly he burst into tears. When I asked what was wrong, he explained to me that he has been going through a tough divorce which is also the reason why he is not cooperating with anyone properly. He even apologized for not treating his co-workers nicely, but that he just had to let out his frustration somewhere. I then felt super bad about gossiping and badmouthing him. You never really know what someone is going through or what's going on in someone's personal life.

Studies show just how addictive gossip can be and the physiological effect it has on our brains. But while it feels good to vent and let out steam, the good feelings we gain from gossiping and complaining are short lived. Since these highs are addictive, we are tempted to keep coming back for more and gossip even more. "Like just about all addictions, we're feeding the spin of a destructive, never-ending cycle. The release of pressure—the good feeling—is ephemeral. In fact, the more we complain, the more likely the frustration, over time, will increase," Bregman (2018) explains.

Sometimes, the guilt feelings and negative emotions we experience are strong enough to keep us from gossiping. But there are even more important reasons that may keep us from spilling the tea.

What triggers people not to gossip?

A gossip goes about telling secrets, but one who is trustworthy in spirit keeps a confidence.
—Proverbs 11:13, cited in Capps, 2012

Researchers (Giardini & Wittek, 2019b) have explored the reasons why people do *not* gossip. By examining why people choose to keep information to themselves rather than sharing it, the authors hoped to gain more insights into "individual motives, group dynamics, and collective behaviors," and in this way to better understand why people do gossip.

Giardini & Wittek use goal-framing theory to understand what motivates people to refrain from gossiping. Goal-framing theory explores human motives and how they apply to "norm conforming behavior, and to the conditions favoring it." According to this theory, human behavior is goal directed, and only one goal can be salient, or prominent, at any given moment. This goal, then, determines which action will be taken at that specific moment. Although goal theory is not a theory of gossip in itself, "it can be fruitfully applied to disentangling the motivations behind gossip as a conscious and purposeful decision."

Giardini & Wittek describe three main frames: the hedonic goal frame, the gain goal frame, and the normative goal frame. While one frame can be more prominent than the others at a given moment, they are often interlinked, either in conflict or in combination.

The hedonic goal frame. The main goal here is to "feel better right now." As we have seen, gossiping can provide a lot of pleasure at the moment we do it. "*Schadenfreude*, smugness, a feeling of power, titillation, catharsis, and solving mysteries" are examples of such pleasures. Feelings of bonding and of belonging also make us feel better right now. When this happens, the hedonic goal frame is more salient than the others and is at the forefront.

The gain goal frame. The main goal here is "to guard and improve one's resources." As we previously discussed, another strong motivation to gossip is "to establish and maintain alliances with other group members who might be important sources of support against potential future threats, in particular from others." This action builds trust, and at the same time, brings on pleasure (which also makes the hedonic goal frame more prominent).

The normative goal frame. The most important goal here is "to act appropriately." This frame is sometimes aligned with the others, and in this case, reinforces the act of gossiping. If Marc gossips about Joe's bad behavior at work to protect his colleagues, he will act appropriately while reaping the benefits of creating a stronger alliance with his colleagues, which, in turn, will provide him with a lot of pleasure. The normative goal frame will reinforce the hedonic and gain goal frames.

However, "in situations where background goals are at odds with the foreground goal, the increasing prominence of the former goal weakens the latter ones, which may eventually lead to a frame switch in which the most salient background goal replaces the foreground goal." If Marc feels strongly that people should not talk behind other people's backs (or if that rule is an implicit part of the corporate culture), the normative goal frame will become more salient, and push the other goal frames into the background. For that reason, Marc may decide not to share the gossip about his colleague. Nevertheless, the normative goal could be to warn and protect a colleague about Joe's bad behavior. But Marc may realize that sharing such negative gossip has the potential of damaging his reputation with other colleagues (thus bringing the gain goal frame into the foreground and pushing the normative frame into the background). Of course, context has a lot to do with which goal frame becomes most salient. People's individual moral values and cultures will play a huge role as to which frame is pushed to the foreground.

Using goal-framing theory, Giardini & Wittek (2019b) argue that there are many strong reasons why people choose to keep their mouths shut. Although gossip is often motivated by a hedonic goal, it is easily hampered by a gain or normative goal. Both of these frames give us strong reasons that motivate us to keep our lips sealed.

Salient gain goal frame

If the gain goal frame is salient, competition is often at the forefront. When two employees in an organization compete for the same rewards (such as a bonus or a permanent contract that can only go to one of them), they will tend to not share gossip with each other. Let's say Joe and Sue are fairly new hires in their company. If Joe finds out something about his manager or a client, he may feel that he has an advantage over Sue, and he will not want to share this strategic information with her. Hence, his lips will be sealed.

A gossiper may also decide to refrain from sharing juicy information about a third party if they depend on this third party. If Joe depends on Mary to get his projects done (or if Mary often helps him or gives him advice), he may refrain from bad-mouthing her. If Mary is in a position of power and could find out that Joe spoke ill of her, she would likely sanction him, which would have a negative effect on Joe's work. As the authors observe: "The possibility for future retaliatory action from the third party may be sufficiently threatening to deter a potential sender from spreading the incriminating information to others." Take the case of former Hollywood film producer and convicted sex offender Harvey Weinstein. The authors explain that he got away with sexual harassment for so long as he had such a powerful position in the movie industry. His employees were scared of spreading gossip about him for fear of losing their jobs.

Salient normative goal frame

When we want to fit in and adhere to certain social norms, the normative goal frame is often the most salient. When a gossiper has a good relationship with her listener, she may want to display exemplary behavior by not gossiping. Even though studies have shown that when two people have bonds of friendship and trust, gossip flows easily, in some cases the opposite is true. Let's say Sue and Mary have a good relation at work. Sue may think twice about bad-mouthing Joe, as she does not want Mary to perceive her as someone who talks behind other peoples' backs. Sue wants to show that she is trustworthy and would also not talk about Mary behind her back. The fear of a negative reaction from a listener can prevent many people from opening their mouths to begin with.

Moreover, if the absent third party is a friend, gossipers will often refrain from gossiping about them out of solidarity. If Sue and Joe are friends at work, Sue would not want to jeopardize Joe's reputation and friendship by talking about the mistakes he made on the project. Protecting our friends from harm is a strong social norm.

An even more important reason for potential gossipers to keep the lid on juicy gossip is if the listener and object of gossip are friends. Joe will not want to talk to Sue about Mary if he knows that the two are good friends. Not only would Joe risk facing disapproval from Sue, but he would also risk that Sue might warn Mary about his attempt to badmouth her. Therefore, Joe could easily harm his relationship with both Sue and Mary by gossiping. This reinforces the importance of paying attention to the informal alliances at work in order to avoid gaffes like Simon's (38).

Simon's first internship was with a publishing house in the Netherlands. He recounts: "I usually don't share gossip, and especially not in large crowds, but while having drinks with colleagues, people mentioned one of the teachers from my school. Since I had an opinion on the topic, I decided to share it, telling the colleagues that this teacher was considered a bum by the students, with little brain capacity, and that the female students avoid him because he seeks their attention in a rather unpleasant and inappropriate way. I hadn't spoken long, when suddenly one of the publishers stood up and announced in a heated tone that she was going to the bathroom and stormed to the back of the bar. I hadn't noticed, but several of my colleagues wore grins on their faces as they saw the puzzled look on mine. 'What just happened?,' I asked, and, laughing out loud, one of my colleagues informed me that the insulting gossip I just shared was about the partner of the publisher who had just marched out."

Finding the *sweet spot of gossip*

Studies (Martinescu et al., 2014) show that while we may gossip (or refrain from gossiping) for a variety of reasons, some are more noble than others.

Typically, when gossip can serve the interests of the group as a whole, research shows it is considered to be "good gossip." When people gossip to warn and protect someone from harm's way, or to promote and enforce certain norms "for the good of others," they are gossiping well. In such cases, gossip is a virtue, Robinson (2016) claims.

Amy (19), who comes from Hong Kong, was working in a large furniture store in the Netherlands. "During my first day at work, my manager warned me to be careful about another manager from a different department. Because he's 'you know what,' he said. Others also told me that he's kind of flirty with girls, and people just kept telling me these stories." Did Amy perceive her manager badly for sharing this with her? "I'm really happy that he warned me," she says.

In the wake of the #MeToo movement, Natalie Portman's advice to women in Hollywood has been "Gossip well!" She emphasizes the importance of "spilling the tea" when necessary. In cases of sexual harassment, gossiping about a sleazy boss can

empower and protect potential victims. Keeping your mouth shut about something like that would certainly reflect badly on you (as we have seen time and time again after numerous #MeToo cases).

Also, employees who revert to gossip to gather information, to vent, or simply to entertain, will not be judged too harshly.

But people who gossip to influence, to compete, or to push forward a hidden agenda will be perceived very poorly (Beersma & Van Kleef, 2008; Wilson et al., 2000).

Janet (35), a British consultant, had just started a new job at a large multinational in the Netherlands. She describes how her manager's gossip backfired, and how her opinion of him drastically changed: "I had just started this new assignment, when the external communications manager briefed me about a variety of colleagues that I would soon have to work with. This manager was very harsh about one of them, Olivia, who is Chinese. He told me that nobody could understand her, and that she was unwilling to accept feedback—basically, he said that she was very arrogant and a difficult person to work with. So, I was quite apprehensive when I met Olivia, wondering how our work relation would be. When I actually did speak to her, I was really surprised, as Olivia was actually very nice and receptive. She admitted that her English wasn't very good, and that she needed to work on it. Afterwards, I realized that I did not have a bad opinion of Olivia at all, but rather, of the manager. He suddenly seemed untrustworthy to me, and I couldn't help wonder what his reasons were for trashing her."

How could the manager have gossiped in a better way? "If he had said: 'This was my experience with her' and 'I felt that she was not receptive to my feedback,' that would have given the impression that it was just his experience," Janet explains. "It wouldn't have had such a negative impact on my opinion of Olivia."

Rosnow & Fine (cited in Capps, 2012) observe: "In the medical community there is gossip that is considered proper and gossip that is considered improper; proper gossip is that indulged in by all MDs, which preserves the status of the profession; improper gossip aims at raising the teller's self-esteem at the expense of his professional peers." The authors stress that the "etiquette of what is proper and improper in gossiping is rigidly controlled."

This etiquette, though, is quite complex and not always palpable.

To come back to the study by De Gouveia et al. (2005) and the scenario where Brett was telling his colleagues that his boss was absent due to a death in the family, the type of information disclosed was not particularly private, scandalous, or embarrassing for the boss. Another case showed that if the reason for the boss' poor work performance had been a messy divorce, for instance, the gossiper would have been judged a lot more harshly for divulging that. The main issue here, the authors note, was the gossiper's intention. This is where they draw the line. If the information was disclosed "out of sympathy or sincere concern" or "out of maliciousness or with a hidden agenda as opposed to good intentions"—this changes the nature of the gossip entirely.

Context and tone are also important factors. "If, for example, someone exclaims in a worried tone: 'I wonder why the boss is late,' it can be deduced that the intention is one of concern, but if it is said in anger, the intention could be to cause harm."

As the study illustrates, the way in which gossipers are perceived is far from clear cut, as respondents have quite different interpretations of these scenarios.

It is not only important to consider the intention of the gossiper, but also that of the listener. Martinescu et al. (2014) use achievement goal theory and have distinguished between mastery and performance goals. Mastery goals are focused on developing competence through gaining knowledge and skills, whereas performance goals are focused on demonstrating competence by outperforming others. Whether employees have a mastery or performance goal orientation will influence the way they react to gossip they hear. If employees are genuinely interested in improving their skills, they will want to hear positive gossip and see it as an opportunity to learn. They will therefore not welcome negative gossip as readily. On the other hand, employees who are competitive and strive to outperform their peers will find reassurance in negative gossip, as it has a self-promotion value. If this becomes obvious, though, their reputation will take a serious blow.

When discussing a clip from *The Devil Wears Prada* in class, most of my students could understand why Emily and Serena were gossiping about Andy. She wasn't a very good employee, and her blunders were worth sharing. But after her makeover and flamboyant entrance into the office, Serena says to Andy, "You look good."

Emily sighs in disapproval, disgusted.

"What? She does," Serena insists.

"Oh, shut up, Serena!" she scoffs.

My students all said they found Emily 'bitchy.' She was clearly a lot more competitive and conniving than her colleague. While they didn't judge Serena poorly (as it was clear she was only gossiping because Andy didn't fit in at work), they did perceive Emily a lot more negatively.

According to Giardini & Wittek (2019a), gossipers share negative information (and consequently damage someone's reputation) either out of mutualism or altruism. When gossip profits both gossiper and receiver, it is called mutualism, and when it mainly benefits the receiver or the greater good, it is called altruism. When it is clear that someone gossips for altruistic reasons (and by doing so, puts their reputation at risk), listeners will value them more. But it is a fine line, and a gossiper's reputation can easily be damaged even when their intentions are good.

We have also seen that several factors, like powerful emotions and arousing situations can easily trigger us to spill the beans. But, as we have discussed, there are many reasons for us to refrain from gossiping. Obeying certain social norms, protecting our interests, and avoiding harming our relationships are such incentives. Gossiping or spreading rumors can be severely sanctioned, so many people think twice before opening their mouths.

In terms of reaching the sweet spot of gossip, Robinson (2016) suggests:

> Achieving one's goals can be severely hampered by a wide variety of norm violators, including liars, cheats, bullies, and braggarts. It takes a kind of social intelligence to perceive when and know how to inhibit these norm violations that makes it harder for one to achieve one's goals. Gossiping all the time about any and every norm violation would not be strategically wise. One must gossip at the right time, to the right person, about the right person, and about the right norms. For instance, if I judge that Barry's constant bragging is highly unlikely to ever hamper my goals or those of others I care about, then I generally shouldn't gossip about that person. Alternately, if Dakota's dishonesty seems likely to threaten my achieving a life goal (either directly or indirectly), then strategically gossiping is prudent.

In conclusion, make sure that you are gossiping strategically and for the right reasons. Furthermore, always question the motives of a colleague spilling the dirt on someone else. Are they sharing juicy gossip to help you understand the corporate culture or to give you a heads up? Or do they have darker, ulterior motives?

Tips for managers

1. Use gossip to learn about your employees' concerns.
If they play their cards well, managers can channel gossip in a good way. They could, for instance, use it to test decisions. How will their employees feel about it? They could find out before implementing a new policy.

Burke & Wise (2003) note that bosses could also use gossip as a way to become familiar with their employees' "wishes, expectations, worries and ideas. When management learns to anticipate employees' reactions, it avoids rumors by eliminating potentially misunderstood communication." Managers can also learn a lot from listening to the informal network and gain insights as to how they could hold meetings more effectively, or manage projects and administrative processes in a better way.

When there is a lot of gossip in an organization, Waddington (2012) claims, it is often a sign that there are bigger problems or issues. For that reason, managers could use gossip as a warning system to predict potential disasters and prevent problems from snowballing.

2. Be aware of employees' emotions.
When managers get wind that employees may be angry about certain decisions, they may want to address these before the gossip spreads and eventually turns into harmful rumors. When words like 'pissed off,' 'angry,' or 'mad' surface, this could indicate the likelihood that negative gossip is spreading. It is therefore of upmost importance to address these emotions early, Berger warns.

Libby (52) is British and works in a large international organization in the Netherlands. She reveals: "There was a time when my colleagues and I used to gossip about how our managers were the only ones getting compliments for our project, whereas my team and I were the ones who had done most of the work. So, we talked about how we felt undervalued and unappreciated. But it turned out that two members of the management team got wind of the gossip and managed to turn the situation around. They contacted the partners abroad who were working with us on the project and told them that we also deserved their praise. We were quite unexpectedly surprised and happy with how our management dealt with this!" This certainly fixed the problem quickly and nipped the gossip in the bud before it could turn ugly.

3. Use the power of bonding.

During a workshop about gossip that I gave in Copenhagen, one of the participants described how his sergeant in the navy found a strategic way to use gossip to his advantage. "In the beginning, he was purposefully nasty and rude with everyone in our team. He knew that we would get together and complain about him. Actually, the fact that we all had something to complain about gave us something in common from the start and really helped us bond. It was actually a great team-building exercise!"

While this may seem like a brave strategy, it is also quite risky. Several managers participating in my workshop shook their heads disapprovingly.

"It may work in the beginning," one participant said, "but it will backfire in the end. People will still wind up leaving the organization if their manager treats them badly. The friendships with colleagues will not be strong enough to outweigh the harm done by a toxic manager."

The key then, would be to not do this for a very long period of time. The soldiers working under the sergeant eventually figured out that this was a strategy, since they could later talk about it lightly.

When employees have a common enemy or problem, it helps them bond and even come to terms with disagreement. In the series *Designated Survivor*, this technique is used when the court is having an intense debate about what to do with a Confederate statue. Should the statue be kept as it represents history or is it hard-core racism? As the debate gets more and more heated and hostile, newly appointed Counsel Kendra Daynes (Zoe McLellan) brings in the political director, Lyor Boone (Paulo Costanzo) to address the issue. He tells the room that they've all profited from slavery and the 'Southern legacy,' which nearly causes a riot. Later on, President Kirkman (Kiefer Sutherland) asks Kendra how they all managed to come to an agreement. She says proudly: "I unified them by giving them a common figure to hate." To which Kirkman replies, "Sadly, I'm starting to realize that that's one of the great secrets of good governance."

So, when managers present employees with a common problem, it may give them something good or useful to gossip about and allow them to bond.

4. Tell everyone or no one.
When important decisions need to be communicated, such as restructuring and pension cuts, for instance, De Gouveia et al. (2005) advise the company to "avoid telling groups of people at a time and rather communicate them to all employees simultaneously. This 'tell everyone or tell no one' policy ensures that information is not misconstrued and does not develop into harmful gossip." Such a strategy is good to follow if you want to reduce the amount of gossip that is sure to occur in these types of situations.

5. Provide coaching and/or a platform for employees to voice concerns.
Another way to reduce the spread of gossip is for management to provide coaching to their employees. Coaching may provide a platform where employees can voice their concerns, frustrations, and grievances. Instead of venting these all over the office, they would do so to one main person, the coach.

Tips for employees

1. Learn how to listen.
An essential skill to brush up on is the art of listening. Kate Murphy (2019) observes in her book *You're Not Listening: What You're Missing and Why It Matters* that people listen less and less.

People worry more about selling themselves and making a good impression on others. But by listening, especially to gossip, you not only create stronger bonds and friendships with others, but you also learn a lot about the (hidden) rules of a culture or an organization.

2. Be selective when gossiping.
There is an optimal amount one should gossip. You may be tempted to share a juicy tidbit of information, but know that you may not come across as very trustworthy. Scarcity is important. It's better to choose a few select allies to gossip with, rather than sharing with everyone at work.

3. Accept that it takes time to become part of the in-group.
If you start a new job, it is wise to tread lightly. Lennie (55) had recently started a new job as a primary school teacher in a small rural community in the Netherlands. "When I started the job, I certainly wasn't the colleague who gossiped about other colleagues," she explains. "I am the one who listened and observed how things were. I noticed that if I shared something, my colleagues looked at me like I was an elephant that just stormed into the room. They looked at me, like, 'hello, who are you??'" Lennie realized that the best strategy was to keep a low profile, and she simply kept her eyes and ears open. As a newcomer, and especially because she started off as a substitute teacher, Lennie accepted that she had little power and credibility, at least in the beginning. Sure enough, it takes time to build trust. And even longer to become a part of the in-group.

4. Be mindful of reciprocity!
When it comes to gossip, we often have the feeling that the more interesting information we are willing to dish out, the more likely we will get interesting information in return. Or that if someone shares something juicy with us, we can trust them, and hence, should reciprocate. But this type of thinking can lead to trouble.

Eva (45), French and an employee at a Dutch NGO, learned this the hard way.

> Once, a colleague that I did not know too well confided to me that she really hated the manager. She told me he was an incompetent idiot who also gave her a poor performance review. I felt flattered that she shared this with me, and I also wanted to give something in return. So, I started to gossip negatively about the manager, without thinking too much about the consequences. Only in hindsight did I begin to wonder whether it was so smart to have trusted this colleague. She ended up using the information I gave her to help her case and in so doing, harmed me. I kicked myself later down the road, but the reason I gossiped with her was to reciprocate and gain her trust and friendship.

In this case, reciprocity can be a tricky thing. You need it to gain trust, but can also get burned if you confide in the wrong people. Divulging the right amount of information, and doing it gradually, is key.

According to Murphy (2019), there are certain guidelines to follow. People who don't know each other so well usually start off by revealing small things that are not too sensitive and that would not cause too much harm if they happened to leak. As they get to know each other better, and show they are trustworthy, they will gradually reveal more and more sensitive information, and therefore, more precious and worthy gossip over time. Building such a relationship and trust takes time, and it's certainly wise not to share too much, too quickly.

5.   Be careful when you find yourself in arousing situations.
"Be careful the next time you step off the treadmill, barely avoid a car accident, or experience a turbulent plane ride," Berger warns in his book *Contagious* (2013). Be aware that in such places and situations, we most certainly will have the unfortunate tendency to overshare. Being aware of this can make us more cautious. To

come back to Emma in *Can You Keep a Secret?*, little did she know that the nice man sitting next to her on the plane (to whom she confided in when she thought they were going to crash) would be her future boss!

6. Don't believe everything you hear. Allow yourself to make up your own mind.

Even though it is normal, and sometimes good to do, trying to get information about a new employee or colleague can also backfire. Daniel (45) is an IT architect at a Hungarian bank. "The information that comes to you about a new employee can be distorted, because everyone has a subjective opinion about that person. Previously, I also did that if a new employee came in," he reveals. "I also asked around if someone could give me information about them. You haven't even met him/her, but you already had a picture of that person. It can be a positive or a negative prejudice. I found that it was sometimes best to take the time to make my own opinions!"

While gossip can be a powerful transmitter of important information and corporate culture, how do we know whether it is true? Can you trust what you hear at the watercooler? What about nasty rumors that sometimes fly around, discrediting certain employees or management decisions?

2. Credibility

A question that kept coming up during my research was: How do you know whether something you hear in the hallway is true? Is it a rumor? Is it gossip? What is the difference between the two? Where do gossip and rumor stand in the larger picture of information disorder? We will discuss how a piece of juicy gossip can easily morph into misinformation or disinformation, depending on the gossiper's intention. This chapter also examines the different types of rumors, how they are transmitted and spread, and the havoc such rumors can wreak.

The difference between gossip, rumors, and other types of information disorders

> *Someone must have been spreading rumors against Josef K., for one morning, without having done anything wrong, he was arrested.*
> —Franz Kafka, *The Trial*

The terms 'gossip' and 'rumor' are often used interchangeably. However, there is a big difference between the two, especially when it comes to credibility. Rumors are typically speculative and unsubstantiated, whereas gossip tends to be a lot more accurate, as the core message usually remains intact as it is being transmitted.

If I observe that Joe, one of my colleagues, is flirting with a waitress at the bar, and I tell this to one of my friends the next day, I would be gossiping. Most likely, my account of what happened is fairly accurate. I've seen it firsthand, and although you could accuse me of exaggerating Joe's flirting, my account would probably still be fairly close to the truth. However, if my friend Anne then tells this story to other people, she would be spreading rumors, as she didn't actually see Joe's flirting with her own eyes. The likelihood that she could exaggerate my story, add her own interpretations and twists to it, would be a lot stronger. After a few rounds, the story may even be that Joe is having a full-blown affair!

Gossipers usually give a lot of firsthand testimony: what happened to them, what they saw, what they heard. No firsthand account of an event is ever a rumor, although it may later turn into one.

Several academics (Ayim, 1994; Foster, 2004) also note that rumors cover a wider range of topics, such as events, objects, and people, whereas gossip is predominantly about people.

Rumors tend to be more public and widespread than gossip, which usually occurs in a more private and intimate setting. According to psychologist Robin Dunbar (2004), only 3-4% of gossip is actually harmful. Most people gossip about problems they have with others, or about the status of members from their network, or from their community. Rumors often tend to be a lot more nasty. And a lot less accurate.

When looking at the bigger picture, we may ask ourselves where do gossip and rumor fit into the larger landscape of misinformation, disinformation, and malinformation?

To begin with, it is important to make a clear distinction between the three (see figure 3). Claire Wardle (2019), in *Scientific American*, defines disinformation as content that "is intentionally false and designed to cause harm." Misinformation is false content that is shared by a person who does not realize that it is false. So, a message on Facebook or Twitter that may start out as disinformation, can turn into misinformation when unsuspecting users share it without realizing that it is false. Malinformation describes true information that is shared with the intent to cause harm. When hackers got access to Hillary Clinton's emails, for instance, and leaked certain details to the public, they used malinformation to damage her reputation and campaign.

The most effective disinformation always has an element of truth to it. The message is often true (or partly true), but taken out of context or misleading. Wardle explains that House Speaker Nancy Pelosi suffered from disinformation when a real video of

Figure 3   Categories of information disorder
Adapted by Jen Christiansen from Wardle & Derakhshan (2017)

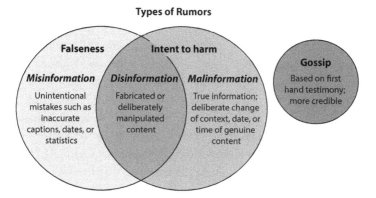

her was slowed down and uploaded to the internet, giving viewers the impression that Pelosi was slurring her words, as if she were drunk. Several people saw it and shared it with their networks. The video spread and was also picked up by mainstream media. Needless to say, Pelosi's reputation was harmed. With deepfake technology becoming more and more sophisticated, recognizing false information is becoming increasingly difficult.

Misinformation, disinformation, and malinformation all intersect (see figure 3). And rumors fit into all three of these categories. The intention to harm (or not) is a distinguishing factor, but all types of rumors tend to be inaccurate. Gossip, in this landscape, is a lot more noble and, generally, more reliable.

Types of rumors

Michelson & Mouly (2000) have also made more specific distinctions between several types of rumors. The pipe dream/wish fulfillment rumors, anticipatory rumors, and anxiety rumors share certain similarities with gossip, as they too strive to make sense of ambiguous situations. Others, such as aggressive rumors and wedge-driving rumors, have a much darker side to them.

The pipe dream/wish fulfillment rumors

These types of rumors express the hopes of those who circulate them. One of my colleagues was complaining to me how many of his students easily spread false information. "It's weird," he exclaimed over coffee. "I told my students that the deadline for my assignment is on such and such a date. I wrote it on the lecture slides, I put it in the course manual, and told them several times in class. But, I regularly get students who ask me whether there has been an extension. 'I heard that the deadline's been moved,' they tell me. Where on earth did they get such an idea?" This is a typical example of a pipe dream/wish fulfillment rumor. Sometimes wishful thinking pushes someone to express their hopes, and after having circulated a little through the grapevine, it becomes a certainty to many students.

Anticipatory rumors

Anticipatory rumors tend to crop up as a result of poor communication. When a situation is ambiguous, employees will try to find the information themselves.

And when a story travels from one person to another, interpretations and speculation twist the facts. When your manager has been laid off, and you do not know who will be the replacement, rumors tend to flourish. All kinds of stories circulate as to why he was let go. Someone's interpretation ("I think he really screwed up with this project and the CEO was pissed"), may quickly become a fact after reaching the fourth person.

After he finished high school, Dylan (24) spent three years working in the marketing department at the German headquarters of an American multinational food, snack, and beverage corporation. "My direct manager there, she was evil," he says. "She kicked a lot of people out of the company by bullying them. I don't know why she did that. She was the highest manager so she was the one hiring them, but also bullying them out a short time afterwards. I think the problem was that all these women that came were younger and better looking, freshly out of university, and new in the company. At first it was always good and then afterwards, she started going around saying to others: 'she's a mess' or 'she's not doing her job right.' It happened at least four times while I was in the company. This can't be a coincidence!" Whereas Dylan is describing how his manager spread rumors as a way to discredit her employees, his account is also fraught with interpretation: that she is behaving in this way out of jealousy is his idea. Maybe she had other reasons? But, as this type of rumor travels around, interpretation and facts quickly intertwine, merge, and blur.

Anxiety rumors

When people are scared and feel threatened, they will be more likely to spread anxiety rumors. If an organization is planning to merge with another or is faced with a major change, for example, employees might not know how this will affect their jobs. This can cause anxiety and prompt rumors. "I heard there will be layoffs" or "there probably won't be enough budget for our project."

Berger (2014) confirms that rumors do flourish in times of conflict, crisis, and catastrophe, due to the generalized anxiety those situations induce.

In 2014, the Dutch newspaper *de Volkskrant* reported on rumors flying around that KLM, the Dutch Royal Airline, would have to scrap 7,500 jobs (Hotse Smit, 2014). This story spread through the media and many other newspapers published headlines such as "Air France swallows KLM" and "7,500 jobs will disappear at KLM." More and more newspapers and television stations picked up the story. Reinier Castelein, the head of the worker's union for KLM, denied these claims but he admitted that this reorganization was a possible scenario. "I've heard the rumor of this scenario so many times now, that I'm now starting to take it seriously." After a few days, the press admitted that these rumored layoffs (and especially the amount of 7,500 jobs) seemed to have "come from nowhere."

On a smaller scale, Heinrich (33), a manager at a large car manufacturer in Germany, explains: "A popular gossip topic at our office was the restructuring of our department which involved a thousand people. The rather low level of transparency sparked speculation and false information about the future setup and the people involved. We wondered whether there would be mergers and which people in which departments would be laid off, and whose job would be in jeopardy." After a while, when various opinions and theories start circulating, it is hard to distinguish between fact and fiction.

In a scene from the Netflix series *The Chair*, Professor Ji-Yoon Kim (Sandra Oh), the newly appointed chair of her English department at (fictional) Pembroke University, says to her teachers during a meeting: "I'm not going to sugarcoat this. We are in dire crisis. Enrollments are down by 30%. Our budget is being gutted. It feels like the sea is washing the ground out from under our feet." But she tries to encourage and inspire her staff: "In these unprecedented times, we have to prove that what we do in the classroom—modeling critical thinking, stressing the value of empathy—is more important than ever and has value to the public good." Suddenly the door flies opens and Joan, a very senior colleague, storms in. "They moved my office to the basement under the gym," she cries. Everyone gasps. "All my books, my ... my stuff, my drawers, dumped into these open carts that are sitting on the floor of the basement over there right now."

"Why would they do that?" someone asks.

"I heard a rumor," one of the colleagues says. "They're forcing everybody over 55 to take early retirement." Everyone starts to talk at the same time. "This is the beginning of the end," someone cries out, over the uproar.

"Okay, people. People, let's try not to panic," says Ji-Yoon.

"Well it's easy for you to say. You're 51," Joan scoffs.

"I'm 46," Ji Yoon replies, insulted, while an uncomfortable silence spreads over the room.

Even though there was some truth to the rumor (in that the dean wants to force some senior colleagues into retirement), the age limit came out of the blue. This scene is a perfect illustration of how fear and anxiety can give birth to unfounded rumors.

Allport & Postman (cited in Capps, 2012) explain: "Whenever there is social strain, false report grows virulent. In wartime, rumors sap morale and menace national safety by spreading needless alarm and by raising extravagant hopes."

This was very obvious during the Covid pandemic, when false information about vaccines and the government cropped up, paving the way for a variety of conspiracy theories. In politics, too, we can see that when there is distrust in government, people quickly try to make sense of events taking place.

Aggressive rumors

Some employees use rumors to push a hidden agenda, to get ahead, or to harm someone. When researchers and psychologists talk about gossip as workplace bullying and harassment, they are actually often referring to aggressive rumors that are used to damage the reputation of a co-worker.

Laura (55), the head of training at a large medical simulation company in Switzerland, recounts that when her CEO had a ski accident, one of her colleagues tried to use rumors to his advantage. "When our CEO had the accident, the information was not communicated very well. So, the story went from him having had a head injury, then, that he was sitting in a wheelchair and that he had open fractures. The whole company was afraid that he wouldn't be able to continue working. The VP Sales then used all of these rumors to strengthen his position and weaken all others. He would tell us that our CEO is very weak, and that he had to take over certain of the CEO's tasks." This VP Sales eventually got fired when all of this came to light.

Nevertheless, rumors can also be a powerful weapon. In *The Girl with the Dragon Tattoo* (2008), Stieg Larsson describes how Swedish journalist Mikael Blomkvist uses rumors to save his magazine *Millennium* from bankruptcy and fight his enemies. He and his team suspected that one of their employees was leaking important information to the enemy and dragging the magazine's reputation downwards, but nobody could prove it. So rather than confronting and firing the colleague, during a team meeting, Blomkvist concocted a plan: "It's important that Wennerstrom [his enemy] believes that *Millennium* is on the verge of collapse because I don't want him to start some sort of retaliation or get rid of the evidence which we mean to expose. [...] So, I want you to start squabbling among yourselves, complaining about me when Dahlman [the colleague under suspicion] is around. Don't exaggerate. Just give your natural bitchy selves full rein." Spreading disinformation was also a part of Blomkvist's strategy: "In a few weeks, we'll call a meeting to warn you about layoffs. You all know that it's a scam, and that the only one who is leaving is Dahlman. But start talking about looking for new jobs and say what a lousy reference it is to have *Millennium* on your CV."

"And you think that this game will end up saving *Millennium*?" one of the colleagues asked.

"I know it will. And Sonny, I want you to put together a fake report each month showing falling advertising sales and showing that the number of subscribers has also dropped."

"This sounds fun," Nilsson said. "Should we keep it internal here in the office, or should we leak it to other media, too?"

"Keep it internal. If the story shows up anywhere, we'll know who put it there. In a few months, if anyone asks us about it, we'll be able to tell them: you've been listening to baseless rumors and we've never considered closing *Millennium* down."

Not only does this strategy help them find the mole, but appearing weak in the enemy's eyes allowed them to get their facts straight and publish the story that proved that their enemy was indeed a crook that conducted illegal activities on a global scale.

Wedge-driving rumors

DiFonzo & Bordia (2007) claim that people often turn to this type of rumor when they feel that their individual or collective senses are threatened. To defend themselves, they will often turn to wedge-driving rumors.

If a boss ridicules or intimidates one of his employees, the latter can use rumors as a way to strike back. When people feel attacked in their sense of self or identity, they will do whatever it takes to defend themselves. The authors recall: "In a recent radio interview on the topic of rumor, one caller—angry at his boss—confessed to spreading a false rumor that his boss had herpes; the rumor lasted at least two years" (DiFonzo & Bordia, 2007).

Functions and characteristics of rumors

Certain rumors, such as the pipe dream, anticipatory, and anxiety rumors, have similar functions as gossip, and there often is a fine line between the two. Like gossip, these rumors tend to crop up "in contexts of ambiguity, danger or potential threat" and they function to help people make sense of these situations.

Like gossip, rumors also have the function to entertain. Capps (2012) explains how something can easily be exaggerated for the sake of telling a good story. "Whether the stories are true or not is less important. Not truth value, but entertainment value—their ability to delight, shock, or move us—is paramount." He describes how humorous gossip could quickly become untrue and turn into a rumor: "Suppose we are discussing our friend's Bob's secret affair with his boss, Rhonda. One of us says: 'What if Bob accidentally ran into his wife at the ski lodge some weekend when he's there with Rhonda?' And off our gossip goes with possible scenarios. We're not saying that he did or will do any of the things we are imagining—we're simply entertaining those ideas for the pleasure they bring."

Still, this can easily become a slippery slope, as interpretation and speculation are mistaken for truth. One of my students told me that there is a saying in Vietnamese: *Thêm mắm dặm muối*. This means: people want to copy an A, but when they paste the A, they paste it differently. They paste the A, plus add dramatic elements. Gossipers want to make their story more interesting and attractive, so that is why they do that.

As Berger (2014) notes, people like to look "interesting, funny and in-the-know" and for that reason don't hesitate to exaggerate things. One study claims that 60% of stories that are told are "distorted in one way or another."

According to DiFonzo & Bordia (2007), gossip and rumors are similar in that they may both be considered as commodities that people exchange for valued assets, and that rumors follow the same rules of reciprocity as gossip does.

Similarly to gossip, spreading rumors may also be considered a virtue in certain cases. In his study 'Character, caricature, and gossip,' Robinson (2016) claims that if rumors are used in order to promote and enforce certain norms, that is fine. If we exaggerate certain facts and someone's character traits to make our point (and therefore spread a rumor), this can still be justifiable. In fact, the author says we tend to do this all the time. Let's say that Paul called in sick one day, and you see him a few hours later, soaking up the sun on a terrace. You might say "Paul lied" about being sick. Or you might say "Paul is a liar." The first statement is true: Paul did lie. But saying that he is a liar gives the message that he does this regularly. Maybe Paul learned that his wife had a serious illness that morning, and that he was having a moment alone on the terrace?

Exaggerating such a character trait to describe Paul is a common fundamental attribution error, according to Robinson. We easily attribute traits to people to "explain all or almost all of the behavior that prompted the attributions." But to say something like "Paul is a liar" is generally false. If Paul never did lie, that would be bad gossip, as Paul's reputation would suffer. But if he did lie, and had done it several times, even though it would be an exaggeration to say that he is a liar, this type of rumor may still have a norm-enforcement type of function and, hence, be justifiable. Paul may be ostracized for a while and then adapt to the norm. In this case, more good than harm is done. Robinson compares such rumors to caricatures of people. "Instead of distorting physical features, they sketch distorted pictures of people's personalities. They magnify the frequency or power of character traits. Political cartoonists exaggerate, but in doing so point out to more important, less readily apparent truths."

Researchers (Kostera, cited in Jemielniak et al., 2018) argue that even when certain rumors are false, they can still be extremely valuable, as they are stories (with a beginning, middle, and end) that often convey a moral.

"According to our view, 'what really happened' is often incidental, while the stories that prevail carry true, or truer, meanings. Just like myths, they can be 'true' from the point of view of human experience and consciousness, and 'untrue' from the point of view of empirical history all at the same time." Therefore, even if the details of a rumor are false, its moral, or lesson taught, is what matters.

Jemielniak et al. argue that such fictional stories can help us truly understand management and organizations, as they often depict emotions and the real nature of relationships that are absent in more rational accounts of what takes place in the workplace.

While the storytelling techniques used in rumors may certainly be a powerful tool to understand organizations, there is a fine line between conveying important lessons about corporate cultures and harming individuals or bullying.

What makes gossip very different from rumors (and all other forms of information disorder) is the manner in which it is transmitted, as transmission is intimately linked to credibility.

Transmission and accuracy

Gossip always leads to poverty.
—Proverbs 14:23

False information—or rumors—can certainly spread very quickly and wreak havoc. This is illustrated in the novel *The Girl Who Takes an Eye for an Eye* (2017) by David Lagercrantz (part of Stieg

Larsson's *Millennium* series). At the end of the story, journalist Mikael Blomkvist writes a damning article, exposing a crime of magnitude, perpetrated decades ago against children of ethnic minorities and involving politicians in the highest of spheres. But something quickly gets in the way of his scoop: a stock market crash. What was unusual about this crash was that there was no apparent trigger for it. "The panic appeared out of nowhere and was self-sustaining. [...] Rumors and allegations raging, all too often gaining a foothold in the mainstream media."

The author continues: "There was talk of automated trading having run amok, about financial centers and media houses and websites having been hacked. But there were also reports that people were about to jump to their deaths from balconies and roofs. [...] News came pouring in from every direction, and not even a well-trained eye like Blomkvist's could tell the difference between what was true and what was fabricated. [...] The herd was already in motion and running for its life, although nobody knew who or what had frightened it."

Although this example may seem rather dramatic, it demonstrates how powerful rumors may be. But how is such a rumor triggered? How are both gossip and rumors transmitted and how do they spread?

The grapevine

To explore how rumors and gossip are transmitted, we must first examine the channel they use: the grapevine. A grapevine is defined as "an unofficial, informal way of getting information by hearing about it from someone who heard it from someone else" (*Cambridge Dictionary*). Several researchers (Ivancevich et al., 2008) describe the grapevine as the "speediest, most efficient channel of communication" in an organization.

Zoltan (52), a manager in a large financial services provider in Hungary, reveals: "At work, we know who the biggest gossipers are. It happened a few times that I wanted to pass some news, so I intentionally told the gossipers and I was sure that within the day everybody would know about it. It was a very efficient way of transmitting information!"

Most employees even consider the grapevine to be "a faster way to transfer information than sending it up the formal chain of command and waiting for a reply," according to Burke & Wise (2003). They also consider that the information transmitted via the grapevine is "more believable and reliable than formal top management communiqués."

Ivancevich et al. (2008) claim that at least 75% of the gossip that travels through the grapevine is said to be true. Certain managers even use this tool as a part of their communications plan, as an early warning about layoffs to come, giving an early hint about the bad news, before officially making an announcement. The grapevine allows managers to see how a new plan may be received before actually implementing it. In this way, the grapevine is a "bypassing mechanism" and is usually "a lot faster than the formal system it bypasses." Since it is face-to-face, the grapevine is quite flexible and transmits information quickly.

The authors point out, though, that while 75% of the information communicated through the grapevine may be accurate, 25% is not.

Credibility

As part of a project on fake news for one of her classes, one of my students, Tina, decided to conduct a social experiment. She would post something fake on Instagram (in an account available to her classmates only) and see how long it would take to travel. She considered saying that one of her teachers was having an affair, but luckily, decided against it, thinking it could harm the teacher in question. So, she went for something more innocuous. Tina posted a picture of her hand with a ring, with the caption: "I said yes!" Very quickly, she got messages from classmates congratulating her. After a few days, Tina started having second thoughts. "I felt like a liar," she told me. "I don't know if I'll be able to wait until next week to tell the truth during my presentation in class. I hope my classmates won't judge me too badly." Tina's rumor even came back to me. During the student Christmas party, one of her classmates came up to me and said: "Can you imagine? Tina is already engaged! She's only 20! That's so young. I'm 21, and still single."

"But you're so young. You have all the time in the world," one of her classmates comforted her. "I think it's a mistake to get engaged so quickly."

I realized how a fairly innocent rumor could start taking on a life of its own. Some people would very likely compare themselves to Tina, either judging her or envying her. Tina started to feel more and more uncomfortable by the whole situation and was wondering whether she would ever be able to take it back and return to the way things were. In the end, she told her classmates the truth during her presentation. A week later, she was relieved to find that nobody was angry with her. "People were shocked, and it definitely raised their awareness about the presence of fake news and misinformation. It feels great to not wear that ring anymore!" she wrote to me in an email.

In this case, the rumor was not very damaging. But it was interesting to see how quickly it spread. And how no one questioned the veracity of such a rumor.

Most of the time, we do not make the effort to verify claims that we hear. Or we wish to believe these claims, or we trust the source, and are therefore less inclined to question her claims. For this reason, several academics (DiFonza & Bordia, 2007) insist that the majority of rumors are false, or wildly exaggerated. Most people spreading rumors will start off with a warning statement along the lines of: "I'm not sure that this is true, but..." or "I heard...."

While rumors are usually untrue, Giardini (2012) has raised the question of how reliable is gossip, actually?

One study claims that the credibility of gossip is linked to two factors: deterrence and transmission. Anonymity is also an important distinguishing factor.

Deterrence

Generally, gossiping, and especially spreading rumors, was always considered a serious offence, according to McAndrew (2014). From the 1500s to the 1800s, gossipmongers (which, for some reason, seemed to be exclusively women) were severely punished. In Europe and colonial America, at that time, when such gossipers were caught, they were forced to wear a 'scold's bridle'—a heavy iron mask that included a flat piece of iron. This piece of iron was sometimes spiked and was pushed into the woman's mouth, over her tongue, so she could not talk. This punishment was approved by the Church and local authorities, and the husband was allowed to drag his wife around the village and subject her to ridicule and humiliation. Such gossipers were also punished by being strapped to a 'ducking stool,' a chair attached to a long beam, and were then plunged into a lake or pond. The amount of times dunked, and for how long, was directly proportional to the severity of the gossip. (As we will discuss in Chapter 4, the idea that it is mainly women who gossip, still clings on firmly today.)

Today, the punishment is different of course. If a gossiper is caught spreading false information, he could potentially experience social punishment such as exclusion, or getting fired or sued. For this reason, people think twice before spreading gossip, or, even worse, rumors. This is called deterrence.

In his crime novel *The Birdwatcher* (2016), taking place in a small town in Ireland, William Shaw describes how a gossiper is punished. Young Billy's dad had just been murdered, and it was the talk of the town. When Billy and his mom were at the butcher's one day, the butcher said:

> "I heard it's something to do with your husband, Mrs. M."
> Billy's mom pulled Billy out of the shop behind her. "Common gossip," she said. "I don't want to dignify them with my business." Even if it was only going to be half a dozen pork sausages and some bacon scraps.

As they walked home, Billy sensed that people were staring at them again, like they had done after his dad had been killed. That night they only had mashed potato and spaghetti hoops for tea, because mum had left the sausages behind in the shop.

Although she wanted to punish the butcher for gossiping, it's not clear whether Billy's mom was punishing herself more by leaving the sausages behind.

From the point of view of the gossiper, Anne (19), a student at a Dutch university, explains how she experienced such deterrence herself: "I remember when I was in high school, how we girls used to share secrets and talk about others. A friend of mine told me she had slept with a guy in our year (who was the love interest of another one of our friends). She said to me immediately after sharing: 'If ever this gets out, I'll know it was you—because you're the only person I'm telling this to.' And even if it was really hard for me to do, I kept my mouth shut. When friends share that kind of information in a group setting, I feel a lot less pressure to keep my mouth shut, as nobody would know that I was the one who spilled the beans."

Transmission

> The cruel 'They say' which goes floating about
> Like a hidden foe, fostering fears,
> Would lose all its force were it firmly shut out
> By the man with the gossipy ears.
> —Anonymous, "Gossipy Ears" (printed in Don McNeill, *The Breakfast Club Family Album* [n.p., 1942], cited in Capps, 2012.)[*]

So why do people still engage in spreading gossip and rumors when the risk of punishment is so high? Giardini (2012) believes that such rumormongers are able to use language in an effective way

---

[*]   *Don McNeill's Breakfast Club* was a variety show on the NBC Blue Network and ABC Radio in Chicago, Illinois. The show aired from June 1933 to December 1968.

so they can avoid taking responsibility for what they are saying, and in this way, protect themselves. People can easily hide behind expressions like 'I have been told that...,' 'I have heard...,' 'People say...,' 'According to my source who shall remain nameless...,' which allows them to transmit the information and maintain their social bonds, without suffering any of the consequences.

It's this transmission that is the biggest distinction between rumors and gossip. Gossip usually has an author. Rumor doesn't.

Anonymity

> *Where there is smoke, there is fire.*
> —proverb

> *The principle street is called 'They Say,'*
> *And 'I've Heard' is the public well,*
> *And the breezes that blow from Falsehood Bay*
> *Are laden with 'Don't You Tell!'*
> —Anonymous, "Gossiptown" (printed in Don McNeill, *The Breakfast Club Family Album* [n.p., 1942], cited in Capps, 2012)

In the television series *Gossip Girl*, each episode starts with an enticing woman's voice: "Gossip Girl here! Your one and only source into the scandalous lives of Manhattan's elite. [...] And who am I? That's one secret I'll never tell. You know you love me. Xoxo, Gossip Girl." Her power is her anonymity. Since no one knows who she is, she can share gossip freely without being held accountable. And as she rightly observes, "you know you love me." The appetite for gossip and scandal is infinite.

What makes rumors especially dangerous is the fact that they can be easily transmitted, without having an author that can be held accountable. And it is not just the gossiper who is anonymous. The listener is as well.

The growth of tabloids and websites like the American sites TMZ and Gawker shows just how increasingly popular they are becoming. The Dutch newspaper *de Volkskrant* reports that TMZ makes an annual profit of tens of millions of dollars and attracts about 25 million visitors a month (Althuisius, 2014). Gawker's slogan is: "Today's gossip is tomorrow's news." So, when TMZ published naked photos of Prince Harry in 2012, the number of hits rose by 220%. It goes without saying that this type of story is very lucrative, indeed. While in the past, newspaper tabloids were popular, people always felt a little bit embarrassed to pick up a copy at the supermarket, or flip through it in front of other people. Now that people can do this online, in the comfort of their own homes, this barrier is gone. Statistics have shown that TMZ even attracts very educated and well-off visitors who, in the privacy of their own homes, are not embarrassed to stoop to lower levels of news consumption. Because people can easily remain anonymous, they have fewer qualms about spreading rumors and posting nasty comments. As Epstein (2011) puts it, "people will say on the Internet things they would never say to another person face to face or over a phone. The blog with its absence of face-to-face contact, provides something like whiskey courage—cyber courage, let us call it—and it cannot be a good thing."

How rumors and false information spread

In an article in *Scientific American*, 'Why we trust lies,' O'Connor & Weatherall (2019) state that the most effective rumors and misinformation start with seeds of truth. For example:

> In the mid-1800s a caterpillar the size of a human finger began spreading across the northeastern US. This appearance of the tomato hornworm was followed by terrifying reports of fatal poisonings and aggressive behavior toward people. In July 1869 newspapers across the region posted warnings about the insect, reporting that a girl in Red Creek, NY, had been "thrown into spasms, which ended in death" after a run-in with the creature. That fall the *Syracuse Standard* printed an account from one Dr. Fuller, who had collected a particularly enormous specimen.

The physician warned that the caterpillar was "as poisonous as a rattlesnake" and said he knew of three deaths linked to its venom. Although the hornworm is a voracious eater that can strip a tomato plant in a matter of days, it is, in fact, harmless to humans. Entomologists had known the insect to be innocuous for decades when Fuller published his dramatic account, and his claims were widely mocked by experts.

So how did such rumors come about and spread so easily, even when scientific studies disproved this? It's because people are social learners. "We develop most of our beliefs from the testimony of trusted others such as our teachers, parents and friends." Even when they are wrong, we tend to believe them, and we don't think twice about transmitting false information. Another reason people transmit misinformation (or rumors) without thinking, is because everyone has the longing to fit in or belong to certain groups. We want to feel connected to others, such as by belonging to a political party, an association of environmental activists, a religion, or a certain ethnic group. By liking and retransmitting messages undermining Trump, for example, we show our allegiance to those people who share our opinions. We feel connected to them. When we are scared (whether it's of crime in our neighborhood, immigration, unemployment, Covid-19, or global warming), and we see a message that reinforces our beliefs, we tend to buy it without questioning it too much. Often, we won't think twice about sharing such messages, according to Wardle (2019).

With the overflow of information and messages we get, we also tend to rely on shortcuts and heuristics to make sense of information. Han (45), a researcher in a large educational institution in the Netherlands, recalls: "I had this friend on Facebook. He once posted a photo of a made-up echography of his liver, as a joke. But soon, everybody started congratulating him on becoming a dad. People just don't read."

Today especially, with the help of the internet, a rumor or a piece of gossip, whether it is true or not, can be spread instantly and reach millions of screens within seconds, according to the Dutch newspaper *de Volkskrant* (Hotse Smit, 2014).

In a webinar called *Facebook and Us: It's Complicated* (2021), Owen Taylor, a professor at the Max Bell School of Public Policy at McGill University, explains that Facebook uses and calibrates an algorithm to determine which information its users will be shown. "It can be calibrated for the things that make us read more. Or the things that give us an emotional response: things that make us angry, things that engage us." Taylor claims that Facebook knew that the angry emoji "ranked five times higher than the like emoji." And the type of story that make us angry will circulate a lot more. In addition, the algorithm Facebook uses does not screen the veracity of such stories.

The medium is the message

In the past, a lot of misinformation and disinformation traveled via social media groups such as Facebook and YouTube. But William Davies (2020) observes in *The Guardian* that private chat groups like WhatsApp have become "unusually effective vehicles" for spreading rumors and false information. Because groups can be formed without others knowing of their existence nor what is being said, it is extremely difficult to challenge false information. Members on WhatsApp groups can feel a strong sense of community with each other, and will be less likely to question or challenge what is being said. Many organizations face the extra challenge of not only informing their employees in a clear, transparent way, but having to fight invisible rumor- and gossipmongers. Davies writes: "There is often a strange emotional comfort in the shared feeling of alienation and passivity. 'We were never informed about that,' 'nobody consulted us,' 'we are being ignored.'" As people rely more and more on WhatsApp to get information about their workplace, a contradictory process takes place.

"The public world seems even more distant, impersonal and fake, and the private group becomes a space of sympathy and authenticity," Davies explains. Therefore, rumors circulate a lot more freely on WhatsApp, and they usually follow a certain pattern. Take Paula, for example. She's a fictional member of a WhatsApp group at work and vents her frustration about her manager, complaining that she was unjustly treated or let down. Tim, a second participant agrees. At this point, it becomes tricky for anyone in the group to defend the manager. So, immediately, the group has the feeling they have a new enemy, and a new resentment is born. "Instantly, the warnings and denunciations emanating from within the group take on a level of authenticity that cannot be matched by [the manager, in this case] that is now the object of derision."

But what if Paula was just having a bad day? What if she had just misunderstood or misinterpreted her manager? Maybe Tim agreed with Paula just to make her feel better, and the others just didn't have the energy or were too shy to say anything. Even if Paula's message doesn't necessarily lead employees to turn against management, it "makes the job of communicating official information far more troublesome than it was just a decade ago."

Contagion

Several scientists (O'Connor & Weatherall, 2019) have tried to understand how false beliefs circulate by comparing the spread of ideas to a contagion. Employing mathematical models and computer algorithms, these researchers observed that ideas are like viruses that spread from one person to the next.

Mathematicians (Fedewa et al., 2013) have come up with models to map out how rumors travel. It all starts with a spreader (S) who knows a rumor. Those who don't know the rumor are called ignorants (I). On day 1, the spreader tells the rumor to one person (an ignorant). This ignorant can either become a spreader in turn, or a stifler (someone who heard the rumor, but decides to keep it to him or herself). Most likely, the number of spreaders grows. Each spreader tells the rumor until everyone has heard it. The authors show that in the beginning, the number of ignorants

Figure 4 Time for a rumor to spread
Source: Fedewa et al. (2013)

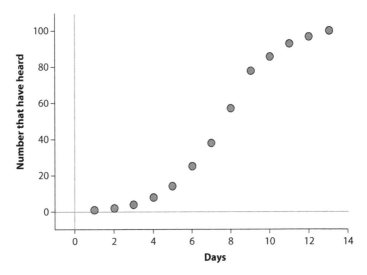

Rumor spread among 100 persons

turning into spreaders grows exponentially, but after about 10 to 15 days, the number of people in the know remain the same. The same trends occur whether the rumor spreads between 100, 500, or 1,000 people (see figure 4).

Psychologists Gordon Allport and Joseph Postman (cited in Berger, 2014) were very interested in what happened to rumors as they spread from one person to the next. They also wanted to see whether stories changed as they were transmitted and, if they did, how exactly. "Were there predictable patterns in how rumors evolved?"

To address this question, they had people play what most of us would describe as a game of Telephone. First, someone was shown a picture of a detailed situation—in one case, a group of people on a subway car. The car appears to be an Eighth Avenue Express and it is going past Dyckman Street. There are various advertisements posted on the car, and five people are seated, including a rabbi and a mother carrying her baby. But the focus of the picture is two men having an argument. They are standing up, and one is pointing at the other, holding a knife.

> Then the game of Telephone starts. The first person (transmitter) is asked to describe the picture to someone else (receiver), who cannot see it. [...] The transmitter then leaves the room and a new person enters. That new person becomes the receiver, and the original receiver becomes the transmitter, sharing what happened in the image he never really saw with the new receiver. [...] The game is repeated to a third, fourth, fifth, and eventually sixth person. Allport and Postman then looked at which story details persisted along the transmission chain.

The researchers found that the amount of information that was passed along dropped drastically every time the rumor (according to our definition) was shared: about 70% of the details were lost in the first five to six transmissions of the story. But they found that the stories did not get shorter. The transmitters tended to focus more on the main points and key details. As the story got retold, many of the unimportant details got left out. While the first transmitter may have described where the subway car was heading and that there was a rabbi and a baby on board, the later storytellers focused more on the argument itself.

This experiment suggests that people retain the critical elements of a story and tend to leave out the less important details. However, the authors do not explain why rumors can be exaggerated, blown out of proportion, or even deliberately falsified. Maybe they do not take into account the intensions of a transmitter who may have a hidden agenda or bad intentions.

Rumors as weapon

Philosopher Mladen Dolar (2019), in a talk called *Gossip, Rumors and Philosophy*, describes a scene in Rossini's opera *The Barber of Seville*. Don Bartolo wants to marry his protégée, Rosina, who is a lot younger than him. Yet Count Almaviva is also very much in love with Rosina and is actively pursuing her. So, Don Bartolo asks his friend, Don Basilio, for advice on how to get rid of his rival. Don Basilio has only one advice: use calumny. Say things about Count Almaviva that are not true in order to damage his reputation. 'Calumny can destroy anyone,' Don Basilio claims. Calumny here is disinformation in full swing. The aria 'La calunnia è un venticello' (Calumny is a little breeze) is, according to Dolar, a veritable eulogy for this type of rumor. It starts pianissimo:

> The calumny is a little wind, a very gentle little breeze which nimbly, softly, lightly, kindly, begins to whisper. (And then there's a crescendo.) Little by little, mildly, in a low voice, hissing, it goes flowing, it goes buzzing; in people's ears it enters deftly and makes heads and brains stun and blow. Getting out from the mouth the clamor grows: it slowly strengthens, it already flies from one place to another. It seems like the thunder, like the storm. [...] In the end, it spills over and blows up. It spreads, it doubles and provokes an explosion like a canon shot, an earthquake, a rain storm. [...] And the miserable one who is defamed, degraded, trampled, scourged by the public opinion by good fortune, falls to death.

(In this case, despite the power of rumor, Don Bartolo's plan failed miserably; true love and reason still triumphed in the end.)

Another, darker example that Dolar brings up in his talk, is in Kafka's *The Trial* (1925). The novel starts: "Someone must have been spreading rumors against Josef K., for one morning, without having done anything wrong, he was arrested."

The story starts with "a rumor, of an unspecified author, a word coming from nowhere, yet overpowering. [...] The rumor, the slander that started it all is mentioned only once in the first sentence. There are no clues as to who this someone might have been. No clues during the trial. The whole novel is presented from the view of Josef K. Only this first sentence is written in the third person, from the point of view of an objective narrator, who also affirms that Josef K. has done no wrong." Spoiler alert! In the end, Josef K. was slaughtered with a knife, like a dog. He was killed because of something that started out as a mere rumor.

Also, in the film *Just Mercy* (2019), death row inmate Walter McMillian (Jamie Foxx) recounts how people first started to talk about the fact that he had an affair. He was first considered a cheater, then a criminal, and then a murderer. No one then had any trouble believing that he killed an eighteen-year-old girl (which was a false accusation in the end, but that still landed him on death row).

What makes rumors particularly dangerous, is that once one circulates about someone (even if it's later proven untrue), the damage is done. To come back to the example of Joe flirting with the waitress, a rumor about him, after some time, could have it that he is having a real affair or that he was sexually harassing the waitress, which, obviously, could wreak havoc on his personal and professional life.

Patrick (27), a Belgian-Peruvian who is employed at an electric utility company in Belgium, confides: "A couple of months back, we had an office party on a Friday, and well, the next Monday, there were a lot of talk. I was a bit shocked because, apparently somebody heard one of our managers snort in the toilet, and then everybody started saying how he was snorting cocaine even though nobody had actually seen him. Apparently, a co-worker was in a toilet close by, and heard the manager speak and then heard a snorting noise. For all we know, he was just blowing his nose or something but, yeah, everybody started talking about it."

Patrick says that many of his colleagues doubted that his manager would have snorted coke. "He's, like, in his 40s, has a wife and kids, so it doesn't really fit the image of the guy who would do drugs at an office party," Patrick explained. "But I've worked in a couple of offices since I graduated, and you'd be surprised: a lot more people than you think do drugs, and even people you would never suspect!" So, even though the rumor died down after a while, some doubts still stuck.

Zoltan (52), who works for a large independent financial services provider in Hungary, recalls how he was the victim of a rumor himself: "Recently, somebody came from the head office and told me that they heard gossip that I was talking in negative terms about the organization. They heard that from a Transylvanian Hungarian when I was supposedly traveling there. The truth is that at the time, I was not traveling in Transylvania and I was absolutely not talking negatively at all. Some ill-intentioned person invented this rumor about me, which was just not true. The biggest problem is that you look really stupid when you start defending yourself. You cannot defend yourself when it's happening behind your back and, unfortunately, in many organizations people take [rumors] at face value."

According to a study by eleven researchers at the Vrije Universiteit in the Netherlands, people don't tend to question gossip and rumors they hear and "see the gossip they receive as very believable." So, if they hear that Tom is not a good person to work with, they simply won't work with him and won't question whether the rumor is true or not.

As Mladen Dolar points out, even when they are unfounded, "rumors always leave a stain. And the stain is nearly impossible to erase." People will always believe that there must have been some truth to these allegations. *There's no smoke without fire.*

There's a great scene in the film *Doubt* (2008). Philip Seymour Hoffman plays Father Flynn, who gives a sermon about the evils of gossip (actually, about rumors, if we stick to our definition). He talks about a woman who asks for God's forgiveness after having spread rumors.

The priest told her: "I want you to go home, take a pillow up on your roof, cut it open with a knife, and return here to me." So, the woman went home, took a pillow off her bed, a knife from the drawer, went up the fire escape to her roof, and stabbed the pillow. And then she went back to the old parish priest as instructed.

"Did you gut the pillow with a knife?" he says.

"Yes, Father."

"And what was the result?"

"Feathers," she said. [Feathers are shown flying everywhere, all over the alley].

"Feathers," he repeated. "Now I want you to go back and gather every last feather that flew out in the wind."

"Well," she said. "It can't be done. I don't know where they went. The wind took them all over."

"And that," said the priest, "is gossip."

In the film, Father Flynn is accused of having sexually harassed a young altar boy. Sister Aloysius (Meryl Streep), the strict principal of the church's parish school, suspects him without ever having solid proof. But after talking with many people around and spreading the seeds of doubt into others, she demands for his resignation. Father Flynn was never able to prove that it was untrue, and does ask for his transfer. Needless to say, his reputation took a deep blow.

Researching gossip: Organizational ethnography

Delving into many quantitative studies on gossip, I felt that they missed out on many of the nuances of the art of gossiping. Also, I thought, most respondents filling out a survey will most likely not tell the truth about their behavior and motivations. Therefore, since I wanted to study my participants in their own environment, I was immediately drawn towards organizational ethnography. Observing people in their own environments, like a fly on the wall, seemed extremely appealing to me.

According to Yanow et al. (2012), "organizational ethnographers can potentially make explicit often overlooked, tacitly known, and/or concealed dimensions of meaning making." As the authors note, "ethnographies can have a direct, critical, even shocking quality, laying bare otherwise hidden and even harsh social realities."

However, Watson (2012) points out that many organizational ethnographers quickly run into ethical problems, and have difficulty publishing their work in academic journals. Indeed, when I wrote about my experiences of trying to conduct an ethnographic study in another department at my university undergoing change, the reviewers at the journal were extremely fearful that people would recognize themselves. "What ethical permissions do you have?" "Is the manager recognizable?"

Since there were still no official ethical committees for universities of applied sciences in the Netherlands (according to De Knecht, 2017), the director of my research group, two senior colleagues, and a few members of the steering committee of the project reviewed my research proposal and agreed with my approach. It was relatively simple for me, in comparison to North American researchers who do similar projects. They need to submit a proposal to an ethics committee (Darmon, 2018).

Finding the *sweet spot of gossip*

Rumors can be extremely powerful and dangerous if used with the intent to harm. In the series *Designated Survivor*, such rumors are used during the presidential campaign. Spoiler alert! One morning, President Kirkman (Kiefer Sutherland) wakes up to a story on the front page of the newspaper accusing him of having murdered his wife, who had died in a car crash a few months back.

"They're saying that I had my wife murdered?" Kirkman fumes to his team, with disbelief and indignation. "That she was a Russian spy? This is an all-time low and that's saying a lot, given that our politics have become so poisonous, so rancid."

After a bit of deliberation, Lorraine Zimmer (Julie White), the president's political strategist, says: "But there is a silver lining. More voters are going to sympathize with you rather than believe this ludicrous bullshit."

"There is no silver lining to this crap!" Kirkman explodes. "It's an affront to anything decent."

When Seth Wright (Kal Penn), the White House press secretary, asks the president how they should handle this rumor and suggests that he provide a statement, Kirkman refuses vehemently. "No! I'm not going to dignify this with a response! And spare

me the lecture on how we need to retaliate every time we're attacked. We're not giving this any oxygen. The administration says nothing. The campaign says nothing. Understood?"

Was this the best strategy? Is silence really the best defense?

When Seth faces journalists from various media outlets at the press conference, he is not able to get them to talk about anything else other than the rumor. "Does President Kirkman have any response to the release of the photos of the late First Lady's car accident?" one asks.

"Guys, we're not addressing this, okay?" Seth answers.

As the journalists show no signs of backing off, Seth explodes. "You should be ashamed of yourselves. All of you. This is 100% trash. This is fever-swamp clickbait for moral degenerates and conspiracy whack jobs. I'm sure whoever created this filth thanks you for being his or her accomplice in trumpeting this revolting desecration. Whatever happened to standards? What happened to ethical practices? What happened to concern for the First children? Guys, that's their mother! That's his wife! [...] This is not journalism! We're disgusted with every single one of you. There's your answer. Are you happy?"

While Seth's outburst may have felt therapeutic at the time, not only was he met with an angry president, but as Mars Harper (Anthony Edwards), the new chief of staff, observed: "Instead, you gave this story three more days because you couldn't control your emotions."

In this case, silence isn't the best strategy, but neither are emotional outbursts. This illustrates how harmful rumors can be and how difficult it is to dispel them once they have been launched.

Tips for employees and managers

When it comes to spreading and listening to rumors, sticky situations can easily occur. Firstly, what should you do if you are the victim of (false) rumors yourself? And secondly, what should you do when you hear damaging stories about others?

If you are the victim of a nasty rumor
1.   Talk about it. Face the situation.
In the French series *Lupin*, it is the bad guy, Hubert Pellegrini (Hervé Pierre), who has the right strategy. Assane Diop (Omar Sy), the gentleman thief, wants to expose his enemy, Pellegrini. With the help of a journalist, Assane gets hold of a VHS tape revealing how Pellegrini sold arms to terrorists, who then blew up the French embassy in Kuala Lumpur in 1996. "He betrayed his country," Assane says to the journalist. "The blood of those victims are on his hands. [...] I'll have this posted on Twitter in the next 24 hours." Assane drops the bomb using the fake name Salvator813.

At the press conference, Pellegrini reacts to these accusations: "France is a country we can be proud of. [...] I pay my taxes in France. I'm a philanthropist. But despite all that, someone launched a rumor that was nauseating and anonymous. And this rumor endangers my integrity and that of my company. Normally, the one who calls himself Salvator813 would not deserve my attention nor my energy. But the reason I'm standing here before you today is because my lovely daughter here and the foundation she'll be launching in order to help young people are threatened by this odious rumor. And I cannot accept that." So, Pellegrini confronts his anonymous attacker. "If this Salvator wants to create a scandal, if he's convinced that what he is saying is the truth, that people need to know, then I have only one question. Why lurk in the shadows? Put down your computer and show yourself. I have nothing to hide. And if you don't either, prove it then!" For this battle, Pellegrini's best defense was indeed to confront his anonymous enemy, and it did work out well for him in the end.

In the Canadian novel *A Better Man* (2019) by Louise Penny, Chief Inspector Armand Gamache was victim of an online smear campaign because of a botched mission. Gamache had just been demoted, but came back at work to face his colleagues. Rather than ignoring the rumors and toxic tweets, he decides to face them, full on. "Truth be told, he had not expected the air to be so foul."

Gamache takes place at the meeting and says:

> "We're not going to start out by hiding the truth from each other, are we? [...] I'd rather colleagues didn't talk behind my back." He met their eyes, then smiled. "I know this's awkward. I've read some of the posts. I know what they're saying. That I should've been fired. That I should've been put in jail. That I'm incompetent, perhaps criminally so. Is that right?" He was no longer smiling, but neither was he angry. Armand Gamache was simply stating facts. Clearing the air by exposing the crap.

And he does just that. He asks various colleagues to read out the posts and responds to each. Although this felt awkward to his colleagues, it was good to provide the space to address the rumors. Gamache was being transparent.

2.   Confront the rumormonger if you can.
Nicholas DiFonzo (2011) writes in *Psychology Today* that there is an old saying that one shouldn't try to defend oneself against

slander. "Your enemies won't believe you anyway and your friends don't need to hear your defense." While this may hold some truth (at least the first part of the statement), I would still advocate for openness and transparency.

Sometimes, you suspect or even know who is talking behind your back. Even if they are not the originator of the rumor, it is worthwhile to confront them. And the sooner you do it, the better. Anita (48), who works for a large educational institution in the Netherlands, recalls: "When you work in education, students are sometimes quick to complain when things are not clear or when they do not get immediate answers to their questions. One day, during a team meeting, one of my colleagues, Sylvie, said: 'One student was complaining about you, saying that you responded rudely to one of his emails, saying: "Don't bother me."' I denied this vehemently, as there is no way I would have ever responded like this to a student. Sylvie insisted: that's what the student told her, so she believed him. I was flabbergasted. I knew that Sylvie was sometimes hostile towards me and was talking behind my back, but this was really damaging, as she was undermining my reputation. After fuming a bit, I decided to confront Sylvie, and asked her which student had said this. 'Do you have the supposedly nasty mail I sent him? Can I see exactly what you are talking about?' Sylvie fumbled, saying she didn't, and finally admitted that maybe she had interpreted things in the wrong way. I was happy that I was able to set the record straight with her, but still, the damage was done. The colleagues she told this to didn't fact check. They'll just remember that I wasn't very professional in this case, and will never know that it wasn't true."

Anita had the right reflex to confront Sylvie and ask her for the evidence and facts. She was able to nip some of these rumors in the bud by holding the author accountable. Even though she probably was not able to erase the stain that was left behind, she was able to stop it from growing and spreading further.

To come back to the nasty rumors against President Kirkman in *Designated Survivor*, the best strategy was certainly not to ignore the rumor, like the president first wanted to do. Kirkman actually had a brilliant response. He suspected that his opponent, Cornelius Moss (Geoff Pierson), was the originator of the rumor that he was responsible for his wife's death. During the televised debate, he not only addresses the rumor but confronts his opponent openly. "I know many of you have read the outrageous conspiracy theories surrounding my wife's untimely death," the president says calmly. "And as vile as I might think they are, and as hurtful as they've been to my children, like it or not, they too represent a free people's right to a protected speech. Having said that, you do not have to condone the content. Cornelius Moss has failed to make any statement of condemnation. So, I have to ask you, sir, can you say to me or the American people that you repudiate those lies and that you do not want the vote of anyone who traffics in such filth?"

As Moss gives a wishy-washy answer, Kirkman administers the final blow: "I didn't hear him say it." Needless to say, he wins the debate, quashes the rumor and comes out with his head held high. Whether such a strategy would always yield such results is to be seen, but it is certainly worth a shot!

If you hear a nasty rumor
1.   Ask yourself whether what you hear is credible.
According to Kurland & Pelled (2000), it is essential to always consider whether the juicy story we hear is actually true. To start with, we should ask ourselves whether it is a gossip or rumor?

Hakim (36), a Moroccan-Dutch employee at a large appliance store in the Netherlands, remembers: "One time, one of the workers stole from our store, assigning fake sales to the name of another colleague. At first, our whole team started to suspect this colleague, and we all gossiped about it for almost a month. We thought that it was extremely strange that he had gotten so many sales in only one month, and when we commented on it, he told us that he was only having a good month."

"Finally, when the investigation about fraudulent sales came to its end, it was discovered that another employee was the real thief. He had to return the money and he was immediately fired.

As you can imagine, it was very embarrassing because we all had wrongly blamed our colleague for a month. I think the best thing is that we learned not to spread rumors without confirming them first."

Therefore, one must always apply critical thinking skills. Burke & Wise (2003) recommend that people look carefully at "matters of source, credibility, substance and consistency." You should be asking the gossiper questions along the lines of: "From whom and in what setting did you hear this? How privy are you to discussions among key company players? Does this rumor contradict other rumors, and if so, why?"

Also, think about the gossiper's credibility. Did he spread stories with evil intent in the past? Is she actually a part of the circles where the information is coming from? How does he know what he is telling you is true? Another important question to consider is what are the gossiper's intentions? Does she want to get even with a certain colleague and is looking for ways to discredit him? It's important to consider all of these questions before believing something and especially before spreading it further.

2.   Address the rumors quickly.
Employees, and especially managers, should do their utmost best to address rumors quickly, as soon as they get wind of them. "Allowing the rumor mill to continually grind away can lead to festering employee concerns. [...] When managers receive word that someone is spreading dangerous, premeditated rumors, they should discover and confront the source, meeting directly with those involved to determine the damage and correct the situation," Burke & Wise advise.

Erik (39), a team manager at a large distribution center in the Netherlands, recounts: "We once had a new part-timer who started working in our team. He was sick right off the start. That's nothing really special: these things can happen. But then, one of our interns made a joke one day, in the cafeteria, that this part-timer was caught for drug trafficking. So, some people didn't hear that it was a joke, and started talking about it. When the part-timer finally returned to work, nobody wanted to work with him. I didn't understand it at all. After a month, I finally got wind of the rumor. I immediately sent out an email that the rumor was absolutely not true. Another time, we had a receptionist who came to work with a black eye. It was nothing special; she just hit herself while moving. But she had just broken up with her boyfriend, and everybody thought that he had hit her. They didn't break up on good terms, that's why. Luckily, I noticed it quickly and was also able to quash that rumor early on."

These anecdotes illustrate how important it is for managers to keep their eyes and ears open to rumors and to address them as quickly as possible. While Erik was able to do so, his poor part-timer still struggled for an entire month to fit into the team and gain his colleagues' trust.

3. Cultivate your credibility as a professional.

In order to gossip successfully, an important factor is to cultivate one's credibility. As in most communication professions such as journalism, PR and marketing, credibility is essential. If you lose it, you lose everything.

Hence, credibility should be a quality that all employees should cultivate, and not just communication professionals. When we gossip, a lot is at stake. Not only do we have the ability to damage a colleague's reputation, but we can harm our own very easily. So, you must convince your listener of your competence and reliability. This will determine whether your colleagues will listen to you and trust you.

To come back to the example of Joe, who I see flirting with a waitress at the bar: if I gossip about this with a colleague, she may choose to believe me totally, or question my version of the facts. "Are you sure he wasn't just having a nice chat with her?" she may ask. If she knows that I have a tendency to exaggerate or believes that I have malicious intentions, she will consider my gossip as not very credible. If she trusts me, she will believe my story.

Jade (21), a Dutch university student, remembers: "Last year, one of the male students in my class told me and my friends that he went out with one of our teachers (who I am not going to name). They got really drunk and at some point the teacher (who is male as well) was hitting on him and trying to convince him to go to his place. The student had a picture with the teacher in which they were both holding a pint of beer and smiling. However, a picture does not prove the rest of the story. Obviously, none of us dared to ask the teacher about it." It seems like, in this case, the gossiper lacked credibility and his listeners wanted hard evidence before believing his story (luckily for the teacher).

If you lose credibility, you will be perceived negatively and risk being kept out of the loop at work. Therefore, it is essential to tread carefully before spreading rumors. As with gossip, make sure your intentions are good before spreading anything.

Questioning the credibility of a juicy story is a good step to take in order to gossip well. But also, understanding the mechanisms of gossip is equally important to becoming a skilled gossiper.

3.   The Mechanisms of Gossip

So, how does gossip work? What do we gossip about? Whom do we tend to gossip about? By understanding the mechanisms, we will be able to avoid certain pitfalls and will be able to channel gossip in a more positive way. In this chapter, we will attempt to answer these questions.

What we gossip about

In this section, we will examine what people normally like to gossip about at work. Are there certain themes in the topics that keep coming up? Epstein (2011) claims that universities are "unimaginable without gossip." People talk "about who is to be promoted, whose ambitions have been denied, who is making what salary, who secretly loathes whom, or what new positions are about to be on offer, not to mention who is bedding down with whom." I am quite sure this applies to most workplaces and not just universities!

To begin with, do we prefer negative or positive stories? Sharing positive gossip, like saying that Judy's performance on the project was awesome, would certainly make you come across as a good team player. According to certain studies, you'd even be more likeable. Still, I would dare to say that if you only share positive stories, you won't come across as very interesting. Let's face it: people like to hear negative stories. Would you enjoy watching a movie for two hours about a happy, rich, successful, beautiful couple with not a worry in the world? No. You would like to see them having difficulties and would like to have a full view of their character flaws (even if, at the end, you may probably long for a happy ending). As Gail (58), a high school principal in Curaçao, puts it: "Most things I gossip about are negative. I don't remember gossiping about someone doing a great job—I wouldn't even consider that gossip."

And indeed, social psychologist Charles Walker (cited in DiFonzo, 2011) notes that a far "greater percentage of gossip is critical rather than laudatory."

Epstein (2011) observes that even when we speak about people we like, we are more inclined to share negative stories. As the Talmud proclaims: "Don't speak well of your friend, for although you will start with his good traits, the discussion might turn to his bad traits."

People rarely gossip about others' qualities. "A tells B about an extraordinary act of selflessness on the part of C, who is much too modest to tell it herself," Epstein explains. "Yet even in these instances it is the nature of gossip to find behind the most altruistic acts low motives—expiating guilt, moral exhibitionism, tax write-offs." Consequently, "saying nice things about people can lead, in the natural rhythms of intimate conversations, to negative gossip."

During the course of my research, where I interviewed employees at my university about a change they were going through, I saw how positive gossip could even be used as a way to get negative gossip. Without even being fully aware of it at the time, while interviewing one of the colleagues involved in the project, I found myself subtly nudging the conversation towards one of the managers (who had been rather hostile towards me and my research). During the interview, I mentioned that this manager was quite impressive and had worked on quite a big project. My interviewee replied with some disdain: "I don't know him that well, but I heard someone say that he's a friend of the other manager, and that's why he's here."

I am quite sure that my interviewee would not have gossiped about him had I said something negative about the manager. He may even have defended him by saying something positive. (But as we will see in Chapter 4, this reaction may have been typically Dutch.)

Research also shows that sharing negative stories can make a gossiper look more intelligent and knowledgeable. Film and restaurant critics seem more expert when they write negative reviews than when they write positive ones. The same can be said about employees gossiping about their managers on the work floor. By being critical, one comes across as more competent than employees who would speak highly of their managers. Martinescu et al. (2019) observe that "negative gossip is a way of presenting oneself to gossip recipients as a qualified judge, which may increase one's status and informal influence. Gossipers boost or protect their reputation by making implicit social comparisons between themselves and targets."

In a more systematic way, Kurland & Pelled (2000) examined what people gossip about at work. They made a distinction between work-related and non-work-related gossip. The authors found that work-related gossip focuses on an individual's work life, such as performance, relationship with colleagues, and general behavior in the workplace, whereas non-work related (or social) gossip would include information about a colleague's marital problems, for instance, or that Mary just had plastic surgery done over the summer holiday.

Work-related gossip

De Backer et al. (2016) distinguish between two main types of work-related gossip: strategy learning gossip and reputation gossip.

Strategy learning gossip is all about the third party's behavior—the *what*. What did they do? What happened? Here, gossipers discuss and learn about successful behavior, appropriate behavior, and cultural norms. Usually, people like to talk shop at work. Employees want to know what is going on. Who is getting promoted or fired? Why? They want to voice their hopes, fears, and concerns about what is going on in the organization (Burke & Wise, 2003).

Reputation gossip, on the other hand, focuses more on the person—the *who*. Who is gossiped about? When talking about the reputation of a third party, Martinescu et al. (2014) note that topics discussed at the office tend to fall into three categories. People usually talk about their appearance, their personality and peculiarities, and their competence. But some of these topics are more accepted than others.

Appearance

Does a colleague dress badly? Inappropriately? Does he have a big nose? Is the new hire hot? These are all topics that would fall under this category.

Brigitte (22) works for a French information technology consulting services company. She describes how her colleagues talked about a new employee that had just been hired: "She's Swedish, she's tall, she's blonde. There was a lot of gossip about her because [the male colleagues] are super excited about her! We are between fifteen and twenty employees in Angers, and she would be the fourth woman to work here. I see it as ordinary sexism, but in our team, there is just one really sexist guy and the rest are really nice. So, one day, we were in a weekly meeting, and my boss arrived and heard we were talking about the new woman who just got hired. The first reaction of my boss was to ask: 'Does she have big boobs?' But it was more he was just playing the fool and trying to make people laugh. He was just being provocative by imitating the usual boneheaded engineer colleague. Nobody answered his question, but the ones who had seen the new colleague described her briefly."

This type of gossip may have gone down well in France, but in the US or Canada, such comments would probably have been seriously frowned upon.

Eleonora (49) used to work for a large transportation company in Estonia. "There were two companies that both operated in the same building complex. One company offered warehouse services and the other, a newer company, worked in international transportation. So, the newly appointed CEO of this new company was a young guy named Leo. He was very energetic and became quite chummy with Tom, the CEO of the older, warehouse company. And because, Leo was younger, he was, you know, a more fashionable guy than the older CEO. He had quite an influence on the older guy, so much so, that the older guy started even buying the exact same clothes as him, and there were days when they both showed up to work in the exact same outfit." Naturally, employees gossiped about their CEO's clothes and appearance, especially when Tom started having affairs with women at work, despite the fact that he was married with three children.

Personality and peculiarities

Is someone at your office loud? Irritating? Arrogant? Or funny and charming? Employees may discuss other colleagues' personalities over a drink at the bar. Such conversations can help identify which personalities "fit best with the firm and which do not," Burke & Wise (2003) claim.

If one of your colleagues has a limp handshake, you may be tempted to gossip about this peculiarity.

Even in the highest spheres of mathematics number theory research, when researchers couldn't make up their minds as to who was right about a mathematical claim, they gravitated towards gossip as a last straw. Michel (53), a math professor at a Canadian university, explains how the peculiarities of two mathematicians ended up playing a crucial role in the debate:

> For about six years, we had an extensive debate in the math community about whether a Japanese colleague had managed to prove the ABC conjecture (a very important open question in number theory). He had written a 500-page report—a series of papers, amounting to close to 1,000 pages in length—claiming to have solved this extremely complex problem. The exposition was unusually dense and hard to understand, so for a long time, nobody was able to validate or refute his claims with much certainty.
>
> One day, two professors from German universities—one had won the Fields Medal—claimed that they had found a gap in his proof. A debate then followed between the Japanese mathematician's followers and those of the German scholars. Mathematicians from all over the world were participating in the discussion, some of them expressing their ideas in blogs. Naturally, the reputation of the mathematicians in question played a huge role in how they were perceived—having a Fields Medal represents a pinnacle of achievement in the

subject and the reservations of the German mathematicians could not be ignored. The Japanese mathematician also had impeccable credentials, having studied and taught at Ivy League universities and an excellent track record.

But since it was very difficult to get to the bottom of the mathematical claims, given their complexity, many relied on gossip related to the personalities and perceived peculiarities of these mathematicians as a basis for forming an impression. The German Fields Medalist's work has created a revolution in the subject in recent years, and he is viewed as powerful, rigorous, and reliable. The Japanese one had the reputation of being a little out of touch, since he had isolated himself for several years, and had declined all outside speaking invitations. Those who couldn't knowledgeably talk about the work itself thus relied instead on these other, more superficial aspects to make up their minds. So, because of this gossip, in the end, the German mathematicians won the debate.

A more common peculiarity that often comes up is drinking behavior. If an employee gets sloshed outside of work hours or during the Christmas party, they will be sure to be a hot topic of gossip.

Ton (54), a Dutch IT architect at a large international computer company, reveals: "Generally, we like to gossip about peculiarities of certain colleagues. Like people who get a little drunk at work or at home, who misbehave, or are easy with relationships. For example, we had this colleague (let's call him Max) who got really drunk one night and then had to go home by bike. He got rained on, and because he was soaked, he took off his pants and shoes and left them outside, at the entrance of his house. He came in and fell asleep on a chair. He couldn't close his door because the shoes were in the way. The shoes and pants made it look like there was actually a man lying on the ground. A little while later, the police woke him up. A neighbor had called as she thought someone was lying there, dead." Ton explained that, although the story was rather funny, people considered Max to be a rather sad character, as there were more stories of this type circulating about him. Eventually, Max's behavior and reputation seriously affected his performance on the job. "Even though he was quite a smart guy, he wound up getting fired." Ton admits that after having heard such stories about Max, he avoided working with him.

Competence

Competence-related gossip is typically the most common within an organization, especially in the Netherlands (but, as we will see in Chapter 5, that may vary greatly depending on culture).

Take Jan (23). He works in the distribution center of a large Dutch textile company: "When I gossip, it is about the way my colleagues do their work. I talk about colleagues who do a lot of other things besides working. I gossip because I want to know if people think the same about someone, I like the idea that I am not the only one with a certain opinion."

Kim (29), who is employed at a large food corporation in the Netherlands, explains: "We had a colleague that got hired by the commercial director. I won't name any names, you know. But this person came into the company easily, and took up a new position that didn't exist previously. So, many colleagues were wondering how she got this job. She also regularly works from home—something that generally isn't done within our organization. So, many colleagues were talking about her behind her back. For example, she always works from home on Fridays, so people are joking that she's laying on her couch or shopping—that she doesn't have to work very hard, because she doesn't need to prove anything to the commercial director. And if the commercial director is also absent, we joke that he's probably sitting on a terrace with her, enjoying the good weather. As you can imagine, the commercial director is also not very popular within our group."

In this case, working from home was a sign that this employee was slacking off and not doing her job very well. (This was before the Covid pandemic, of course.) The fact that she landed the job in an unconventional and non-transparent way made her colleagues even more inclined to discuss her performance.

Bogdan (21), an employee at an international financial organization in Bulgaria, also adds: "I remember, we had this colleague who did not come to work for a month because she had a toothache. The whole office started gossiping about her, and people started to speculate whether she got fired, or whether she went missing. All kinds of stories from A to Z came up. In our organization, a lot of the times people take days off without actually being sick. When that happens, people at the office start to gossip about the colleague and whether he really is sick, what is he doing if he is not sick, etc."

Even during the pandemic, when working at home was the norm, employees found other ways of noting and gossiping about colleagues' absences. Sammy (27) is from Curaçao and works in a Dutch drugstore. "A lot of people at my store have gotten corona," he explains. "I think it's because the store is so small and there isn't a lot of room to move around so people come into contact with other people faster. One day, a colleague of mine called in sick complaining of corona symptoms. Since that was when a lot of people were getting infected, that wasn't anything strange. A couple of weeks later, I got sick too, and stayed home for a little over two weeks. But when I got back, this colleague still hadn't returned to work, and by then it had already been over a month that he hadn't come in to work and he wasn't answering his phone at all. So, there were rumors going around that he was faking it to get out of work because everyone who got corona was back at work within three weeks. It took three months for him to come back to work, but the managers couldn't really say anything because they couldn't prove that he didn't have corona at that time since everyone who had symptoms had to stay home. Even though this happened a couple of months ago, people still talk about it and about how he probably had faked it for that long." (Maybe the poor colleague had long Covid?)

Non-work-related gossip

Naturally, people are also interested in their colleagues' private lives. Who is having an affair? Who is getting a divorce? Who lost a lot of weight over the summer? These topics tend to come up quite frequently at the watercooler or at the bar.

In *Bridget Jones's Diary* (1996) by Helen Fielding, Jude, one of Bridget's friends, ran out of a board meeting, because "she was about to burst into tears and was now trapped in the ladies' with Alice Cooper eyes and no make-up bag." Her boyfriend, Vile Richard, described as a "self-indulgent commitment phobic," had just dumped her yet again. Afterwards, Jude meets her friends at the bar, and they gossip viciously about all the "fuckwits" they know of in their circle of friends and colleagues. One lists all of the cases of "emotional fuckwittage" she knows of: "[O]ne whose boyfriend of thirteen years refuses even to discuss living together; another who went out with a man four times who then chucked her because it was getting too serious; another who was pursued by a bloke for three months with impassioned proposals of marriage, only to find him ducking out three weeks after she succumbed and repeating the whole process with her best friend." And Bridget who is having an affair with her boss, Daniel Cleaver, spends an inordinate amount of time gossiping about him. If you have a vested interest in one of your colleagues yourself, the odds are, you will have your eyes and ears open and will likely gossip a lot more!

In the series *Lucifer*, one scene takes place at the police office. Lucifer (Tom Ellis) has been Detective Chloe's (Lauren German) assistant for a long time (and even though he denies it, visibly has feelings for her). Unfortunately for him, a new colleague has started to develop a closer relationship with Detective Chloe. Ella Lopez (Aimee Garcia), a mutual colleague, who also works with them at the laboratory, gossips with Lucifer about Detective Chloe and her potential new crush, as these two are in a room together, talking:

Ella: "They totally boned."
Lucifer: "Miss Lopez, please, don't be vulgar. The detective doesn't... bone."

Ella: "Seriously, do you not see the epic fireworks? There's more chemistry over there than in my lab. And they just went to the Axara concert. It's a natural aphrodisiac."

Lucifer: "Well, if you're a pimply millennial, perhaps, but the detective is a grown woman with sophisticated taste. Trust me, she's not so easily won over."

Ella: "Oh, my God. You are totally freaking out right now."

Lucifer: "What?"

Ella: "About this coming between you and Chloe."

Lucifer: "Don't be preposterous. I'm not freaking out about anything."

Ella: "It's okay. Okay, I... I get it. You're afraid that they're gonna start spending all their time together. You know, joining each other at crime scenes, bantering over dead bodies. And where does that leave you, right?"

Lucifer: "I assure you, Miss Lopez, that is the least of my worries. The chemistry in there is just a... a flash in the pan."

Even when you don't have such a vested interest in your colleagues' personal lives, knowing about them may provide us with useful information and help us determine how trustworthy they are.

Anita (29) is Polish and works for a Dutch construction company. She travels a lot for work, and explains that quite a few of her colleagues have affairs during these trips. "Obviously, we gossip a lot about that," she admits. "We were once working on a project in Costa Rica. One of our colleagues, a Serbian guy, always painted a beautiful picture of his family. He would Skype everyday with his wife during working hours. He would even call us to wave to his wife. He was always showing pictures of his sons. But at the same time, he was living with a Costa Rican lady, and she was coming every night to meet him after work. So, he wasn't even hiding her or anything. So, yeah, of course, we were gossiping about it."

Anita says that she couldn't help judging her cheating colleague poorly. "For me, if he is cheating on his wife, and he is cheating on the person that is closest to him, that means that I cannot trust this guy. At work, you need to trust people to cooperate. So, knowing this about him does influence how I perceive him."

Pietro (21), a marketing consultant in Spain, also remembers: "We used to have a boss who had just come back to work, but who was still on probation after having been in prison. (He went to jail because of a very important corruption case.) So, whenever he invites one of us out for coffee, we joke about how he is paying it with the money of the Spanish people." Knowing that the boss had been in prison for corruption is useful information, indeed.

Who we like to gossip about

We have seen what people like to gossip about. But are there certain people who attract gossip more than others, because of their function or position? Studies show that managers are very often the topic of gossip. And if we look at celebrity gossip, we can see just how big our interest is for people who have it much better than us. Yet while we have a great thirst for dirt on our bosses and colleagues higher up the ladder, we are also extremely interested in our equals.

The manager

> *There is something powerful in the whispering of obscenities, about those in power. There's something delightful about it, something naughty, secretive, forbidden, thrilling. It's like a spell, of sorts. It deflates them, reduces them to the common denominator where they can be dealt with.*
> —Margaret Atwood, *The Handmaid's Tale* (1985)

Ellwardt et al. (2012b) show that within organizations, supervisors and managers are very popular topics of gossip. There often tends to be "a heightened thirst for negative news about people with high status in the organization." Because managers tend to have more control and authority, there is "by definition a negative element in the relation between boss and workers." Employees therefore tend to push back and resist this control by forming coalitions.

Robert (51), a Dutch hairdresser, reveals who his clients usually gossip about when they talk to him about their work: "People nearly always talk about their managers. Like 'the manager is incompetent,' 'he has no vision,' 'he has no backbone,' or 'I could have done this or that if it weren't for the manager.'" Talk is much more often about a boss or manager rather than about a direct colleague.

Kees (58), who works for a large telecommunications company in the Netherlands, also admits that management is a favorite topic of gossip. "We often discuss how we're expected to do our work. We had a few changes in the way we have to do our job, recently. We don't really see how this is an improvement, or how this is efficient, so we talk a lot about that. We often discuss management and ask ourselves whether they know what they are doing. It often seems like they have no clue."

At my university, it was interesting to see what happened when certain colleagues were promoted to team leaders. The relationship with these colleagues suddenly changed: while nobody was particularly interested in gossiping about them when they were our equals, this changed drastically the moment they became our superiors. Their competence, the decisions they made, what exactly they were doing all day—were suddenly topics of conversation at the coffee machine. After a year or two, several of these team leaders decided to come back to teaching and, almost instantly, ceased to be a topic of conversation.

Resisting change
Ellwardt et al. (2012b) allege that employees of a subordinate status tend to gossip more negatively about their managers in order to resist change. "Gossip is a weapon of the weak," they claim.

Clegg & Van Iterson (2009) describe gossip as "background conversations that provide the murmurs of discontent to which change projects are often a reaction. 'Lower order members' cool out those projects of the authorities that they find disagreeable, using the resources of their background conversations to gossip, make mockery and show cynicism in 'hidden transcripts' of counter power." The authors compare this to tavern conversations or carnivals, where members of the lower social order "mock and subvert the dominant order and authorities."

By doing this, subordinates try to resist power and push and probe for weak spots. "Moments of resistance such as these will rarely if ever overcome the system, but these small bursts of pleasure do serve to make domination more bearable and less injurious," the authors note.

Lack of trust

When subordinates resist change by gossiping, they do so without immediately harming their relationship with their boss. However, Ellwardt et al. (2012b) found that resistance to change and rank alone were not the main factors contributing to negative gossip. Lack of trust in management is an important ingredient. As information usually tends to travel from the top down, employees at the bottom of the organizational flow chart are usually the last to receive information and, by then, it's often too late.

This lack of information, the authors warn, undermines the trust in management, and this leads to a greater urge to take part in negative gossip. "The more management succeeds in presenting itself as trustworthy, the more likely positive news travels through informal channels. On the contrary, beliefs in untrustworthy behavior provide a fertile soil for negative gossip." Several studies (cited in Ellwardt et al., 2012b) show that employees who felt badly treated by their supervisors reverted sooner to gossip than to a direct confrontation. For some, badmouthing the boss and harming her reputation was a major strategy to get even with her.

If, on top of not trusting management, co-workers also have a good relationship with each other and trust each other, the more negative gossip will be spread about the managers. This is the ideal recipe. Ellwardt et al. claim that negative gossip occurs twice as much when there is a lack of trust in management, than when colleagues just have a trusting relationship with each other. So, having negative experiences with your boss will be a greater driving force to spread negative gossip. Even if you don't know your colleagues that well, chances are you will still vent your frustrations.

The ones who have the most difficulty, the authors observe, are the middle managers. Even if they do not make the important decisions within the organization, employees often blame them, as they associate them with management in general. Unlike subordinates, middle managers are less likely to gossip about their managers, as it would not only harm their superiors' reputations, but also theirs.

Sour grapes and envy
You know the fable of the fox who tried to eat the grapes from a vine but couldn't reach them? Since he couldn't get them, he rationalized his failure by saying he didn't want them anyway— they were sour. In the same way, for certain employees who would like to achieve a higher position in their organization but cannot, watching their managers struggle (and even fail) provides them with consolation. You'd have to be crazy to want to be a manager, anyway, they'd say.

In a video talk, Andreas Wismeijer (2020), a psychologist at Tilburg University, explains that it is exactly this feeling that applies to the way we gossip about celebrities. When we compare our lives to that of a famous actor who spends his holiday on a yacht while we are at home ironing our clothes, our lives seem pretty drab in comparison. But when the celebrity is photographed as he pukes over the side of his yacht because he is seasick, we are suddenly content that we stayed at home to do the ironing.

Jealousy and envy are great triggers for gossip. Dylan (24), who used to work in the marketing department of the German headquarters of an American multinational food, snack, and beverage corporation, recalls: "There used to be a lot of chitchat going on in the smaller positions, basically talking about bigger positions and how they got the big positions. If it's a woman, it was like, 'she definitely used her connections to make her way up.' And then obviously, who was deserving what. Like, 'this person really does not deserve this position.' I think that was because quite a number of people were unsatisfied with their own positions, or with their life in general."

Propinquity

While managers and celebrities are popular topics of gossip, other researchers (Clegg & Van Iterson, 2009) argue that people often prefer to gossip about people who are similar to us, or are close to us in proximity. We are more interested in our direct colleague, who has a similar function to ours, rather than someone who is a lot higher up in the ranks. This is what Freud called the 'narcissism of minor differences.' "We gossip about those whom we rub up against rather more than those whom we spy from afar. For the latter, we allow others, who claim closeness, to do it for us, giving rise to the whole industry of the gossip columnist and celebrity magazines."

Generally, envy is more easily aroused by someone close to us that is slightly better off, than by someone more distant who is much better off. The proximity effect is a result of the greater visibility of one's neighbor. Hence, envy can provoke more negative feelings and more gossip. The researchers argue that propinquity, that is, nearness in time, place, and social relations, even increases the animosity of gossip. Since organizational members work in close proximity with other members, they are more likely to experience this narcissism of minor differences.

Joelle (27), an assistant in a nursing home in a rural area in the south of France, recounts: "I moved in the south of France with my boyfriend six years ago. We are both quite young, so when my colleagues found out that we had decided to build our own house, they started talking a lot, but without asking me anything. That is the main problem. We were 21 and 24 when the construction work started. At this time, I only talked about this to one of my colleagues. I thought we were good friends. It has never been a way to show off. I just wanted to update her about my life. Building a house is a pretty big achievement. So, I was proud, and I think it is normal. But then, she probably told someone else, and in the end, they all were wondering how we did pay for this. Or even worse. At some point, I have heard that they were gossiping about the fact that my boyfriend and I were going to break up one day, and we will be in deep shit because of the loan we probably took on. It was like, they almost wished me to break up!"

Other studies (McAndrew, 2014) show that people are usually most interested in gossip about others of the same gender as themselves and who also happen to be around the same age. The author found that college students were not very interested in hearing about (nor talking about) academic awards being given to one of their professors. But similar information about a peer was considered quite interesting and was a lot more likely to spread.

Researching gossip: Using autoethnography?

After running into all kinds of ethical issues when trying to use ethnography as a research method, I considered using autoethnography. When working on the research project at my university and started to experience setbacks, I started to reflect on my own gossip behavior. I started to analyze my emotions and reflect on what pushed me to engage in and respond to gossip, and I soon realized that the focus of my research had shifted. By trying to observe how people gossip, I found myself reflecting more and more on my own role and behavior in the process. I therefore wondered whether it would not be more authentic to reflect on what triggers me to gossip. Would conducting an autoethnography, "an approach to research and writing that seeks to describe and systematically analyze personal experience in order to understand cultural experience" (Ellis et al., 2011), not be a better method to understand the mechanisms of gossip within my organization? Contrary to ethnography, rather than being in the background, I would place myself in the foreground.

As an insider, the researcher becomes better positioned than an outside ethnographer to reveal the true story, as s/he has a natural access to his/her surroundings. Researchers (Brown, 2014) have used autoethnography to analyze the role of teachers or to reflect on immigrants' experiences in academia (Popova, 2016). Because of their privileged position and access, and due to the reflexive nature of their work, such accounts provided insights that few studies on similar topics could ever provide.

And as a researcher, am I not in a better position (and more willing) to analyze and reflect on my feelings and actions than any of my interviewees would? I could definitely provide a truthful account of what was going on in my mind. However, I soon began to question how valid my observations were. To what extent are my perceptions and reactions justified? For instance, I had the impression that one of the colleagues from my research group was less friendly to me and that s/he may have caused my setbacks. But was this perception solely the figment of my imagination? Would another researcher in such a situation have felt the same way I did? How would researchers conducting autoethnographies address such questions when making their methodology choices and how can they ever be certain of their conclusions?

Initially, a very appealing reason for using autoethnography (other than regaining access and a greater authenticity) was to protect my interviewees. I found it a lot easier to expose my feelings and experiences than someone else's, as I felt that I did not have to worry as much about overstepping boundaries when it came to protecting my subjects' privacy. Moreover, getting consent from my interviewees and having my research approved by my research group would be less of an issue, as Forber & Pratt (2015) put it: "Do I have to provide consent for me to study myself?"

But I soon realized that I was not just talking about myself. By documenting how I responded to a gossip situation, I had to talk about others, even if I did so indirectly. Could I really mask the identities of the colleagues in my research project, since some were close colleagues from my research group and others were managers? Even if I remove the names and fictionalize the accounts significantly, certain colleagues would still be able to recognize them. Autoethnographers in similar situations have either asked for their subjects' permission or let enough time go by so the likelihood of recognition would be very slim. Certain authors even chose to remain anonymous themselves. I also soon realized that I started to worry not only about my interviewee's privacy and reputation, but also my own. Would I really want to confess my moral shortcomings? Would any scholar admit to feeling jealousy towards more successful colleagues? Or to having gossiped negatively about others to get ahead? You know the answer! (Darmon, 2018).

While it is clear that we have good reasons to gossip about our peers and managers, the art is to remain discreet and subtle. Not only do we not want to be labeled as the office gossip, but more importantly, we really don't want to get caught red-handed (especially by our managers).

Getting caught: When the third party is no longer absent

There's a hilarious scene in the film *Johnny English* (2003) with Rowan Atkinson. The clumsy, rather daft, secret agent tries to mingle at millionaire's Pascal Sauvage's party and flirts with an attractive woman, who introduces herself as Lorna Campbell (Natalie Imbruglia). He does not recognize Pascal Sauvage (John Malkovich), who creeps up behind him. Johnny English grabs his Bloody Mary, assuming Sauvage is the waiter: "Can you get some of those cheesy nibbles?" he asks him, and turns back to Lorna. "Now, where were we?" he asks her, plunging his eyes into hers.

"You obviously haven't met our host, Monsieur Sauvage," she says.

"No, thank God! You know, I think I'd rather have my bottom impaled on a giant cactus rather than exchange pleasantries with that jumped-up Frenchman. As far as I'm concerned, the only thing the French should be allowed to host is an invasion."

English turns to face the man he believes to be the waiter, standing right behind him. "Sorry can I help?" he asks.

"Pascal Sauvage, the jumped-up Frenchman," he says sarcastically, shaking Lorna's hand. Johnny English's awkward reaction and Lorna's mortification are priceless. It's not that English was gossiping that added humor to the scene, but the way in which he got caught.

This illustrates the importance of the *absent* third party. The person we are gossiping about should definitely be out of earshot!

When confronted by a television host on Dutch national TV about gossiping with Trudeau, Macron, and Johnson at the NATO convention, Prime Minister Mark Rutte shot back: "It's good to gossip. As long as it stays a secret!"

Nevertheless, as Rutte can testify, keeping gossip a secret is not as easy as it seems. Soon after he had been reelected for the fourth time, during the cabinet-formation talks, comments were made about Pieter Omtzigt, a highly vocal and critical MP. Attendees suggested giving Omtzigt another job to keep him away from parliament. One of the informants present made notes of the discussion, and when she walked out of the meeting and left Parliament, a photographer took pictures of the notes she was holding. He was able to zoom in on the comments and, suddenly, conversations that were supposedly held during a private meeting were out in the open for public consumption. Mark Rutte got into serious trouble and his position as newly elected prime minister was instantly on the line.

But as columnist Bert Keizer (2021) wrote in the newspaper *Trouw*, "[m]inisters should still be able to say somewhere that they're going crazy because of Saint Omtzigt. Can't politicians or ministers gossip about someone who they feel is a ticking time bomb or a volcano waiting to explode?" While Keizer explains that it's absolutely human to gossip, the biggest problem is getting caught.

And it is a problem. Just google "getting caught gossiping" and you will see that the situation happens a lot. Many employees have lost their jobs because of it. In a column in the Canadian paper *The Globe and Mail* (Galt, 2007), where readers share their experiences of having been caught gossiping, one man recounts: "My boss wants to fire me because I commented on his big teeth and bad breath. I was really just a sideline man who heard these conversations and chimed in on occasion. One specific employee told the boss that I was the main contributor to the gossip, and my boss has had it in for me ever since."

"What should I do?" the reader asks Michael Stern, an expert on workplace culture.

The main advice to people who find themselves in such sticky situations is to, first of all, stay clear of gossip altogether. But as the author notes, "[t]he offices and factory floors would be pretty empty in Canada if employees were routinely fired for gossiping about their bosses."

Most experts agree that malicious gossip can sink a career. Your boss may not explicitly tell you why you are let go, but you wouldn't be too far off to assume that it was because she caught you gossiping.

Cathy (21) used to work in the restaurant of a large department store in Ireland. She remembers how one of her colleagues had been told off by her boss for not working very hard: "That made her really angry. So later on, she started ranting to me, saying, 'Ugh, I hate that manager,' but what she didn't know was that the manager was walking by behind her. I was, like, 'Fuck, we're screwed.' But, luckily, she was the one talking, not me. Two months later the manager approached my colleague and she said something like, 'I'm so sorry, I'm not renewing your contract.'" Cathy is certain it was because her manager had overheard her colleague gossip.

Also, if you get caught, you can also be sued for defamation (or for spreading harmful rumors). Looking at the amount of law firms offering counsel for such cases, we can see that the problem is certainly considerable (especially in the US).

Finding the *sweet spot of gossip*

It goes without saying that getting caught gossiping off guard by the supposedly absent third party will get you in trouble. But

your reputation could already take a blow with your listener(s) if you cross the line by gossiping about the wrong thing or person.

To begin with, negative gossipers are generally less liked than positive gossipers, according to a study by Farley (2011). The negative gossipers who gossiped a lot were most disliked of all. What is paradoxical, is that negative gossipers are considered more interesting and more knowledgeable than positive gossipers. So, while it is important to not dish out too much negative gossip, you also don't want to come across as a bore or a Goody Two-shoes. Navigating this is delicate, to say the least.

An important consideration to think about is: What are the consequences our gossip may have? In an article called 'Are they mad at me… or are they just blunt?' in the *Harvard Business Review*, Alice Boyes (2021) recalls receiving instructions from a colleague quite bluntly. "Their directions were along the lines of, 'make sure you do this, this, and this' and 'make sure you don't do this, this and this.' I felt my anxiety spike," she reveals. "Collaborating with this kind of blunt communicator can cause you to waste time and emotional energy ruminating over whether you've done something wrong or worrying that you're too sensitive."

This is a typical situation where one would be tempted to gossip, to get the emotional support and the validation that it's not you, it's them. Nonetheless, the author stresses that such gossip could harm the blunt colleague considerably. "The legend of the colleague's behavior and personality can quickly overtake the reality and lead to them being unfairly labeled as difficult and potentially being excluded," Boyes (2021) warns. This type of gossip can also backfire as your colleagues may start siding with the blunt colleague. So, before you open your mouth and share your feelings and insecurities, it's wise to be mindful of the consequences. And if you can't help yourself, make sure you talk to someone you can trust!

In the Netherlands, employees do not gossip so readily about other colleagues' appearance, unless they are very close to each other. Therefore, discussing this is usually a quick way to cross the line between what is considered acceptable or not. In Brazil or Portugal, this would probably not be considered a cardinal sin (see Chapter 5).

I remember once gossiping with a few colleagues about a co-worker, Trevor, that we all found extremely arrogant and incompetent. We were sharing anecdotes about some of his blunders and laughing together. Suddenly, one of the colleagues, Ginette, commented on Trevor's bad teeth and how repulsive she found him. There was suddenly silence in the group, and I could sense that Ginette was being judged poorly.

Tijs (22), an employee at a housing corporation in the Netherlands, reveals: "I have a colleague who often makes comments about people that makes me think: 'That wasn't necessary.' These comments are predominantly about personal characteristics and traits that people have, like what others look like. When he does that, I feel a strong aversion towards him. I don't hate him, but I certainly don't trust him, and would never share things with him."

Naturally, there are certain situations where gossipers would be judged very severely, instantly. Jan (23), who works in the distribution center of a large Dutch textile company, explains: "Sometimes the gossiping gets out of hand. For example, we have a Dutch co-worker who converted to Islam a few years ago. There are a few colleagues who do not like Muslims in general and they will not hold back when giving their opinion. They say things like: 'How is it possible that someone wants to be a Muslim? Muslims are bad. Muslims are responsible for the terror attacks.' Whenever someone talks to me in this way I will say something about it. It makes me feel sick."

Daniel (45), an IT architect at a Hungarian bank, recounts: "We do business with occasional suppliers. They are not always involved in the life of the bank, but are often the topic of gossip. There was once an account management transition, where we worked with Indian colleagues. And we gossiped about everything; what they eat, how stinky they are, how drunk they were from the Pálinka (a very strong Hungarian alcohol), and how they behaved at the project closing party. We talked about with whom they were trying to build a closer relationship within the company while they were drunk. However, one of our colleagues listening to this was not comfortable with these comments and ended up going to the HR department to complain about our conversation."

As these last examples show, when gossiping turns into bullying and discrimination, then, obviously, it is no longer acceptable.

Carla (28) works for a large furniture retailer in the Netherlands. "It's okay to share your (negative) opinion about a person or situation," she says. "But when your behavior towards the person changes, it could easily turn into bullying. I think it's bullying when there is a whole group of people who are just gossiping to make fun of someone, instead of only sharing some negative thoughts about a certain situation. When you are constantly talking negatively about someone, it might change the way you and your colleagues see him/her. I also don't think it's acceptable when it's not just about one situation anymore, but about more personal things."

Such bullying can poison a company's culture. Stacey (22), employed at a large appliance retail store in the Netherlands, reveals how her colleagues' and manager's gossip became very toxic for her: "In the beginning of my employment, my colleagues told my manager everything that I did wrong. They gossiped that I was slow in counting and that I couldn't count. Later on, I noticed that they started to gossip openly. So, it was noticeable that my colleagues were gossiping in front of customers. Later on, the manager also started to gossip openly about me. They also spoke badly about my country [the Antilles], where I came from. Finally, even though I had a private conversation with my manager, I found out later on that she told others about it. She also continued making discriminating slurs."

Bullying and making racist comments are clear ways of crossing the line. But, usually, making a faux pas is much more subtle. One can be perceived negatively fairly quickly even without committing such sins as overt bullying. Wayne (27) works for a small Dutch consultancy office: "Somebody once told me that Laura (one of my colleagues) was pregnant," he recalls. "I thought: 'Ah, this person just thinks Laura is pregnant because she is getting a belly. It was around Christmas time, so it can happen.' But she [the gossiper] went around telling it to everyone. She didn't know for sure; she just guessed. She saw a belly and started this rumor that Laura was pregnant. When she [the gossiper] told me, I said: 'Ask her if she is.' Then she said: 'You cannot do that. It's not nice. Imagine if she isn't pregnant.'" Wayne admits that he really did not think highly of the gossiper: "I don't like the person professionally. I think it's very immature to talk like this."

Yordona (47), a manager for a construction company in Bulgaria, remembers: "At my previous workplace, we used to collect money for coffee, filters, and sugar. One colleague was responsible for that and was keeping track of the money. So, she used to comment on how many coffees one was drinking, and what amount of sugar people put in their coffee. She even used to gossip about what my colleagues were eating. This was ridiculous. I don't think I ever paid that much attention to the things she was saying, but it certainly wasn't very pleasant to know that someone is talking behind everyone's back in such a way."

Coming across as petty and as someone who meddles in other peoples' business is a sure way to cross the line.

It is important to keep in mind that, in general, managers hate gossip. According to one study by Grosser et al. (2010), while managers may rely on gossip themselves, they do not particularly value it from their employees. Managers are made to feel insecure by gossip and do not make the distinction between positive and negative gossip. The more a person engages in gossip activity, the lower the supervisor rates that person's work. In certain cases, they are certainly justified.

Mark (31) is a manager for a real estate platform in the Netherlands. "Recently, three of our Dutch colleagues suddenly got closer to each other because they did not agree with a specific policy," he says. "First you saw them gossiping in the hallway. Everyone could see that they were discussing something regarding a management decision because when someone from the management (me, in this case) walked by, the conversation stopped. Later on, I noticed that these colleagues went to lunch together and separated themselves from other colleagues. Everyone noticed this, and this had effect on the company atmosphere. I think they didn't even realize it themselves. So, gossipers should realize that this behavior reflects on them as well. By separating themselves in this way, they isolate themselves from the rest of the organization."

Although it is understandable that in such cases, managers hate gossip, in other cases, they should learn to appreciate it. A study (Ayim, 1994) shows that quite a few managers at the top do rely on gossip to get crucial information that they would not normally get. It's even essential for their work. Mark acknowledges that he sometimes learns a lot from the gossip going around at work. "Sometimes, it happens that a decision is made that goes against our company's mission and, rather, goes more in the direction of making more profit. I noticed that, when this happens, our employees start to gossip. They won't say it directly to the CEO that they disagree with the decision, but they try to find support with other colleagues. That's actually a good thing, if you ask me, because most of the time the gossip does reach management and the CEO. So, then they are informed and can act on it. This keeps the company values very much alive in our organization!"

Tips for employees and managers

1. When you hear negative gossip, consider the source and the motivation they may have.

Especially when employees are discussing someone else's poor performance, question their motives. Could it be that they have a hidden agenda? That they feel insecure about themselves? In some cases, certain people may spend a lot of time criticizing others' performance in order to distract their colleagues from the fact that they are not necessarily doing very well themselves.

Darlene (45), a producer at a Canadian television station, recalls: "We were a small team working on a show. We had a colleague, Jean, on the team who kept bad-mouthing one of our team members. Jean would gossip about how incompetent he was, and liked to point out the mistakes he made. Everyone spoke about this guy and didn't pay as much attention to anyone else. We were really surprised when we discovered that Jean wasn't meeting her deadlines and wasn't functioning all that well herself. It's like she used this gossip to distract everyone from her own inadequacies."

This example illustrates that while such gossip may be informative and entertaining, it may just be a smoke screen to hide the truth. Taking the credibility of the author into account and having a critical approach to gossip is of upmost importance.

2. Avoid being (too much) the topic of gossip yourself.

Needless to say, having an exemplary behavior at works minimizes the gossip that could be said about you. Avoid having affairs, stay off the bottle, and don't get involved in corruption scandals. However, Ted Jenkin, author of a blog called 'Why Your Co-workers Talk behind Your Back' (2014), insists that there are certain (less spectacular) topics that are sure to attract gossip:

-   Spending too much time on a coffee break. If you spend hours in the office kitchen, your colleagues will notice that

you are wasting a lot of time and will assume that you are not very productive.
- Having a messy office. The author guarantees that if your office is a bomb, your desk will certainly "make Instagram and Vine with more fun being poked at it than a piñata."
- Being the office "drama queen or king." People are quick to gossip about a colleague who is constantly running in and out of the office, taking private calls on their cell phones, and always having emergencies at home.
- Taking too many sick days. Being frequently absent will not go unnoticed. Especially if this increases your colleagues' workloads.

Even though you may not want to be the hot topic of gossip at work, if no one ever talks about you, good chances are, you are considered boring. As Oscar Wilde put it: "There is only one thing in the world worse than being talked about, and that is not being talked about."

3. Confront the third party rather than talking behind their back. Rather than talk about someone behind their back and risk getting caught, why not confront them directly with the issue? Peter Bregman (2018), in the *Harvard Business Review*, believes that this is the best solution. "It's a scary, more risky thing to do," he says. "But it's why it's worth developing your emotional courage—because, while scary, it's far more likely to be highly productive." Most people complain (or gossip) because they feel powerless. Employees are scared that if they confront their bosses, they will suffer the consequences. "It's a risk," the author concedes. "Or it may gain you their respect and, in one sentence, change the direction of the leader and the organization."

This may be a strategy worth looking into. If your managers and colleagues are open to constructive feedback, this may be the best way to go. Nevertheless, people from many cultures are a lot less direct than Americans or Dutch people would be and would never think of confronting someone directly (see Chapter 5).

Tips for employees

1.   Managers hate gossip.
Managers who notice their employees gossiping will tend to rate them poorly. So, beware! Managers have the impression that a worker gossiping is wasting time and creating a negative atmosphere. And they may also have the feeling that they are the topic of gossip (which, indeed, is very often true). Even if you are sharing positive stories at the watercooler, you can be pretty sure that your manager will not see the difference.

2.   Gossip about celebrities. It's a lot safer.
Andreas Wismeijer (2020), a psychologist at Tilburg University, claims that a celebrity can feel like a type of common friend to everybody. We know them but they do not know us. It's safe to gossip about Angelina Jolie or Brad Pitt. They will never know (or care) that we gossiped about them. Unlike a colleague or a manager, they will never find out. And, as we have seen, not getting caught is of the essence!

3.   If you are caught, don't deny it or lie—especially if the gossip is in writing.
Mark Rutte saw that the consequences of lying were even worse than getting caught. Most experts agree that the best strategy is to own it. "Like mold in the basement, the damage caused by being linked to gossip continues to grow if left unchecked," Michael Stern, an expert on workplace culture (cited in Galt, 2007), explains: "If you know you've been caught, don't pretend you weren't. You need to have a face-to-face talk with the other person and attempt to put the comments in context and apologize if necessary."

Jane Burnett, author of the article '3 ways to move forward when you get caught gossiping about a colleague' (2018), says it's best not to do it too quickly, as the apology may come across as insincere: it will look like you are more sorry for getting caught. Wait a bit, then promise the third party that this will never happen again, and that you will handle such situations differently in the future.

4.   So... don't get caught.

When gossip originating from the Dutch political party Democrats '66 came into the open that, apparently, politician and informant Johan Remkes had a drinking problem, Sigrid Kaag, the leader of the party, immediately took responsibility and came clean. "The words have been withdrawn immediately," she claimed at the start of a parliamentary session.

But the damage was done. She and her party still came under fire. Politicians called them 'cowards' and described the gossip as 'sad talk.'

Keep in mind that once you get caught, the damage may be irreversible. So, the best thing is not to get caught!

Tips for managers

1.   Don't try to eliminate gossip—use it to your advantage.

Gossip is inevitable, and managers will very often be a topic of choice. Instead of taking offence, managers should keep their eyes and ears open and even encourage their employees to gossip with them.

Annie (60), the principal of a Canadian high school, believes that by gossiping, she has become an even better and more humane manager. She explained that once, two of her teachers who had been in a relationship for a long time suddenly broke up. "When school started again, I saw them at the introduction party. The woman was happy and glowing, but her partner was standing alone, looking very depressed. I had heard the gossip, so knew what was going on. I went over to speak to him and asked him if he was okay. He shared his problems with me, and I told him that I would be there if ever he needed to talk. I think he really appreciated that. I would have never noticed him if I had not heard the gossip previously. That's why I love to gossip!"

A study by Ayim (1994) shows that those managers who are left out of gossip circles have a lot less power, eventually lose control, and are unable to remain at the top.

2. Understand what triggers your employees to gossip.
Resistance to change, uncertainty, and fear are good reasons for employees to gossip. The more quickly a manager responds to these fears, the better. Transparency and accountability are key.

3. Be fair.
Employees look at each other and compare themselves with each other. So, it is key to remain fair and transparent.

Tina (26) is Indonesian and worked at several luxury hotels in Bali. "At one of the hotels I worked for there were a lot of trainees working there. They would usually be hired if they did a good job after the six-month trial period. But, in certain cases, some would receive a contract straight away, after only a short period of time, just because they got along well with their superiors. This gives an unhealthy atmosphere, as the seniors who have worked there longer as full-time employees, who have dedicated a lot of hours to the property, suddenly get bumped by newcomers."

So, if one team member gets a promotion or a privilege, it is important to explain why. If the decision is fair, others will be less bitter about it and less likely to gossip. Not only is the manager protecting herself, but also her subordinate who just got promoted.

4. The Who

As we have seen so far, we have plenty to gossip about, and certain people, just by their rank or position in the organization, are sure to be hot topics of conversation. We have also discussed how easy it is to cross the line by saying the wrong thing or by making a joke that comes across as not funny at all. Another extremely important factor to consider in order to gossip well is whom to gossip with. Whom can we trust? What makes us gossip with certain people at work and not with others? Sometimes the stereotype that certain people are bound to be good gossips just because of their profession or gender may give us the wrong impression and lead us down the wrong path. Other times, such stereotypes are simply harmful.

Professional gossips

There's a funny scene in the comedy series *New Girl*. Nick (Jake Johnson) says to his roommate Schmidt (Max Greenfield): "Please tell me you're not dressing up as Santa this year?"

Schmidt replies: "Of course, I'm going to dress up as Santa! I like it. Plus, I get all this dirt on my co-workers. They get drunk, and they whisper what they want for Christmas in my ear. So, I can use this information to subtly undermine them and control them for the rest of the year!"

This scene illustrates that we are more inclined to gossip with certain people. Short of dressing as Santa, certain professions seem to go hand in hand with gossip.

Judging by the dozens of hair salons from all corners of the globe with names like 'Gossip Hair,' 'Hot Gossip Hair and Nail Salon,' or 'The Local Gossip,' it is clear that hairdressers and beauticians have mastered the art. The book *Confessions of a Hairdresser: Gossip, Gossip, and More Gossip* by Robin Daumit (2009), illustrates this perfectly. Take my hairdresser, Robert. Every time I go for a haircut, I am impressed by the conversations he has with his clients. They seem to share all kinds of intimate things with him, and he always listens compassionately, laughing at their jokes. I once asked Robert: "I can see that your clients speak to you very freely. Do they gossip a lot with you?" He laughs. "Do they ever!"

Robert quickly told me that he never gossips about other clients with his clients. "If I gossip with you about someone we both know, you will leave and probably wonder whether I talk about you with other people. So, I am really careful not to do that."

In popular culture, beauticians and manicurists are very often depicted as gossipers. No one is surprised when Elle Woods (Reese Witherspoon) goes for a manicure in *Legally Blonde* (2001) to gossip about her unpleasant Harvard classmates and ex-boyfriend.

Or in *Seinfeld*: Elaine (Julia Louis-Dreyfus) arrives late to her appointment at the nail salon, so one of the manicurists tells her she will have to wait for another one to be free. "Well, how long will it take?" Elaine whines. "I have a million things to do." The manicurists start to gossip about her in Korean. "*Princess in big hurry. Mustn't keep princess waiting. Poor princess.*"

"What?" asks Elaine.

"Not long." (They all laugh.)

"*Princess wants a manicure,*" one informs her colleague. "*You got the princess.*"

"*Oh, lucky me!*"

Receptionists and secretaries are also talented. Take Leonie (63), who works as a receptionist at a municipality in the Netherlands. "Because I'm sitting at the reception desk," she explains, "a lot of people come to talk to me, so I hear a lot. When people have something they want to get off their chests, they often come to me. Once there was this colleague in my department who was really boy crazy. I think she was looking for a boyfriend. So, there was a lot of gossip about her and, as receptionist, I could see a lot. Even when she was not supposed to be present, she was there. And when certain male colleagues had an evening shift, she would stay behind to be with them. So, of course, we would talk about that."

John Demos, in *A Little Commonwealth: Family Life in Plymouth Colony* (1970) (cited in Capps, 2012), claims that in Colonial

America midwives played a crucial role as professional gossipers. They were expected by the town authorities to persuade a pregnant woman out of wedlock to reveal the identity of the father of the baby. The midwives would manage to get this information when delivery was actually taking place and the woman was least likely to resist. "Such information would be used to punish the father and to make him financially responsible for his child's maintenance. The midwife, then, became a 'tattler,' an 'informer,' a role that served the interests of the community if not the biological father of the newborn."

But while certain professions, such as hairdresser and manicurist, may be good at attracting gossip, others may be more selective. In Lee Child's thriller *Night School* (2016), army cop Jack Reacher walks into a bar in Hamburg hoping to find information about a suspect who, he knows, is a regular patron. We may think the bartender may be a good person to begin an investigation with, but Reacher knows better: "Bartenders never spill the beans. Why would they? Who came first, the sixty people they had to live with every night of their lives, or the lone guy they had never seen before?"

I couldn't help wonder whether Reacher was convinced of this, more or less consciously, because the bartender happened to be male. Interestingly, many of these gossipy professions tend to be dominated by women.

What does gender have to do with it?

The tongue is the sword of a woman—and she never lets it get rusty.
—Chinese proverb

A question that comes up a lot when I talk about gossip is whether women gossip more than men. Do they gossip differently? Academic studies are quite divided on this question. As we will see, the entire notion of gossip (and all of its negative connotations) is often very much linked to women. Hence, the rules vary greatly depending on gender.

Figure 5 *The Gossip* (c. 1922) by William Penhallow
Source: Smithsonian American Art Museum

Today, many studies (Rosnow & Fine, 1976; Clegg & Van Iterson, 2009) claim that there is still a strong perception that gossip is mainly a 'woman thing,' and that men would not normally engage in 'such petty activity.' Within an organization, the concept of gossip tends to be linked to women, especially to secretaries.

Just look at popular culture. The gossips are nearly always women. In the series *Virgin River*, the (female) town mayor Hope (Annette O'Toole) is shown running around, gossiping and meddling in everyone's business. In the Canadian-American series *When Calls the Heart*, we see that it is the women in the village who are gossiping and whispering in each others' ears. You wouldn't see men engaging in such activities. As for the series *Gossip Girl*, the title and the woman's voice imply that the anonymous gossiper is a woman. Stereotypically, you would expect it. Spoiler alert! Gossip Girl is actually a boy!

In art, too, when a gossip is depicted, it is typically always a woman. Look at the painting *The Gossip* (circa 1922, figure 5) by William Penhallow, showing two women from the Sangre de Cristo Mountains in northern New Mexico actively gossiping.

And this is not new, as is illustrated by the painting *The Village Gossips* from 1828, by Rolinda Sharples (figure 6).

In the book *The Family Upstairs* (2019) by Lisa Jewell, Henry, a teenage boy living in a household where strange things occur after a new family moved in to stay with his, observes: "I was as ever, hanging around the kitchen with my mother, eavesdropping on her conversation with the women who now seemed to live in our house. I'd subliminally determined at this point that the only way to really know what was going on in the world was to listen to women talk. Anyone who ignores the chatter of women is poorer by any measure." Here, too, the implication is that women gossip more.

But is this really true?

Quite a few researchers (Dunbar, 2004; Foster, 2004; Luna & Chou, 2013; Michelson & Mouly, 2000) have found that women actually do not gossip more frequently than men, despite the expectations that they do.

Lea (27), who works for an international wholesale chain based in Austria, notes: "In my department, there are mostly women, so I witness female gossiping more than male gossiping. But the two men that we have in the department gossip just as much as the women, if not even more. I would almost say they completely make up for the lack of males with how much they gossip!"

Laszlo (26), a Hungarian project manager at an American engineering company, also says: "I would even say that men gossip more than women! Especially older men really love to gossip!"

Bitchy or assertive? Stereotypes and expectations

Even though several studies prove that men gossip just as much (and, in some cases, even more) than women, it is clear that women suffer from huge prejudices. According to Clegg & Van Iterson (2009), when gossip is seen as positive discourse within organizational studies, it is often represented as being masculine. Women, on the other hand, are often considered to engage in "idle talk," "tattle," and "run about," whereas men "shoot the breeze" and "talk shop," Michelson & Mouly (2000) observe.

Heinrich (33), a manager at a large car manufacturer in Germany, observes: "Females tend to gossip more about female colleagues, men rather about career topics and work-related topics, like how something is done and that it could be achieved more efficiently in another way or by use of a different technology."

It's well known that gender stereotypes dictate how men and women are perceived at work. In an article in the *Harvard Business Review*, Evans et al. (2019) claim that men are often stereotyped as having "high achievement orientation, ambition, and focus on task accomplishment." Women, on the other hand, tend to be considered as less ambitious and having "lower levels of achievement orientation," which is due to their increased family responsibilities. Such stereotypes affect how women are perceived in a variety of situations and, naturally, how they are perceived when gossiping.

The article claims that men who use humor in a presentation are considered as funny and as having more status and prestige compared to men who do not use humor. But when a woman used the same jokes in the same presentation, her audience considered her as having less status and as being less capable. Several participants had the feeling that she was even using humor to cover up her inadequacies and her "lack of real business acumen by making little jokes." The male speaker, on the other hand, was seen as witty and using humor to "break the monotony of his presentation."

In William Shaw's crime novel *The Birdwatcher* (2016), Detective Sergeant Alexandra Cupidi was assigned a murder case on her first day of the job. She quickly took control and, during a meeting, assertively assigned tasks to her male colleagues. Afterwards, a few officers remained in the room, staring at the list of tasks on the whiteboard, and started to gossip.

"That new one. She's very...," one of them said.

"Assertive," another completed.

"Dominant."

If DS Cupidi had been a man, most likely, she would have been considered very competent. A man who is ambitious and assertive is considered to be strong, while a woman with these qualities is considered to be bitchy. In her book *Nice Girls Still Don't Get the Corner Office* (2014), Lois Frankel notes that when a man is impatient, he's considered to be a "go-getter, always on the go, or ready to move ahead." When a woman is impatient, it means that "she expects too much, has a sense of entitlement, or doesn't understand how things work around here."

When it comes to gossiping, women are judged even more harshly. "You know how girls love to talk behind each other's back all the time, then act like they are best friends when talking to each other?" Patrick (27), a Belgian-Peruvian who works at an electric utility company in Belgium, laughs. "Well at my job, I'll see some women talk shit. They'll be like, 'Oh, did you see the dress she has on? You can see her breasts!' or 'It's too short,' or 'Did you see her lipstick? It's really ridiculous!' I think that between us men, we never say anything about how anyone looks like, like 'Oh, look at his jeans, they're too tight' or 'His shoes aren't clean enough,' or whatever."

After a bit of probing, Patrick does admit that men also like to gossip. "Men definitely gossip, but about different things, maybe a bit more work related. But, hmm, women also gossip about work-related stuff. Come to think of it, I've recently overheard a couple of men talking about how the girls look."

In Margaret Atwood's *The Handmaid's Tale* (1985), Offred, the narrator, describes what happened when she caught the women in the kitchen gossiping about her: "Their faces were the way women's faces are when they've been talking about you behind your back and they think you've heard: embarrassed, but also a little defiant, as if it were their right."

In popular culture, women are too often portrayed as 'busybodies,' meddling in everyone's business, spying on their neighbors behind closed curtains. Even if there seems to be a type of hierarchy for women gossipers, they are always portrayed in a negative way. In the detective novel *Liar Liar* by Mel Sherratt (2020), Mary Stanton is a widow who had retired seven years previously. She lives in a block of flats where criminals operate fairly freely. "We wouldn't say she was a busybody but she did know a lot of what went on. People liked to offload to her, share gossip too. Of course, she never said anything to anyone, so she had garnered a certain trust among the regular tenants, often being seen as a confidante."

'Confidante' is certainly better than 'busybody.' Nevertheless, Mary was still killed because the perpetrator suspected she had seen too much and didn't trust her to stay silent. When the police arrived at the scene, Detective Sergeant Grace Allendale shook her head. "Poor Mary," she says. "She seemed a lovely lady, even though a bit of a busybody. And where would we be without people like her?" Even though Mary had been brave and contacted the cops when all of the other tenants in the building were too scared to come forward, she was still labeled a busybody. Rather than recognizing her courage, she was perceived as an indiscreet gossiper. If Mary had been a man, would she also have been labeled a busybody? I would dare to bet not!

When it comes to women in the workplace, perceptions are not much better.

Farley et al. (2010) claim that while women at work are stereotypically seen as warm and nurturing, women who gossip are not. They are seen as opinionated and willing to take the risk of ruining relationships, hurting someone's feelings, or being vindictive.

Kim (29), who works at a large food corporation in the Netherlands, recounts: "Last year, this young woman, 25 years old, was hired. She must have been standing in front of the line when God was busy distributing beauty, because she is truly a good-looking woman! But the women at work were extremely jealous of her and spent time making fun of her clothes and make-up. Whereas the men made rather dirty comments and jokes about her."

In this case, women are seen to be jealous, petty, and nasty. Men make jokes.

Many academic studies also reinforce such negative stereotypes. For instance, McAndrew (2014) claims that "women are more likely to use gossip in an aggressive or socially destructive manner." Although men may be interested in the doings of other men, women are "obsessed" by the doings of other women. "And that is not benign." Women are more likely to use gossip to exclude and ostracize others. "The motivation for this relational aggression can be as trivial as simple boredom, but it more often transpires in retaliation of perceived slights or envy over physical appearance or males." Women will try to exclude competitors from their social groups and "damage their ability to maintain a reliable social network of their own," according to the author.

Another study (Farley et al., 2010) claims that women who gossip a lot are perceived as having a greater need to control others. Also, not a particularly desirable characteristic!

Others (Vaillancourt & Sharma, 2011) use evolutionary psychology and biology to show that it is in a woman's DNA to gossip and display "bitchy behavior," as she is competing for males and needs to dismantle the competition.

But as Soraya Nadia McDonald (2013) from the *Washington Post* observes, such studies are usually based on flawed research. "These claims aren't just irresponsible because they reinforce sexist and pernicious stereotypes about women. [...] Too many researchers merely end up providing pseudo-scientific justification for the status quo."

In *Nice Girls Still Don't Get the Corner Office* (2014), Lois Frankel explains that during her coaching sessions, she had heard numerous complaints from women that other women tend to backstab them more than men. Women are more often perceived as conniving and catty, especially when dealing with their female peers. But this isn't necessarily true: "Backstabbing is gender blind." But everyone has different expectations of women. Because they are seen as more nurturing, we expect women to treat us better than men would. When this doesn't happen, we feel that an attack coming from a female colleague is a lot worse than from a man. It's also "more socially acceptable to point out the foibles of women than to do the same with men. Men do it to women all the time, so the less enlightened woman follows suit."

Different gossiping styles

While women suffer from many gross generalizations and stereo-types (that are often untrue), several researchers found that there were still notable differences in terms of how men and women gossip, what they gossip about, and why they gossip in the first place.

Several researchers (Rabeau, 2008; Watson, 2012) found that women tend to gossip more about intimate matters of other people as well as physical appearance and clothing.

A woman's attention to detail also distinguishes them from their male counterparts.

Koos (31), a back-office manager at a sales company in the Netherlands, observes: "Women tend to go into a lot more depth. They're a lot more detail oriented than men are. Women turn every stone instead of ploughing the entire garden, like men do."

Monika (22), an event manager in Lithuania, also notes: "Women like to hear more details. With men, you have to be more concrete when gossiping; they are very direct and the gossiping is shorter."

The underlying reasons to gossip differ as well: women are more prone to use gossip as a way to establish group solidarity and make social comparisons.

Watson (2012) believes that men and women have different attitudes towards friendship and that influences the way they gossip. Women tend to have greater needs for intimacy and closeness in their friendships, while men try to gain power and status. Therefore, men are more interested in achievement gossip, as being in the know is a way of gaining status. The author claims that women are usually less self-involved and tend to talk more about others, as they are more interested in building and maintaining social networks.

Who we gossip with

In Margaret Atwood's dystopian *The Handmaid's Tale* (1985), she describes a totalitarian and repressive society where dissenters

Figure 7   Gossip alliances
Source: Wittek & Wielers (1998)

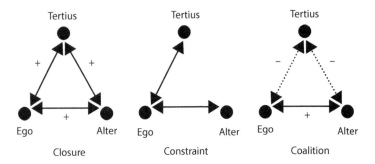

are executed and hanged at the Wall. Even if you don't know whom to trust, and making a mistake could cost you your life, people still talk. "There can be alliances even in such places, even under such circumstances. This is something you can depend upon: there will always be alliances, of one kind or another."

We have looked at gender stereotypes and professional gossipers, but another essential question is: Whom are we drawn to when we feel the need to gossip? Are there certain people whom we are more likely to confide in? Whom should we talk to and whom should we avoid? What are the best alliances for gossip?

Wittek & Wielers (1998) examined the typical social interactions that lead to gossip. There are always three players involved: the gossiper (which they call 'ego'), the listener (called 'alter'), and the person being discussed (called 'tertius'). The authors describe three types of triads that describe different gossip scenarios: closure, constraint, and coalition (see figure 7).

Alliances

Closure triad

In the closure triad, the gossiper, listener, and target all have good relationships with each other—for example, two siblings may be gossiping about their mother, whom they both love very much. Or two employees who are friends, exchanging positive gossip about their manager, whom they both like. Although people regularly gossip about common friends and relatives, this is much less interesting than gossip coming from the other two triads. But even gossip about a friend that starts off as positive, may easily morph into something more negative. You may discuss that you are worried about Mary—she's such a nice person. It's too bad she didn't get that promotion. She really deserves it. But maybe she was not diplomatic enough with her manager, maybe she didn't do so well on the last project she worked on. Gossip in this type of triad can also lead to juicy stories, especially since the gossiper and listener are good friends and trust each other.

Constraint triad
In the constraint triad, the gossiper knows the third party, but the listener doesn't. To come back to Robert, my hairdresser: "People tell me all kinds of things about their work, because it is totally safe," he explains. "They don't have to worry that I will discuss their issues with other colleagues. For many, it's actually a great way to let off steam! Even if they don't know me that well, you would be surprised at how much they share!"

This is a perfect example of a constraint triad.

Knowing that your listener doesn't know the target increases the feeling of safety. I am pretty sure that Robert will never talk to my colleagues or manager about what I have said about them. So, like many people, I suppose, I often walk out of my hairdresser's not only in awe of my new haircut, but of how loose-lipped I have managed to be. Some of the things I told him, I would never dream of sharing with my colleagues.

Even if my hairdresser may lend a good ear to my woes at work, Wittek & Wielers (1998) claim that someone like Robert won't be as interested in hearing my work gossip as my colleagues would. Even if the gossiper and listener have a good relationship (like I do with Robert), the listener won't be as interested in hearing gossip about an absent third party they do not know. For this reason, the constraint triad is less strong than the coalition triad.

Coalition triad

When the gossiper and listener have a good relationship with each other and they both know and dislike the absent third party, this is called the coalition triad. So, two colleagues who are friends and trust each other gossiping about another colleague or manager they dislike will provide the best type of gossip. The coalition triad, the authors believe, is the one leads to the juiciest type of gossip.

Not mutual friends but mutual enemies make the best topic for gossip, as is well illustrated in the video spoof 'The Secret Joy of Having a Mutual Enemy,' by US comedians Akilah Hughes and Milana Vayntrub (2020). Two workmates, start talking cautiously:

"So who's on your team?" Akilah asks.

"I have Warren, Melina, Charlie...," Milana answers.

"Charlie? Hmmm."

"You know Charlie?"

"Yeah," Akilah says with a reserved smile, hinting ever so slightly about her feelings. "Yeah, I like Charlie."

"Uh huh."

"Do you... also like Charlie?"

"He can be interesting..."

"Yes!"

"Just sometimes..."

"He might be..."

"... just a..."

"tad..."

"a bit..."

"much!"

"OK. Honestly, I fucking hate him!"

Then the two women seemed to have reached an epiphany, a revelation. As they throw their initial caution to the wind and share their true feelings, they start dancing, as in a trance. Big letters flash on the screen: "We have a mutual enemy!"

This feeling is delicious and very recognizable.

Brigitte (22), a French student, used to work for a student organization, securing contracts with companies. She remembers just how bad her workplace was when she first started: "It was a *catastrophe*! It was going really bad between colleagues, there was a bad atmosphere, we were always fighting about everything, so, obviously everyone was talking behind everybody's back! When I first started working in the organization, I had the feeling I was alone in thinking that the president was doing a bad job. But by talking with others and hearing some of the remarks about him, we started to talk more and more about it. First, it was with three, four, and five people. In the end, every time we met, we were talking about the president because the organization was doing badly. We realized we were not alone in thinking that! Here, I think the gossiping was a form of delivery. Honestly, I was feeling so good by talking, listening, or sharing gossip I heard about him!" In this case, gossip really helped to bring the colleagues together!

Yao et al. (2014) have also found that we tend to gossip with people who know the same targets as we do, especially when these are involved in "interesting" and "socially relevant situations" to us.

Optimal amount of people

Even if all of these triads feel exclusive and seem to involve only three people, Giardini & Wittek (2019b) show that, very often, information does not stay inside the triad for very long. Listeners will typically tell the information to somebody else and will then go from being the listener to becoming the sender, in the next gossip triad.

We have discussed how gossip and rumors can spread and eventually reach a large number of people. According to Yuval Noah Harari in *Sapiens: A Brief History of Humankind* (2014), "gossip helped Homo sapiens to form larger and more stable bands." Yet, even gossip has its limits. "Sociological research has shown that the maximum 'natural' size of a group bonded by gossip is about 150 individuals. Most people can neither intimately know, nor gossip effectively about, more than 150 human beings."

Dunbar (cited in Murphy, 2019) claims that the best gossip usually takes place face to face: a gossiper and a listener talking about an absent third party. But it can also take place with a group of four people: one gossiper and three listeners. If the group is larger than that, at a party, for instance, people usually break out into smaller groups to talk. With the internet and social media, rumors can travel a lot more quickly and reach a much larger audience, but as we have seen, the accuracy and quality of the information suffers.

Relationship between gossipers

It would be safe to say that co-workers who know each other well and have a friendly relationship will gossip more with each other. But this is not the full picture. Gossiping with strangers also has its appeal. And while we talk about friendship and trust, what role does gossip play in building (and losing) these?

Friendship

> If people really knew what others said about them, there would not be two friends left in the world.
> —Blaise Pascal (cited in Epstein, 2011)

When the gossiper and the listener know each other well, trust each other, and are good friends, they will be more open with each other and more likely to share their true feelings. So, it is not a huge surprise to hear that friends are much more likely to exchange negative gossip than two people who only share instrumental work ties (Turner at al., 2003).

Ellwardt et al. (2012a) claim that friendship and gossip are strongly linked. The more people trust each other, the more negative gossip will flow. There is always a strong risk in sharing negative gossip with a colleague, especially if it is about a superior. You need to be sure that the colleague in question will not leak the information you share.

Kristel (29), an account manager for a multinational software company in Germany, recounts how she once told a close colleague that her boss had approached her to apply for a better position at work. "I told that person: well, I might change teams, if that happens, and if it's going well, I will switch teams. So, the only people who knew this were my boss and this colleague. But one week later, someone came up to me and asked if I wanted to do a project, even if I am leaving the team. And I was like: 'What? How do you know that I am leaving the team? I am not leaving the team now! I don't know if I am leaving the team at all!'" Kristel fumed: "My colleagues knew more about me than I did myself and I didn't want or like that. If you tell someone a secret, that is private and when someone else knows about it, you know that someone is talking behind your back." After this incident she felt uncomfortable and sad, and felt that her close colleague had broken her trust and, most certainly, their friendship.

This example brings up the question whether friends can even exist in an organizational setting. Ferrari (2014) believes that "in the workplace there are no friends" and that's why gossip is so widespread.

While there is a clear link between gossip and friendship, it's not clear what comes first: gossip or friendship. There are two schools of thought on the topic: one, that you have to be friends before you can gossip, and the other, that you need to gossip first in order to become friends.

Friends first

According to Ellwardt et al. (2012a), certain researchers believe that once people, or co-workers, are friends, then gossip starts to flow. "This is because senders need to be tied to receivers who can be trusted not to reveal the source of the gossip." The friendship and trust are first built, and then gossip occurs. You know your friend, you know she thinks pretty much like you, so you know she won't judge you too harshly if you talk poorly about another colleague. Most importantly, you trust your friend and know she will not share your information to someone else. "The trust embedded in friendships reduces potential drawbacks of gossip behavior, such as rejection and damage of reputation."

Gossiping first
On the opposite side of the spectrum, other researchers (such as Dunbar, 2004) believe that friendship is a "product, not a precondition, of gossip." Gossiping with someone first may eventually lead to friendship. "Individuals establish and maintain informal relationships through gossip: providing discrete information on third parties works as a signal of trust and interest in a durable relationship." If you gossip with Tim (someone you don't know very well at first), you will most likely share something relatively unimportant. If you see that your gossip doesn't come back to you, you start to trust Tim more and will share more with him. If you discover that Tim also shares your views about certain absent third parties, you'll probably get bolder and share more, openly and honestly. Tim will trust you more, so he will reciprocate. After a while, you will trust Tim and consider him to be a friend. This process happens gradually (Ellwardt et al., 2012a).

According to social penetration theory, each individual has an onion skin: the outer layers are easily accessible and fairly public, whereas the inner layers and inside core are private and hard to reach. By gossiping with someone and gaining their trust, you progressively gain more access to the inner layers and you become friends. Gossip, in this case, is used as a sounding board to get to know someone and see whether they have the potential to become a friend.

In their study, Ellwardt et al. (2012a) find that it is generally gossip that leads to friendship and, less often, the other way around. Gossip is often shared between employees who are not friends (yet). The authors also claim that simply being in close proximity to someone will be enough to increase the likelihood of gossip.

However, gossiping with strangers or colleagues that we do not know well enough can be quite tricky.

Strangers

One study by De Backer et al. (2016) shows that if gossipers and listeners are not close, or do not know each other, gossiping may seem "awkward and unwarranted, thus decreasing perceptions of liking, trust, and expertise," especially if the gossip is negative.

Nevertheless, the authors found that even sharing negative information about a stranger to another stranger "may positively influence first interactions" between two people who don't know each other very well. In a social experiment, three groups of participants were put together to see whether they would cooperate. In the first group, the participants were told not to speak to each other. In the second group, an actress who pretended to be one of the participants, told the following story to the others in her group: "Oh my god, I know that experimenter! I saw her last week in our parking lot. I was sitting at my desk at our bedroom window, and she was just leaving the parking lot. She hit another car when she was driving out of the parking spot, and she surely noticed because it was quite a hard smash, but she just looked around, did not notice me or anyone else and she drove off! She did not even get out of her car to see how bad the other car was damaged, or leave a message or anything. I thought it was just so mean of her!"

In the third group, another actress told a similar story, saying that she had committed the hit and run herself in order to get there on time. (Only the actress from the second group is actually gossiping.)

The researchers looked at how the actress playing the role of the gossiper in the second group was perceived, compared to the actress in the third group, who confessed to have done the hit and run herself, and to the actress who stayed silent in the first group. Out of the three, the gossiper was rated the most positively. She was considered more trustworthy, more friendly, and even more honest than the other two. This confirmed previous findings that sharing even negative gossip with others positively influences the relation with new acquaintances. Yet, the study (De Backer et al., 2016) finds that when it came to cooperation, participants were a lot less keen to work with the gossiper, compared to the other two. The study very well illustrates the precarious balance that gossipers find themselves in.

Hierarchy and gossip

Another study by Martinescu et al. (2019) shows that the hierarchy of the organization strongly influences how employees gossip with one another.

Gossiping with subordinates

People in higher positions usually do not have much interest in gossiping with their subordinates. Doing so could even be harmful to them, as it could make them lose some of their authority and status. In some cases, it could even endanger their position at work: "bonding with a lower partner may damage one's reputation or the power relation."

Jane (51), who works at a large educational organization in the Netherlands, recalls: "We used to have this manager who was friends with a few people in our team. We would often see him gossiping with the people from his in-crowd. We all felt that he was quite unprofessional and, of course, it created a lot of division within the team. As you can imagine, this manager didn't last too long."

Marleen (56) used to work in a governmental organization in the Netherlands. "I remember how one of our managers used to gossip about one of my colleagues, Nell. Nell used to work as a cleaner, but when she was in her 50s, went back to school to get a degree and got hired to work at the archives of our organization. I really admired her for that, but my manager kept putting her down. He would make fun of her (when she wasn't there) in front of our team. 'Can you imagine Nell used to be a cleaner and now she makes more money than you?,' he would say to some colleagues. I was really shocked! To begin with, I found it really unprofessional for a manager to gossip with his subordinates. Also, the role of a manager is to help a team bond. But this one used his power to divide us by creating jealousies and encouraging us to bad-mouth each other."

Normally, though, Martinescu et al. (2019) believe that the powerful are less likely to be interested in the insights offered by their low-power conversation partners.

Pim (28), a manager at an engineering firm in the Netherlands, claims that he changed his way of gossiping after he was promoted: "I mainly stopped now, because I am in a management position at work, so not many people gossip with me. I also do not start it because it would portray a bad image."

Since gossip relies so much on reciprocity, and because the power imbalance creates such an asymmetrical relationship, it makes it even more unlikely for managers to gossip with their subordinates.

Tirana (30), an Albanian who grew up in Greece, works as floor manager for a large clothing store in the Netherlands and oversees about 30 employees. "When one of my employees comes to me and says something negative, I am there to be their manager," she says. "I am not there to be their friend with whom they can share these things. Of course, when it's something really big, I give them advice. But then it depends a lot on the gossip. It depends on what they tell me and then I adjust my behavior according to my position. Usually, I have to respond by saying, 'If you have a complaint, then just go to that person and tell them, not me.'" In certain cases though, Tirana finds it difficult to stay neutral. "Currently, everyone is talking about one of the assistant managers—he just got this position but he is not capable of doing his job. There's a lot of gossip that the only reason he got the position is because he is the store manager's best friend." Even though Tirana agrees with the gossipers, she keeps her feelings to herself. "I just don't tell my opinion. I keep a neutral position and don't comment on it."

Yordona (47), a middle manager for a construction company in Bulgaria, reveals: "Sometimes I want to know things about my subordinates. Who is late for work, who is skipping work very often. I also want to know about their working habits. In this case I will sometimes go and talk to one of my employees, and have a brief talk, ask them how are they doing, how is it at work.... Usually they start talking to me easily, sharing news and gossip. That's how I get the information I need."

Gossiping with colleagues of the same rank
Even though Yordona is eager to get information via her subordinates, she herself is very careful when speaking to her superiors. "Sharing gossip with my boss is a completely different story. I don't want to be as direct with him. I share my opinion when we start talking about work and try to do it in a very discrete way. This is completely different from the way I gossip with my friends. With them, I'm used to being very straightforward and would have no problem saying something like, 'OMG, I don't like George because he did this and that.'"

Bonding with equal partners may be a lot more functional, according to Martinescu et al. (2019). The study shows that employees at the same level tend to gossip in order to gain information and receive social support. As they are usually dependent on each other, they are in a better position to trade information and support each other.

Gossiping with colleagues of the same age
Jan (23), an employee in the distribution center for a large Dutch textile company, says: "Most of the time I gossip with co-workers that have the same age and background as I do. When someone thinks the same about the person I gossip about I feel connected and I do not feel like I am on my own. It gives me a feeling of security within my group of colleagues."

Many of our interviewees said that they usually tended to feel comfortable talking with people who are about the same age as them.

Kees (58), an employee at a large telecommunications company in the Netherlands, confides: "I usually tend to gossip with people my own age. I wouldn't gossip about management with younger colleagues, for example. For one, I don't want to demotivate younger employees and, also, I think they would quickly see me as an old fart. I would have done the same at 30; if a guy of 50 came to me, saying, 'nothing is good around here,' I would also think, 'what an old whiner.' So, I don't want to come across as an old bat who's always saying 'things were so much better in the good old days.' That's why I don't gossip with younger colleagues. It's not because I don't trust them or think that they would rat me out to the management."

Beau (25), a forklift driver at a gardening company in the Netherlands, adds: "I'm the youngest person at my work. The others are all 35-40 years old, so we're in different stages of our lives. So yeah, I don't know, that may cause differences in our communication. So, because of that, there's not much gossiping."

Gossiping with managers
Would you ever gossip with your manager or supervisor? Dave (22), who works at a green energy supplier in the Netherlands, responds vehemently: "No, no! I never gossip with managers or supervisors! Basically, it's not even because I don't think they'd want to or they wouldn't want to participate in the gossip. But they're obliged to report stuff like that happening, especially if it gets out of hand. So, I mean, I wouldn't take any risks. Most of the time, I gossip with direct colleagues about other colleagues."

Lea (27), an employee at the HR department of a multinational wholesale company in Austria, also admits: "I'm usually very careful with gossiping with people in higher positions because it makes a very bad impression. I'm not as close to them as I am to my peers and can't anticipate their reaction."

Emma (23) is an Austrian intern at a large technology company specializing in internet-related services. "I don't gossip at all with my managers," she explains. "Unless they start it, of course. I never initiate, but once they start, I follow, because I want to fit in, but also because it's interesting to hear what is going on from their point of view."

Martinescu et al. (2019) show that in upward relationships, when employees gossip with their manager, their goal is usually to inform and influence the high-power listener "who has formal control over resources and the authority to take action." As a way to make themselves less vulnerable, to obtain certain rewards or resources, to bypass the formal channels of communication, to ensure that they are treated fairly, or to make sure the transgressors are punished, employees will revert to gossip.

We see this in the series *Suits*. Harvey (Gabriel Macht) and Louis (Rick Hoffman) have entered law firm Pearson Hardman at the same time. They are both lawyers at the same rank, and have been competing viciously ever since. In one scene, Louis is talking to Jessica Pearson (Gina Torres), his boss: "I'm not saying that I haven't been charmed by Harvey, but it's just so patronizing when you say that he can handle those things and 'Louis, you can only handle this.' Jessica, I could have handled Gerald Tate [a very important client of the firm]."

It is not clear whether this strategy works, as Jessica replies: "And I told you I disagree." In any case, we do not get the impression that Louis got the upper hand by gossiping with his manager, but he certainly tried.

Finding the *sweet spot of gossip*

Gossiping with the right person may be very tricky. To begin with, whom can we trust? Who may be considered a friend? Should we gossip in order to make a friend or wait to gossip once we have this friend? As we will see, the very definition of friendship is very subjective. When are we opening too much and too soon? The relationship between friendship and gossip is very much a chicken and egg relation: What comes first? While you can gossip freely with a friend, you need to start gossiping in order to make that friend. Yet, it is very easy to lose the trust of a potential friend by gossiping in the wrong way.

Hierarchy at work also plays a huge role in finding the right allies. The majority of our interviewees claimed that they much prefer to gossip with people who are their equals. It is also wise for

managers to keep their ears open to office gossip (knowing that their subordinates will certainly hold back), while being careful not to overshare themselves. As we will explore in Chapter 5, attitudes towards hierarchy are also very much influenced by culture.

Furthermore, women still suffer from heavy prejudices and misconceptions when it comes to gossip. On one hand, we may have the erroneous impression that women are good gossips, which could lead us to confide in the wrong person. On the other hand, we tend to judge a female colleague more harshly when she gossips than we would a male colleague, which is really not fair! Therefore, we should think twice when gossiping about female colleagues. Robinson (2016) argues that "gossip is clearly impermissible when it serves to reinforce an unjust social order." If employees gossip about a negatively stereotyped group, this may work to reinforce the stereotypes. "For instance, gossip about a woman as being a gossip, ambitious, or weak is pernicious precisely because of existing stereotypes against women. Such gossip, especially when the subject is a member of a marginalized group, reinforces oppression."

Tips for female employees

1. Tread lightly when gossiping at work.
You will be judged more harshly than your male colleagues. As women are easily perceived as bitchy and petty when they talk about others, it's wise to keep this in mind before engaging in gossip. Tone down the amount of gossip a bit and speak in a more diplomatic tone (especially if you are talking to colleagues you do not know so well).

2. Make your colleagues aware of the prejudices and stereotypes about female gossipers.
In the article 'Making jokes during a presentation helps men but hurts women,' Evans et al. (2019) conclude that women should not stop using humor altogether. Rather, organizations and managers should make people aware of this prejudice. "Research shows that when people who value equality learn about situations that lead to bias, they become more vigilant and can refrain from succumbing to the bias," the authors claim. With gossip, too, making your colleagues aware of such biases might help them look at female gossipers differently.

3. Be more gentle when gossiping about other women.
In her book *Nice Girls Still Don't Get the Corner Office* (2014), Lois Frankel urges women in the workplace to avoid "ragging on other women" as they have a harder time than their male counterparts do on the job. Keep that in mind and cut them more slack.

Tips for managers

1. Be wary of gossiping with subordinates. Listen well, share little.
Gossiping with a few select employees will certainly lead to unfair situations and have a toxic effect on the team morale in the long run.

But if it is done well, managers can gain a lot by gossiping with their subordinates. Even if it is not in the interest of the manager to confide in his employee, he can certainly gain more information this way. Martinescu et al. (2019) state that even when high-power employees take part in downward gossip, they tend to only share information that is "relatively low in elaboration" or not offer any information at all. They may just opportunistically collect gossip from their subordinates, without offering anything in return. Or managers may gossip with low-power employees "in order to help them make certain strategic decisions, influence others through informal channels, or find new friends who might support them if needed."

2.   Share positive gossip with subordinates.
According to a study by Chang & Kuo (2020), by engaging in positive gossip, managers can foster trust in the organization and increase work commitment. "Managers' positive comments tell colleagues that managers explicitly recognize and, at least verbally, reward the subordinate's good behavior and/or performance. This is linked to enhanced commitment toward the manager." By hearing such positive gossip, employees will then feel more positive about their manager, about their team, and about their work in general. The fact that this study has been conducted in Taiwan certainly skews the findings, however (see Chapter 5).

Tips for employees

1.   Keep hierarchy in mind.
Most employees tend to trust and gossip with colleagues of similar rank and function. Tread very carefully when speaking to a superior as, most likely, the information you share may be used against you. If your direct colleagues learn that you have been gossiping with the manager, there is a very high chance you will lose their trust and that they will see you as a rat.

2. Do not gossip with too many colleagues. Choose your allies well.

Again, scarcity is essential. Gossiping with a few trusted colleagues may lead to friendship. But if you give the impression that you are gossiping with a lot of people, your colleagues will not trust you. If you have the feeling that a gossiper is sharing a story with you only, you will value it a lot more than if he is broadcasting it next to the coffee machine.

As one of my Indonesian students, Richard (19), mentioned during a focus group: "If people seem to be talking to everyone and sharing secrets with everyone, I would consider them to be a lot less trustworthy."

Take the time to figure out who your allies are. Divulge a small thing first and wait to see what happens to it. Remember that it takes time to build trust.

3. If you are new at a job, wait for someone to share something with you before you share something with them.

Jessica (42), the manager of a large food chain in Germany, reveals: "In my opinion, gossiping in front of, or with, new colleagues is unacceptable. I have to say that if there was someone new coming to me to talk about another person, I would immediately think this new colleague would also talk to others behind my back."

5. Gossiping Across Cultures

In order to gossip well, it is not enough to only consider what we gossip about and with whom. An equally important factor to take into account is the cultural background of our fellow gossipers. Culture plays an essential role in determining whether we are gaining or losing our colleagues' trust, and whether we are crossing the line.

Several researchers (Wilson et al., 2000; Gambetta, cited in Rooks et al., 2011) note that gossip is universal and occurs systematically, regardless of culture. According to Wilson et al. (2000), "People in all cultures gossip with an appetite that rivals their interest in food and sex." Some (Manaf et al., 2013) even claim that gossip in organizations is universal, and that it occurs despite the "boundaries of time, culture and geographical constraints."

We can safely say that gossip is universal.

Not only do we all gossip, but we do it for the same reasons. Manaf et al. (2013) show that gossip has the function of building group solidarity, entertaining, and enforcing group norms. Even though their studies were conducted with Malaysian employees, the authors conclude that the function of gossip is the same everywhere in the world.

This may be true. Everyone gossips with equal enthusiasm and they do it to fulfill similar needs. Nevertheless, as most of the studies on gossip were conducted either in Western Europe or North America, how can we be sure that the findings apply to all cultures?

Looking more deeply into this, I was surprised to find that very little research was done about cross-cultural gossip. Watson (2012) claims that "there are no systematic comparisons of the cross-cultural aspects of gossip."

We asked many of our Dutch interviewees whether they adapted their gossiping styles with colleagues from different cultures. Most said they didn't. Erik (39), the team manager of a large distribution center in the Netherlands, states: "I don't really notice any difference. At least not with the people I work with. We don't really pay much attention to cultural differences."

This is a big mistake.

Zoltan (52), who works in a large financial services provider in Hungary, observes: "I often see that people don't take culture into account, whereas they really should. I do because I'm an expert in national and corporate cultures, and I always consider the mindsets and backgrounds of people I talk to. I notice that usually people don't do that."

Zoltan points out the dangers of ignoring cultural differences when gossiping: "I have experienced situations where my Hungarian head office colleagues came and told things about Romanian head office colleagues to the local Romanian employees. This is not something that is done in the Romanian culture. The local colleagues were shocked because in their culture, people don't talk about such things. It really can be a dangerous thing!"

Laszlo (26), Hungarian, a project manager at an American engineering firm, explains that he feels more comfortable gossiping with colleagues from a similar background and culture. "When someone has a completely different culture, they can certainly interpret things quite differently. They might perceive a certain gossip negatively, while we think we're just saying something that's pretty neutral."

Ida (24), a Greek-Albanian manager at a large international fashion company in Greece, admits: "It would be risky to gossip with colleagues from a different cultural background for the simple reason that they might feel offended or uncomfortable."

The fact that we tend to be more comfortable gossiping with people from our own culture says a lot. Femke (55), who is employed at a large educational institution in the Netherlands, claims: "I don't really gossip with people from different cultures." Although more than half of her colleagues come from different cultures, and the language at work is English, she feels more comfortable in her own language. "It's a lot easier and quicker for me to come up with gossip in Dutch than it is in English. Also, you really have to trust who you're gossiping with."

Although it is tempting to stick to colleagues with the same cultural background, it is a big loss. By being aware of the cultural differences and attitudes towards gossip, not only can we learn more, but we can also bond with a greater variety of colleagues.

To start with, we will examine the cultural codes that may influence gossiping styles and how certain intercultural theories apply to gossip. What are the hidden codes of conduct? Secondly, how do gossiping styles change from one culture to the next? Which topics are acceptable or not? How do we express ourselves when gossiping? How direct can one be as a gossiper? Is it better to confront the third party directly rather than talking behind their back? Finally, even though everyone talks about gossiping only with friends or with people they trust, the very definition of friendship and trust varies from one culture to the next.

Researching gossip: Using gossip as an ice breaker

A study (Dreby, 2009) explores how gossip affects Mexican families that are separated when one family member emigrates to the US to find work and provide for the family left behind in Mexico. The author explains: "Given the sensitivity surrounding migrants' separations from their children, parents were often more comfortable talking first about their friends or other family members before broaching their own experiences. Many times, my interviews began with mini gossip sessions. Sharing stories about others with me seemed to put parents at ease, making them subsequently more comfortable in disclosing personal details about their own lives."

Cultural codes

Sometimes the language of gossip seems universal. Jenny (19), a student at a Canadian university, recalls: "I once went to a café with my roommate to study. We sat at a table and soon after we noticed that a woman he had gone out with and dumped in a nasty way was sitting at the table next to ours. I could hear her talking to her friend in Chinese. Even though I don't speak Chinese, I had the feeling I could understand what she was saying: just by her tone of voice and the looks she was giving him. It's like I could suddenly understand Chinese!"

Most of the time, though, various cultures have very specific and invisible codes. Since most of these codes are hidden, they are difficult to learn, so people can very easily overstep boundaries and put their feet in their mouths.

In Elena Ferrante's *Those Who Leave and Those Who Stay* (2014), the third book of her Neapolitan Novels series, a few hidden cultural codes of gossip are made explicit. When Lenu runs into Nino, one of her male friends, they talk about his ex-girlfriend, whom he avidly criticizes: "She's really made badly, even when it comes to sex." Lenu is shocked that he mentions her sexuality: "No one in the neighborhood would have [mentioned her sexuality] in speaking of the woman he loved. It was unthinkable, for example, that Pasquale would talk to me about Ada's sexuality, or worse, that Antonio would speak to Carmen or Gigliola about my sexuality. Boys might talk among themselves—and in a vulgar way, when they didn't like us girls or no longer liked us—but among boys and girls, no."

This example illustrates how certain rules and codes of conduct are hidden and not readily obvious to people of different cultures. Similarly, within an organization, certain people may readily divulge stories or gossip that may seem acceptable to them, but could be considered shocking or inappropriate in other cultures. Talking about sex at work, for instance (especially with colleagues of the opposite gender), may be acceptable in some cases, but would certainly be taboo in others.

Note that organizational differences are not only due to cultural differences, but also to corporate cultures. Various organizations within the same country can differ considerably. An engineering firm would certainly have different codes of conduct than would a law or marketing company, even if they all are from the same country.

In order to get a better grip on many of the invisible cultural codes that exist, it is essential to examine intercultural communication theories and see how they apply to gossip.

Several well-known interculturalists such as Geert Hofstede, Edward Hall, Fons Trompenaars, and, more recently, Erin Meyer, have drawn up models and frameworks to describe and compare various cultures in order to crack some of these hidden codes of communication. These models are regularly used in business and in various areas of life. I have chosen the dimensions that best apply to gossip, like Hall's dimension of high-context vs. low-context, and Hofstede's dimensions of individualism vs. collectivism, power distance, masculinity vs. femininity, uncertainty avoidance, and information flow. We have also found that other factors, such as whether someone is of a dignity, honor, or face culture, or whether they adhere to a mainstream religion, will not only influence their attitudes towards gossip, but the way they express themselves when gossiping.

High-context versus low-context

I had just started a new job in the Netherlands. One day, I was having lunch with two Dutch colleagues, Jan and Peter. Jan was telling Peter that he had to work with Susan again on this new project. As he said this, he raised an eyebrow and the tone of his voice sounded slightly sarcastic. Peter said: "Oh, Susan, eh?" I looked at both of them, and asked them what was the problem. Did they not like Susan? Both men started to snicker slightly. "Let's say, she's not the most competent," Jan explained.

"Why not?" I asked. "What did she do exactly?"

Peter and Jan looked at each other. I could sense they were becoming slightly uncomfortable, but I kept on pushing. I really wanted to know why they thought Susan was incompetent.

Jan looked at me, annoyed. "Do we really have to spell everything out? Can't you just get the hint?"

I was embarrassed. But this incident made me think. I saw that in these few moments, I had dropped down considerably in Peter and Jan's esteem. I was being too pushy and too nosy for their liking. However, I really wanted to learn from their experiences with Susan and maybe avoid some of the pitfalls she fell into.

In his book *Beyond Culture* (1976), anthropologist Edward Hall made a distinction between high-context and low-context cultures. In low-context cultures, like Canada and the US (and many individualist cultures), communication tends to be very explicit, direct, and elaborate. People do not share a common history and background, so they must spell things out explicitly. Messages are interpreted nearly solely on the spoken words. In high-context cultures, where members share more of a common history and background, communication often relies on less direct verbal communication as well as on non-verbal communication. People may use a small hand gesture or facial expressions to convey meaning, or use certain metaphors (which would go completely unnoticed by someone coming from a low-context culture). People from high-context cultures learn how to "read the air" and read between the lines. Contrarily, people from low-context cultures need things to be spelled out clearly and explicitly for them to get the message.

Looking back at my conversation with Peter and Jan with hindsight, I realized that as a Canadian, I was in a much lower context position than my two Dutch colleagues, who were far better than me at getting hints and understanding vague insinuations. I like things to be spelled out without ambiguities. I had always gossiped in this way with Canadian colleagues and never felt I was out of line.

A colleague of mine told me that she went to Peru to give a workshop to local educators. She observed that their style of gossiping was often cryptic (high-context) and was always misunderstood by the Dutch colleagues who attended the workshop. Rather than criticizing their manager openly and distinctly, the Peruvians would do so by describing a football game. "This player missed the ball or couldn't score a goal." The Peruvian colleagues understood that there were deeper layers to this football game, whereas the Dutch colleagues wondered why they suddenly started talking about football.

Individualism versus collectivism

According to Hofstede et al. (2010), individualism refers to societies where ties between individuals are rather loose. People tend to care for themselves and their immediate, nuclear families. Collectivism, on the other hand, applies to societies where "people from birth onward are integrated into strong, cohesive in-groups, which throughout people's lifetime continue to protect them in exchange for unquestioning loyalty."

Countries like the US, Canada, Australia, and the Netherlands tend to score high on individualism, whereas Columbia, Mexico, Indonesia, and many African countries score a lot higher on collectivism.

People from collectivist cultures tend be a lot more protective of their clans and extended families than people from individualist cultures would be. As their loyalties are different, so is their gossip.

One study (Dreby, 2009) explores how gossip affects Mexican families where one family member emigrates to the US in order to find work. The author shows how social networks, and the accompanying gossip, powerfully shape Mexican migration. Because Mexicans score quite high on collectivism and rely quite heavily on their social networks, the author notes: "It would be rare for families not to be affected by the opinions of others." Social norms and gender roles are clearly reinforced by gossip. Men are expected to provide for their families and women to be good housekeepers and mothers. Affairs are, of course, a prime topic of gossip. I am quite certain that a similar study made on a more individualist culture would yield very different results.

Several academics (Luna & Chou, 2013) have observed how individualism or collectivism influences people's attitudes towards gossip. Minkov (2013) claims that members of collectivist cultures may treat members of their in-groups very differently to people who do not belong. He distinguishes between exclusionism and universalism. Exclusionism is the tendency to treat people on the basis of their group affiliation and to reserve favors and privileges for friends, relatives, and other groups with which one identifies.

Outsiders are excluded. "While exclusionist cultures strive to achieve harmony and good relationships within one's in-group, they may be indifferent, inconsiderate, rude, and sometimes even hostile toward members of out-groups," according to Hofstede et al. (2010). Universalism is the opposite: here, people are treated primarily on the basis of who they are as individuals. Their group membership or family ties are much less important. (This trait is more often associated to members of individualist cultures.)

Therefore, if you are part of the in-group in a collectivist society, you will certainly gain access to gossip that you would not hear if you do not belong. De Backer et al. (2016) writes that members of collectivist cultures may use reputation gossip by "slandering rivals and foes, and boosting the reputation of family, friends and allies." If you are part of an in-group there, you will certainly enjoy the protection from your group, and you may rest assured that they will not gossip about you to the outside world in a negative way.

Compared to the US, Belgium scores higher on collectivism, especially Wallonia. There is a great example of collectivism at work in the French-Belgian crime series *La Trêve* (*The Break*). Inspector Yoann Peeters (Yoann Blanc) arrives to the small town of Heiderfeld and is soon called to investigate a case of suicide. He quickly feels that there is more to this than suicide, and notices that the chief of police is very eager to close the case, which he finds suspicious. During a car ride with his partner, Sébastian Drummer (Guillaume Kerbusch), Yoann asks: "Do you know the chief well? What do you think of him?"

"Well, I owe him my job. Without him, I'd be in Brussels or Charleroi—in a bad area. That's where they send cops straight out of school. Some cops have to wait ten years before they get a job in their home town. [Chief of Police] Geeraerts intervened so I could get posted here. He knew my father."

"Oh, yeah?" Yoann replies. This gossip seems to satisfy him, and he goes on to follow other leads. If he had been from a more universalist, individualist culture, he probably would not have lowered his guard and still considered the chief of police a potential suspect.

In collectivist societies, personal relationships tend to be more important than the actual task when working with others. If you become part of an in-group, that will probably be more important to your career than your actual qualifications. As Hofstede et al. (2010) put it: "[T]he personal relationship prevails over the task and should be established first." In individualist societies, though, the task is much more important than personal relationships.

Anna (41), who used to teach at a Russian university and now teaches in South Africa, explains how such cultural differences cropped up at work and generated gossip. "In both [Russian and South African] cultures, you see a lot of habits of tribal communities where tribal laws often seem to be the strongest. And the tribes are always fighting among themselves. At the university, there is a professor who employed both of his children at his faculty. So, there is a lot of stuff where families are very close at work, and that has a lot of bad implications on the organizational culture. You also see husbands who employ their wives, parents who employ their children. For instance, one professor who used to be the head of the department had his wife as his right hand. His daughter was also employed in the same department. And these people tend to be very aggressive. When we have meetings, they're so loud. And the other people tend to retreat, because they don't want to get into a conflict with them. So that causes a lot of problems. And, of course, people gossip about that all the time. All the time!" Especially the colleagues coming from more individualist, universalist cultures.

Individualism/collectivism also strongly influences the level of cooperation between colleagues. A study (Wu et al., cited in Giardini & Wittek, 2019) looked at how gossip had an impact on the cooperation level between students from a collectivist culture (Beijing, China) and students from an individualist culture (Boston, US). The researchers found that when a gossiper provided negative gossip about an absent third party, this type of gossip was interpreted as a form of punishment and negatively influenced the Beijing students' cooperation. However, such negative gossip did not disturb the Boston students so much. The authors attributed this to culture: gossip as a form of reputation building helped increase cooperation in individualistic cultures, but it had the opposite effect on members of collectivist cultures.

How does all of this apply to hierarchy? As we will see, the way we gossip about our managers will not only differ greatly whether we come from an individualist or collectivist society, but also from a high- or low-power distance society.

High-power distance versus low-power distance

Geert Hofstede defines power distance as "the extent to which the less powerful members of institutions and organizations within a country expect and accept that power is distributed unequally." In countries that score low on the power distance index, such as the Netherlands, Sweden, Austria, and New Zealand, employees look at their bosses as equals and are not afraid to contradict them if need be. Managers from low-power distance cultures also tend to consult their subordinates before coming to a decision.

In countries that score high on power distance, organizations tend to be extremely hierarchical, and there are wide gaps between salaries at the top and bottom. In low-power distance cultures people try to minimize inequalities as much as possible, whereas in high-power distance societies inequalities among people are expected and even desired.

In low-power distance countries "the hierarchical system is just an inequality of roles, established for convenience," according to Hofstede, "and roles may be changed, so that someone who today is my subordinate may tomorrow be my boss." Organizations are fairly decentralized, with flat hierarchical pyramids. Salary ranges between top and bottom jobs are relatively small.

Looking at attitudes towards political leaders already speaks volumes. Mark Rutte, the Dutch prime minister, can simply go to work riding his bicycle. No one pays particular attention to him. This would seem mind-boggling to people from other countries (especially those that score higher on the power distance scale), where politicians are driven around and escorted by body guards.

The way we gossip about celebrities and royals also varies greatly. The British tabloids have an endless appetite for dirt about the British royal family. In the Netherlands, the royals agree to be photographed during their ski holidays once or twice a year, on the condition that the journalists and photographers then leave them alone. So far, this gentlemen's agreement, dating back to 1965, seems to work. Celebrities and politicians are not hounded by paparazzi in the Netherlands. There just seems to be less interest in their private lives.

Attitudes towards age and position within an organization are also more important in high-power distance cultures. Pietro (21), a Spanish marketing consultant (whose culture scores higher on the power distance index than the Netherlands), explains: "When I am talking with my bosses or other managers who are 30 or 40 years old, I do not talk in the same way that I do with the companions that are my age. I try to be more respectful."

The high-power distance dimension plays an even greater role in Asian cultures.

Nguyen (26), a sales executive at a large hotel in Vietnam, admits: "I feel like even though my manager and I work in the same office, the distance is very high. I rarely talk to her about intimate issues. We subordinates gossip with each other a lot more often!"

Hence, in organizations of low-power distance cultures, subordinates who treat their managers as equals will certainly be more prone to discussing problems with them directly, even if it concerns a colleague. In high-power distance cultures, employees tend to fear their managers a lot more and would never consider gossiping with them. Viktoriya (26), a Bulgarian working for a large international health organization in the Netherlands, reveals: "I don't gossip with managers because I don't want to inflict something bad on another person. I think that if gossip about someone's performance reaches the manager's ears, it would be really bad for the person."

Even gossiping about a manager can instill fear. Minh (25), an employee at a Malaysian temp agency, thinks twice about gossiping about a manager. "We think that when we talk about the manager, something good may be okay but something bad [is not]. You'll be in a lot of trouble when somebody tells your manager. We don't want to get into trouble so we just talk about work!"

In countries that score high on the power distance scale, like Malaysia, Russia, or India, employees tend to be afraid of disagreeing with their superiors. Bosses are seen as "autocratic or paternalistic" and many of their employees expect them to reach decisions without consulting them or their subordinates. Subordinates expect to be told what to do. They would probably lose respect for their managers if the managers asked the subordinates for advice. That would be a sign of weakness.

Needless to say, gossip in high- and low-power distance cultures would definitely reflect the very different expectations people have of their managers.

For my research, I presented a scenario to German, Dutch, and Chinese students where the secretary at work tells a colleague during an office party that her date, Jack, a married man, is a sleazebag. While Jack is out getting some drinks, the secretary informs her that he had slept with her, along with four other women at work. We asked the students what they thought of Jack. What if he was just a regular colleague? What if Jack was the manager? All agreed Jack was bad, whatever his title. "Having affairs at work is not a good idea," many said. Jack's greatest sin was that he was cheating on his wife. Where the students greatly differed was in their expectations of a manager. The Dutch students (who come from a low-power distance culture) said that it didn't matter whether Jack was a manager or their colleague. He was simply misbehaving. The German students expected that a manager should be a good role model, and step up to his responsibilities. So, Jack was judged a bit more harshly if he were the manager instead of just a colleague. Interestingly, the Chinese students (who come from a high-power distance society) weren't all that surprised by Jack's behavior. "Managers behave badly because they have the power to do so," one student said.

Researching gossip: Taking power distance into account

When I first started doing the research where we interviewed German, Dutch, and Chinese students, I was working with two student research assistants. In the beginning, I wanted to interview some of the students myself, as well. But we soon noticed that we were putting our interviewees in the role of gossipers. Even if they were discussing fictional scenarios, our interviewees were still gossiping about the characters. We then thought that the Chinese students, who score higher on Hofstede's power distance scale, might feel more shy about talking to me, as I am a lecturer and significantly older than them. Therefore, we decided that the interviews would be conducted by the two student research assistants (who were trained to follow the same interview process), so that all of our interviewees could speak more freely (Darmon, 2019).

The way managers are expected to deal with gossip is strongly influenced by their culture. According to a study (Chang & Kuo, 2020) conducted in Taiwan (where power distance is quite high), managers tend to follow the "conventional wisdom that managers should cultivate a distance from subordinates to preserve their dignity and authority." The authors recommend that managers, instead, build trust by gossiping positively about an absent colleague in front of their subordinates. They claim that rank plays an extremely important role in the way managers are perceived. The higher the rank difference between manager and subordinates, the more influential their words will be. So, by gossiping in a positive way about their subordinates, managers will increase work commitment, "improve team dynamics and make subordinates feel better."

I am quite certain that this would not be the case in a country with a low-power distance culture, where managers have less influence and authority. In Denmark and the Netherlands, for instance, such a strategy may even backfire. In some cases, the subordinate being gossiped about in a positive way could even suffer from the resentment of others.

Masculinity versus femininity

Another dimension of Hofstede's that should be considered when looking at cross-cultural gossip is whether a society is masculine or feminine. "A society is called masculine when emotional gender roles are clearly distinct: men are supposed to be assertive, tough, and focused on material success, whereas women are supposed to be more modest, tender, and concerned with the quality of life. A society is called feminine when emotional gender roles overlap: both men and women are supposed to be modest, tender, and concerned with the quality of life."

Culture definitely influences the way men and women are expected to behave and, also, to gossip. What is interesting in this regard are different cultures' attitudes to status. In masculine cultures, such as Switzerland, the US, Venezuela, and China, it would be normal for people to put themselves forward. If they are wealthy, they will show it by having an expensive house and car. Employees will use superlatives to describe their achievements on their resumes. In feminine societies, like the Netherlands and the Scandinavian countries, people are a lot more modest. Those who are well-off tend to be much more discreet about their wealth, and don't drive particularly flashy cars.

This dimension has a huge impact on the way people gossip.

Hannah (55) comes from Malaysia, but has been living in the Netherlands for a long time. "I certainly gossip differently, depending on whether I am speaking to Dutch friends or to Malaysian friends," she says. "With Malaysians, we love to name drop. For example, I know the wife of a minister, and I had some juicy gossip about her, so it's always a good way to break the ice at a party." Hannah explains that sharing such gossip with someone she doesn't know that well is a way for her to gain the listener's trust and show that she has status and is well connected.

At a Dutch party, this would certainly be quite different. The Dutch don't get overly excited about what politicians and celebrities do, so, gossiping about a minister's wife would certainly not be a way to impress potential new friends. "A Dutch person would probably wonder why I'm talking about this, find me indiscreet, and would probably trust me less (unless she was already a friend)."

This clearly is because the Netherlands is a lot more feminine than Malaysia, where showing that you have status is a good way to impress your listener.

Contrarily, in Denmark (a country that ranks highly on the femininity index), bragging or showing off is considered a cardinal sin. During a workshop I once gave about gossip at a business school in Copenhagen, several students quickly pointed out that *janteloven* plays a huge role in how and why Danish people gossip. People who stick out or brag about their achievements will quickly become the object of gossip, they told me.

Janteloven means 'the law of Jante,' and was coined in 1933 by Danish-Norwegian author Aksel Sandemose. In his book *En flyktning krysser sitt spor* (A fugitive crosses his tracks), he lists the rules that dictate how Scandinavians should think about one another. The main ones are: "You're not to think you are anything special," "you're not to think you are smarter than us," "you're not to think you can teach us anything," and "you're not to think you are more important than us."

All of the students agreed that *janteloven* does play a role in the way they and their colleagues talk about others. "People gossip when somebody is working hard to be promoted and is doing it in a maybe 'too' self-confident way," one student explained.

"If someone sticks out too much, or talks about himself too much. They shouldn't think they are better than us," another chimed in. "When people talk about how good they are, we will find examples to bring them down and make comments on their mistakes."

"Also, if the boss makes a lot of money, or has an au pair," another said.

"I believe, that the lower your income, the more you bitch about others who have things like an expensive car," a participant noted. "A colleague of mine got a new fur coat, and some people started to talk about how she could afford this with her salary and that it was a bit over the top to wear it."

In many feminine cultures, people who stick out or give the impression that they are better than others are quickly shot down. So, when someone from a more masculine culture breaks these invisible rules (without realizing it), they will be sure to be hot topics of gossip. On the other side of the equation, someone from a feminine culture gossiping negatively about a colleague's success will come across as jealous or envious to someone from a masculine culture.

Uncertainty avoidance

Uncertainty avoidance, according to Hofstede, is "the extent to which the members of a culture feel threatened by ambiguous or unknown situations." People from high uncertainty avoidance cultures need predictability and clear rules. Countries that score high on the uncertainty avoidance index, such as Russia, Japan, Germany, and Uruguay, value job security and clear directions at work. At the other end of the spectrum, countries like the UK, Canada, and China do not mind more ambiguous situations. Employees from such countries will be more drawn to working freelance or starting up their own businesses with all of the risks that that entails. Employees from low uncertainty avoidance cultures will not mind taking initiatives themselves when their manager's instructions are more ambiguous.

Therefore, topics of gossip coming from high uncertainty avoidance colleagues will likely be about unclear or vague instructions given by their managers, for example. If there is any uncertainty about the health of their organization, these employees may be even more quick to worry and to gossip about it. Wondering whether there will be layoffs will trigger a lot more stress and anxiety than for colleagues coming from low uncertainty avoidance countries.

Employees coming from low uncertainty avoidance countries may find rules and red tape cumbersome and may more readily gossip about that.

Information flow

Another interesting factor to consider is the speed in which information (and, in this case, gossip) flows in the workplace. Edward Hall (cited in Nunez et al., 2014) explained that in certain countries, like the Netherlands, information tends to be more compartmentalized—it stays within departments and doesn't flow freely. Employees share juicy stories with colleagues from their own departments and not with others. This is called slow information flow. In countries with a fast information flow, like France, China, Turkey, or Morocco, however, information and gossip travel more freely. It would be normal for a colleague from one department to share information with his friends and colleagues from other departments. "All it takes is one visit to the coffee machine, watercooler or restroom for an employee from one department to be up to date on what is happening in another department," Nunez observes. For Dutch people, who have a tendency to keep information "compartmentalized, controlled and planned," this way of sharing information would likely be seen as "unprofessional gossip." Such a gossiper would probably be deemed indiscreet and not very trustworthy.

Honor, dignity, and face cultures

According to one study (Severance et al., 2013), people from different cultures may perceive, to varying degrees, gossiping as aggression. Pakistanis, for instance, belong to an "honor culture," where people go to "great lengths to uphold the reputation of oneself and one's family." Reputation is vital—it can be earned and it can be lost. For people coming from such collectivist, honor cultures, an assault to their reputation is considered to be a serious attack to their self-worth and, hence, very damaging. In contrast, the US is a "dignity culture." People there believe that everyone is created equal (as reflected in the Declaration of Independence). Dignity cultures tend to be more individualistic as well. While certain behaviors could lead to a loss of dignity, many tend to believe that "dignity can never be lost." For this reason, negative gossip doesn't have the same ability to damage one's fundamental sense of self as it would in an honor culture. And someone gossiping negatively will be perceived as less threatening or aggressive to members of dignity cultures than they would to members of honor cultures.

Certain cultures, like that of Japan, are described as "face cultures." Here, someone's sense of positive image is very much linked to the context of social interaction. Severance et al. (2013) define face as "the respectability and/or deference which a person can claim for himself from others by virtue of his relative position in a hierarchy." In face cultures, "one must not attempt to claim more face than others are willing to grant, as this would disturb the social hierarchy and result in social sanctions against the individual." Therefore, people from face cultures usually follow norms of modesty and humility to "avoid overstepping status boundaries." Maintaining harmony and preserving others' face is also extremely important. So, one can imagine that gossip in such cultures may pertain to people who break these rules. At the same time, the way in which such stories are told may be more mindful so as to not humiliate the object of gossip. Since public image is extremely important, a gossiper attacking someone will be perceived as being a lot more aggressive to someone coming from a face culture than to someone coming from a dignity culture.

The influence of religion

Generally speaking, gossip is very much frowned upon in most religions.

De Gouveia et al. (2005) note that readings from the Christian Bible talk about 'the evil tongue' and gossip: "The godless man uses his mouth to destroy his neighbor but the virtuous use their wisdom to save themselves. Gossip reveals secrets, but the trustworthy man keeps a secret."

Capps (2012) explains that Jesus expressed himself vehemently against gossip. This can be seen in the Gospels after Jesus rejected the traditional dietary laws and restrictions. Doing this provoked much criticism and, naturally, gossip. Matthew claimed that Jesus dealt with the situation by calling the people to him and saying: "It is not what goes into the mouth that defiles a person, but it is what comes out of the mouth that defiles." (Matt. 15:11-19, cited in Capps, 2012.) "Do you not see that whatever goes into your mouth enters the stomach, and goes out into the sewer?" Jesus asked. "But what comes out of the mouth proceeds from the heart, and this is what defiles. For out of the heart comes evil intentions, murder, adultery, fornication, theft, *false witness, slander.*"

The Bible also contains many references in which gossipers are condemned. For example, Psalm 101:5 reads: 'Whoever slanders his neighbor secretly I will destroy.'

Islam considers backbiting as one of the Major Sins. According to Giardini & Wittek (2019b), the Koran states: "God has heard the speech of her who wrangled with you about her husband, and complained to God; and God hears your gossip; verily, God both hears and sees" (Koran Sura 58: The Pleader of Madina, cited in De Gouveia et al., 2005).

The Torah also forbids gossip: "Thou shalt not go up and down as a tale-bearer among thy people." (Leviticus 19:16, cited in De Gouveia et al., 2005.) Nicholas DiFonzo (2011) points out in *Psychology Today* that the Talmud speaks in great detail about "the damage that a person can do by gossiping about a person's vocation, likening it to murder."

The influence of religion is powerful, indeed, and will certainly impact one's general attitude towards gossip and gossipers.

Sofia (49) is originally from the Philippines and works in human resources in a German pharmaceutical company. "I grew up as a Christian," she explains. "Ever since I was young, I was always taught to not gossip with someone that isn't part of the solution, since that won't get you anywhere." Even when she had an opportunity to use gossip to her advantage, Sofia felt rather guilty about it. "One time my colleague gossiped with me about how our boss doesn't really get anything done properly and that he's always really unorganized. She told me that she looked through a presentation he prepared for our client the next day and told me that there were some things missing and even some typos. So, in that moment I was quite thankful that she said something, because that gave me the opportunity to still make changes. If she hadn't said anything, then we could have looked stupid in front of our client. In that way, the gossip kind of helped us to avoid mistakes. But I still think that I wasn't the right person to talk to about this."

I once discussed the role of culture when gossiping, with Diyora (30), an academic working and living in Uzbekistan, whom I met at a conference. She told me of a bad experience she had in the past: "When I was working on my PhD, someone—I never knew who it was, but I assume it was a colleague of mine—told my supervisor that I didn't want to work with him anymore, and that I preferred to work alone. I suddenly noticed that my supervisor was quite angry with me, but he wouldn't say why. I insisted, and he finally told me. I was really surprised as I had never said that, so as a last resort, I said: 'I swear by the Koran that this is not true!' This is a serious and solemn oath that you don't make lightly, so my supervisor acknowledged that he had to believe me."

Using the Koran or the Bible to gain credibility and trust may work well with religious people, but with others this would certainly have less impact.

Trust and friendship

It is clear that the rules and codes of gossiping are different from one culture to the next and that building trust can be quite delicate. To start with, whom can we trust? What does it mean to trust a colleague? Many of our interviewees said that they trust their friends at work and feel they can tell them anything without being judged (and vice versa). But what does it mean to be friends? Does it mean, like Ferrari (2014) suggests, to follow certain codes such as "not to speak badly about friends" or "not to publicize their confidences"? We will see that not only do the codes to gain and maintain trust and friendship vary greatly across cultures, but so too do their very definitions.

During my research, when we interviewed Chinese, Dutch, and German students about their perceptions of various gossip scenarios, nearly all of our interviewees said that they gossiped openly with friends and other people they trust. Friends can tell you anything they like—no matter how bad or catty—and they will be excused. This seemed to me to be a universal statement that transcended culture and geographical constraints.

But looking a little more closely, I realized that while all my interviewees spoke about 'friendship' and 'trust,' these notions had very different meanings to each of them. I found that the word 'trust' has different meanings and nuances in different languages. According to Usunier & Lee (2005), in the English language the notion of trust is mainly based on reliance and on how truthful someone or something is. How reliable is a person? In German, however, the word *trauen* is first used in a negative sense: *Ich traue dir nicht* (I don't trust you). There must occur a transformation, indicated by the prefix 'ver-,' *vertrauen*, for the word to be used in a positive sense: 'Ich vertraue dir' (I trust you). For Germans, trust is something you earn. It doesn't come automatically. The French word *confiance* comes from *cum* (which means 'with' or 'shared' in Latin) and *fides* (which means 'faith' or 'belief'). Here, the notion of sharing common beliefs is central to trust. For the Japanese, the word for 'trust' is *shin-yô*, which means "sincere business."

Erin Meyer also claims in her book *The Culture Map* (2014) that the notion of trust is highly influenced by culture. On one end of her trusting scale are task-based cultures and on the other end are relationship-based cultures. In task-based cultures, like the Netherlands, the US, Germany, and Australia, trust is built through business-related activities. "Work relationships are built and dropped easily. You do good work consistently, you are reliable. I enjoy working with you, I trust you." When people change jobs, they often lose touch with their old colleagues. Many Dutch people separate their work and private lives very well.

According to Meyer, employees from relationship-based cultures will often remain friends after leaving a job. Several of my friends from relationship-based cultures have commented with some dismay that their colleagues quickly forget about them once they leave an organization. "I thought I had a solid friendship with one of my colleagues, but a few months later she had moved on and no longer contacted me to get together," one confided.

Relationship-based cultures, like those of India, Saudi Arabia, and China, have a very different definition of 'trust' and 'friendship.' "Trust is built through sharing meals, evening drinks, and visits to the coffee machine. Work relationships build up slowly over the long term. I've seen who you are at a deep level, I've shared personal time with you, I know others who trust you, I trust you."

In order to gain trust and become friends with people from relationship-based cultures, Meyer suggests, the key is to be yourself and "show that you have nothing to hide."

She stresses that in Spain, Brazil, and many Asian countries being too positive when speaking about others may make you look inauthentic and fake. Meyer quotes a Spaniard's perception of Americans: "They don't dare complain or show negative emotion. In Spanish culture, we put a strong value on the importance of being *auténtico* and we perceive Americans as not being authentic."

I clearly remember a moment when I was gossiping with a Dutch colleague that I did not know so well. I was trying to be *auténtico* and criticized another colleague quite vocally and not in the kindest of ways. I tried to convey to my listener that she could trust me since I was being so open with her. But from her body language and facial expressions I could tell that she felt just the opposite and soon realized that I had made a gaffe and damaged the potential trust between us.

In a Dutch study that is typical of a task-based culture, Ellwardt et al. (2012b) looked at the role of trust when employees gossiped about their managers. Surprisingly, they found that employees gossiped more negatively about their managers even when they had low trust, non-friendly relationships with their listeners. The study, which took place in a medium-sized Dutch childcare organization, showed that negative gossip flowed even more freely when employees did have "trusting and frequent contacts" with each other on top. In their study, the authors operationalized trust by using the following statements in their survey: "The organization will always try to treat me fairly" or "Management can be trusted to make sensible decisions." When it comes to defining trust between co-workers: "Most of my workmates can be relied upon to do as they say they will do" or "if I got into difficulties at work I know my workmates would try to help me out."

Such a study would very likely not apply in a relationship-based culture, as the definitions of 'trust' are very different.

Gossiping styles

During a workshop for one of my classes, I presented the students with the following scenario about 'Bob the slob.' Bob is Peter's direct colleague. Peter walks into Bob's office. Bob tells him that he deleted the confidential file Peter has been working on for the last five months. Peter walks out of the office, upset, and runs into a colleague. "What would you say if you were Peter? How would you gossip about Bob?" I asked my students.

I had a Ukrainian and a Brazilian student enact the situation while the rest of the class observed. The Brazilian student, playing the role of Peter, ranted: "That idiot! You would never believe what he did!" Everyone in the class could empathize with Peter's feelings of frustration and anger. However, my Brazilian student soon started to tell her listener that Bob was a jerk, who had a bunch of affairs in the department. "But that's not true!," exclaimed a Dutch student, quite shocked. "I know," my student answered, "but if I am angry at Bob, I want to make sure that the listener will be on my side."

It goes without saying that my Brazilian student would make social blunders if she were to work in a Dutch organization. This type of incident could seriously impact her relationship with colleagues and, ultimately, affect her job performance.

As this short anecdote illustrates, differences occur in the way we gossip, and adapting one's style is of the essence. Kristina (19) works for a large financial services provider in Moldova. She has a Russian and Chinese background and explains that she definitely adapts her style depending on the cultural background of her listener. "When I used to study in London, I used to unconsciously adopt different styles when talking to people from different cultural backgrounds. For example, my Chinese self is much, much, much kinder than my Russian self, while my English self is more sarcastic. So, I can see how culture really influences the way I talk about people and things."

So, what words do we use? How long do we linger on certain topics? Some topics which may be considered interesting across cultures (like sexual relationships between colleagues or a woman's attractiveness) will be discussed in very different ways. How direct should we be? Is it an option to confront the third party rather than talking about them behind their backs, even if they are your manager? How is humor used in gossip across cultures?

Acceptable topics of gossip depending on culture

We saw in Chapter 3 that popular gossip topics at work tended to be about appearance, peculiarities, and performance. These seemed to be of interest to people from all cultures. However, the differences seem to lie in terms of how one gossips about these topics. In the Netherlands, people will readily gossip about their manager's or colleague's performance, even to colleagues they do not know so well. But making comments about someone's ridiculous outfit or bad hair would be considered inappropriate unless the gossipers were very close friends.

In many Latin American countries, however, talking about a co-worker's appearance, even in a vulgar way, would not illicit as much disapproval as it would in the Netherlands.

Once, during a workshop about gossip that I gave in Belgium, I asked the participants to re-enact the following scenario: Anna was just hired at your workplace because of her IT expertise.

She has an alternative punk look. One of your colleagues, Susan, comes to talk to you about Anna. "Can you believe it?," she tells you. "They hired that weirdo? She looks like she stepped out of a science fiction movie!" How would you respond to Susan? Certain participants responded politely that Anna did look strange, and that they were surprised she was hired. An Asian participant said: "Her parents must be very sad that she looks like this." A Dutch participant, though, felt quite uncomfortable by the way Susan was talking and started to defend Anna and contradict the gossiper. "Well, she's very good at what she does. How she dresses is her business." The more the gossiper playing Susan's role insisted, the more the Dutch participant became defensive and defended Anna.

Another example of this occurred during one of my journalism classes. Even though my students had to remain objective when interviewing their subjects about their experiences with gossip, I could see a few had trouble hiding their opinions and emotions. In one case, such an interview illustrated exactly what happens when someone crosses the line. Dan, my Dutch student, interviewed Youri (23), a Ukrainian student who used to work at a theme park in Dubai. Dan asked Youri whether he ever gossiped about his bosses.

Youri: Oh, hell yeah, ha ha, I mean, that's the funniest.
Dan: Well, tell me about the funniest gossip you ever heard.
Youri: Damn, there are so many to choose from. Ha ha, one day, a lot of attractions were not working properly and operators had to close them every hour. I was listening on the radio and had to report information to our base. At one point, one of my supervisors was reporting that an attraction was unavailable and, suddenly, he couldn't put the words together. He was tired from running all over the place and couldn't catch his breath.
Dan: I don't see why that's funny.
Youri: Well, that person was a bit out of shape, ha ha, so I and the guys in the office had a really good time just talking about how fat he was.

Dan: How would you feel if you found out that people spent their workday laughing at you?

Youri: It wouldn't be great, but I don't feel bad about this one. It gave me the joy to survive the rest of my day!

Dan: Are you not ashamed of this behavior?

Youri: No, not really.

Youri went on, trying to convince Dan that the gossip was funny, completely oblivious to the fact that he had crossed the line in Dan's eyes.

In my own experience, I also noticed that when I cross the line gossiping with Dutch colleagues, they will start to contradict me. At first politely, but the more I insist, the more adamant and defensive they get. The best strategy in this case (and in Youri's) would be to change the subject and back off. Avoiding topics such as appearance, I learned, is a sure way to keep my foot out of my mouth.

Viktoriya (26) is Bulgarian and works in a large international health organization in the Netherlands. She, too, admits that she had to adapt her style of gossiping when talking to colleagues from different cultures. "In Bulgaria, when you actually gossip about someone it may appear rude to someone else, so you really have to adapt. The Bulgarian style of gossiping, in my opinion, is mostly negative. You never gossip about someone doing something great, but always gossip about something bad. Compared to most of my international colleagues, the Bulgarian style is really negative. I find that Dutch people are 'colder.' They don't really seem to care about your business that much. Whereas in Bulgaria people are much more interested in other people's lives."

Viktoriya explains that she has made mistakes several times: "You burn yourself once, twice, and then you get used to it. For example, Dutch people started asking me why I was talking behind people's backs and why I didn't just talk to them directly."

Viktoriya took the advice. But still, is confronting the third party directly such a good strategy? Especially if they are your manager?

How direct can you be?

In one study (Tucker, 1993), 277 students enrolled in an under-graduate sociology course at a state university in the southeastern US were asked how they dealt with conflict with a supervisor. Most had part-time or temporary jobs working as waiters, cashiers, cooks, busboys, and salespeople, among others. The author found that 29% sought direct contact with their supervisors or managers and tried to resolve the conflict directly. For many of the students, this was considered too risky, especially considering that they had no permanent contracts or job security. Half of the students turned to gossip instead, trying to gather support for their cause or asking colleagues for advice.

I am certain that the percentage of employees reverting to gossip would have been even higher had the study been conducted in high-power distance countries, where people fear their managers a lot more.

In the Netherlands (low-power distance), people may pride themselves on having the courage to confront their bosses directly rather than talking behind their backs. But for people coming from high-power distance cultures, it could be suicide to do so. Even for employees in low-power distance cultures, it may still be safer to talk behind the manager's back. Other factors (like job security) play a huge role in how direct one chooses to be as well.

Another predictor as to whether people from different cultures will seek confrontation or choose to gossip may be found in Erin Meyer's evaluating scale on how people give negative feedback, in general. The author of *The Culture Map* (2014) notes that people from different cultures vary greatly when dishing out negative criticism. People in France, Russia, Israel, the Netherlands, and Germany, for instance, tend to be extremely direct, whereas people from many Asian countries, such as Indonesia, Thailand, and Japan, will provide criticism in a very indirect way. Another important factor to consider is whether a country is high- or low-context. Therefore, Meyer uses two axes to map out how people from various countries give feedback: direct versus indirect

Figure 8 Meyer's feedback scale (2014)

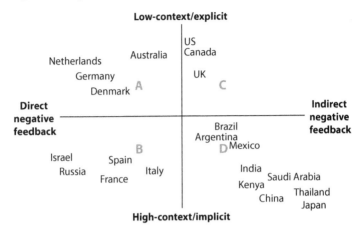

negative feedback, and high-context versus low-context (see figure 8). So various cultures fall into either one of four quadrants:

1. Low-context cultures that value direct negative feedback (like Germany and the Netherlands)
2. Low-context cultures that value indirect negative feedback (such as Canada and the US)
3. High-context cultures that value direct feedback (France and Israel, for example)
4. High-context cultures that value indirect feedback (Brazil, India, and many Asian countries)

So, how does this apply to gossip? How likely are various cultures to dish out criticism directly rather than gossiping behind one's back?

Low-context, direct negative feedback
Elise (20), an employee at the HR department of a large organization in the Netherlands, describes a fairly typical situation: "A colleague of mine tells me how much she hates the boss. She always complains that she is treated poorly and unfairly. I think she is rather annoying. I do understand her, but if she's unhappy, she should tell the boss herself."

This type of comment came up regularly during my classes and research: Why gossip behind someone's back when you could actually be honest and tell your co-worker or manager directly what is bothering you?

In the *Harvard Business Review* article called 'Stop complaining about your colleagues behind their backs,' Riegel (2018) also recommends confronting the third party directly. No matter what you call it, the author says, gossip always remains a "destructive communication strategy that negatively impacts individuals, teams and the whole organization." Riegel uses the example of Doug from accounting, whose colleagues gossip about how difficult it is to get a timely response from him. The author recommends that people adopt a "tell them first" policy with colleagues like Doug. "When someone approaches you with gossip about someone else, ask 'Have you already told her?' to remind them of this policy." The key is to normalize feedback, whether positive or negative.

Giardini & Wittek (2019a) claim that gossipers are often negatively perceived if they violate this major social norm: "[T]hat is, that grievances or problems should be discussed directly with the person in question, and not behind someone's back." This, according to the authors, explains why gossipers are often considered as less trustworthy, "making it more difficult for them to sustain cooperative relationships."

Following such a norm, Margo (48), a nurse in a care home in the Netherlands, decided to confront a colleague who was not functioning well. "She was often sick and cancelled her appointments with clients, which gave us a lot more work. So, my team and I decided to talk to her and stop gossiping. We just decided that we want to talk to her first. Sometimes the reason for a problem is different than you think." Even though the colleague did not take the criticism very well, Margo still felt confronting her was the right thing to do.

In this example, or in Doug's case, whose sin was to be late responding, confronting the third party may be a good way to go, especially if they come from such low-context cultures and are used to receiving direct negative feedback. People from such cultures also don't shy away from addressing even more delicate topics.

Jan (23) is employed at the distribution center of a large textile company in the Netherlands. "I notice that people often gossip about people who smell," he says. "In my opinion, it's better to be straightforward with that person. It should be possible to tell someone when he has a bad smell around him. I had several occasions like this. In my experience, the person with a bad body odor does not like it when you just tell him, but in the long run, he can and will do something about it."

Also, if you are the absent third party and find out that colleagues are gossiping about you, your reaction would certainly be influenced by your culture. If you come from a culture falling into the low-context, direct negative feedback quadrant, most likely, you will choose confrontation.

Leonie (63), an employee at a municipality in the Netherlands, recalls: "I used to have a good job at the municipality, but then I had a stroke. After I recovered, I couldn't function in my old job anymore, as it was too difficult for me, mentally. So, I was placed in a call center instead. Everyone there was nice to me, except for one colleague. This person ignored me for two years and refused to speak to me. I also found out from other colleagues that she was talking about me behind my back. So, at one point, I had enough and confronted her. 'Shall we talk about it like adults?' I asked her. 'Why are you acting this way towards me? Did I do something wrong to you?' Then she said: 'You got this job without even having had an interview. I was hoping a friend of mine would get the job. But she was never even invited for the job interview.' So, I told her about my stroke and how I got the job. We talked about it, and she apologized to me for having been so rude all this time. This happened ten years ago, and we now have a good relationship. I'd even say we've become friends."

In this case, having been direct was the right thing to do by Dutch standards. Had Leonie been from a country where feedback is given a lot less directly, she would probably never have confronted her rude colleague and never would have had a chance to become friends.

Confronting the third party or a gossiper would absolutely not be done in other cultures. Even in the US (where Riegel, the author of the article, is from), which is also low-context, but where feedback is given more indirectly, telling Doug that he has a bad body odor or that you find him completely incompetent would certainly require a lot more delicacy.

Low-context, indirect negative feedback
I was once having a coffee with two colleagues (one Dutch and one Canadian). We were discussing the workshop that we just had, about the quality of education.

"A bit of a waste of time," I said, "and poorly organized. Can you imagine? I arrived to lunch five minutes late and the sandwiches were already gone. It's like the organizers had just a small tray for five people. Registration was also a mess."

"That's pretty blunt for a Canadian to say," my Dutch colleague observed (a little bluntly).

My Canadian colleague laughed. "Yeah, in Canada you would be a lot less direct. You'd raise an eyebrow and say something like, 'The sandwiches did look good. Too bad there weren't any left when I arrived.' People would sort of get the message that the workshop was poorly organized, but you just wouldn't say it straight out."

Even though Canada scores high on the low-context scale, and people tend to be very explicit in their communication, when it comes to giving feedback and confronting people directly, they are a lot less. This example illustrates how easy it is to make a faux pas—even with people of your own culture when you've been away for a long time. When you are a bit too explicit in the way you gossip about others, you may come across quite poorly to members of countries who fall in this quadrant.

Kristel (29), a German account manager working for a multinational software company, admits that she finds Americans (who fit into this quadrant) quite difficult to read. "You don't know what they really think, because they are always nice to everyone. I think that in Bavaria [Germany], if you gossip about someone, you don't act like you like the person, like Americans do sometimes. You just don't talk with them. You just say hello and maybe 'How are you?' but not much else. You don't pretend that you like them if you actually don't." Whereas both Germany and the US are both generally low-context cultures, the Americans have a much more indirect way of giving feedback than Germans would and would sooner talk behind a colleague's back than confront them directly.

High-context, direct negative feedback
In the Netflix series *Emily in Paris*, Emily (Lily Collins), a young twenty-something from Chicago, moves to Paris in order to provide an American perspective at a French marketing firm. She has difficulty adapting to her French colleagues, who are downright hostile to her. Sitting on a park bench, she complains to her new friend, Mindy (Ashley Park), who came from Shanghai to work as a nanny. Mindy exclaims: "I love Paris! The food is so delicious, the fashion is so chic, the lights so magical! But the people: so mean!"

> Emily: "I mean, they can't *all* be mean?"
> Mindy: "Yes, they can! Chinese people are mean behind your back. French people are mean to your face!"

Judging from Emily's experience, the French are a lot more direct than are Americans when it comes to giving feedback, and will tend to tell you straight out what is wrong rather than (only) gossip behind your back. Emily's boss, Sylvie, clearly tells her what she is doing wrong. But that also doesn't stop her from gossiping nastily about Emily behind her back.

People from countries like France, Russia, and Israel, who fall into this quadrant, will most likely make their dislike of the third party clear while still using high-context techniques to gossip about them.

High-context, indirect negative feedback

For people coming from cultures from this quadrant (such as China, Japan, and India), it would be unthinkable to walk up to a manager or colleague to give him negative feedback. As we have seen, people from such high-context cultures tend to 'read the air' and interpret hints. Hearing negative gossip about a colleague may easily take on an extra layer of interpretation.

During my research, using the case study of Bob the Slob, a Chinese student observed that if her manager was gossiping to her about Bob's mistake, she would wonder whether her manager was trying to tell her something about her own performance. Interestingly, this thought never occurred to the German and Dutch students presented with the same scenario.

Because they are not accustomed to speaking so openly, it is certainly not out of hypocrisy or lack of transparency that cultures from this quadrant tend to revert to gossip instead of being so straightforward.

Humor

Another area that could lead to a vast amount of misunderstandings when gossiping cross-culturally is the use of humor.

Peter (26) works for a large international electronics company in the Netherlands. He observes that his colleagues of different nationalities do use humor differently when gossiping. "Belgians tend to be very polite and business-like, so they won't appreciate it if they hear rude or hard-core gossip. I also notice that the French really don't get our sense of humor and tend to be quite strict. We can really laugh with the Brits though. You can talk with them as if you were at the bar!" From Peter's observations, we can see how cultural differences can easily get in the way of a good gossip session. If two people don't share the same sense of humor, they most likely will refrain from sharing humorous gossip with each other. Peter's comments would apply to all cultures, as I am quite sure that Peter's French and Belgian colleagues would also be critical about their Dutch colleagues' sense of humor.

Whereas using humor can easily backfire, used in the right way, humor can be an excellent communication tool. Morreal (cited in Capps, 2012) observes that "when gossip is dominated by the spirit of humor, it tends to transcend the pettiness and viciousness that have given gossip such a bad name for so long." Capps (2012) shows that organizational humor (very often found in gossip), is also a powerful tool for understanding the culture of an organization.

According to Jemielniak et al. (2018), humor is "referred to as a relationship lubricant, and a key ingredient to the social glue that the organizational culture provides." The authors note that "many totalitarian organizations and states recognize jokes and humor as a serious threat." Indeed, humor allows employees to adopt a certain distance from their roles and take the official organizational discourse with a grain of salt. Adding humor to gossip helps employees bond and fit into the work culture even more.

Jelmielniak et al. (2018) collected gossip and funny anecdotes from a Polish organization and were able to come to conclusions as to what employees liked to gossip and joke about. The authors recommend that scholars "study the different uses of humor by people of different cultural backgrounds." So far, very little work has been done to take cultural differences into account in this area.

Needless to say, peoples' sense of humor may be quite different from one culture to the next. Several researchers (Fonseca & Hafen, cited in Dreby, 2009) note that gossip, like humor, can be described as a cultural practice. And understanding these cultural practices can help us avoid many gaffes. What may be considered to be funny in one country may come across as downright offensive in another.

Amy (19), who comes from Hong Kong, explains: "We have a saying in Cantonese: We like to see people *pok gai* [a swear word in Cantonese]—we like to see people fail hard. People will laugh and they will feel better about themselves. When we gossip about someone failing at something: 'Oh! She got fired!' we're like 'Oh!

Too bad!' but we actually feel better about ourselves. This is a very Hong Kong kind of thing. So, at work, there are so many things we can laugh about. Like the new part-time guy or the new intern that we just hired, people might say: 'He's so stupid. He doesn't know how to put price tags on something. And I just saw a manager shouting at him two days ago. I wonder when he will quit the job.' We'll say these things. It's kind of funny."

While laughing at people's miseries or having overt *Schadenfreude* (as they call it in German) may be considered funny in Hong Kong, such humor would certainly go down less well in countries like the Netherlands. Theo (27), who works as a systems administrator in a large bank in the Netherlands, says that if colleagues were to gossip about someone getting fired, the way they tell the story would make a huge difference. "If it's in a nice way, like, if a colleague would tell me, 'Yeah, I heard he is getting fired,' that is respectful. But if it's like: 'Yeah, ha ha ha, he's getting fired, ha ha,' it's not funny. It always depends on how someone says it. Some things are not laughable, like, how is that funny?"

So, there would be a good chance that Amy's sense of humor would be misinterpreted in the Netherlands, and that she would be judged poorly. Theo in Hong Kong would probably come across as quite humorless and stiff.

Also, styles of humor can differ greatly from one culture to the next. Take Jamie (55). He is British and works in financial services in a large, international bank. Even though he claims that he doesn't really adapt his gossiping style with colleagues from different cultures, he does recognize that the British have a special type of humor. "Sarcasm is a big part of the British humor," he explains. "When it comes to gossip, sarcasm is obviously going to be a big part of that. Sometimes, we'll make jokes about Welsh, Scots, and Irish people." But sarcasm is a dangerous thing. "Sometimes you are being funny and other times you are being mean," Jamie admits.

I wonder how many listeners have been offended by such gossip, the humor being lost in translation?

Borislav (20), a Bulgarian national employed at an international outsourcing company in Turkey, explains that a colleague's sense of humor, or lack thereof, strongly influences his trust. "When I see that a person takes everything in a very serious and personal way, reacts in a negative way to something I say, I won't gossip with them. Also, if they don't respond well to irony. Because, in our informal communication, most people talk in such a way, with jokes, and use irony."

Jiang et al. (2019) claim that even if humor is present in all human cultures (as is gossip), there is a huge difference as to how it is used. To start with, attitudes towards humor vary greatly, especially between Westerners and Easterners. "Easterners' attitudes towards humor are not that positive. Specifically, in China, Confucianism has devalued humor. Chinese self-actualization denigrates humor while stressing restriction and seriousness. Chinese are reluctant to admit they are humorous out of fear of jeopardizing their social status. Chinese do not think that [possessing a sense of] humor is a desirable personality trait," contrarily to Westerners, who consider a sense of humor to be a desirable personality trait. According to the study, Chinese respondents were "less likely to think of themselves as humorous."

Moreover, Jiang et al. note that different cultures make use of different types of humor, which they classify as either self-enhancing, affiliative, self-defeating, and aggressive.

Kazarian & Martin (cited in Jiang et al., 2019) explain: "Affiliative humor refers to the tendency to say funny things, to tell jokes, and to engage in spontaneous witty banter in order to amuse others, to facilitate relationships, and to reduce interpersonal tensions. This is an essentially non-hostile, tolerant use of humor." Self-enhancing humor is "the tendency to maintain a humorous outlook on life, even in the face of stress or adversity." Humor here is used as a coping strategy.

Aggressive humor on the other hand, is the tendency to use humor to criticize or to manipulate others. Sarcasm, teasing, ridiculing, or making offensive comments (like sexist or racist jokes) would fall into this category. These types of humor are often considered to be a way of "enhancing one's self at the expense of one's relationships with others."

Finally, self-defeating humor uses much self-disparaging humor in order to amuse others by saying "funny things at one's own expense, and laughing along with others when being ridiculed or disparaged." People revert to self-defeating humor "as a form of defensive denial" or "to hide one's underlying negative feelings." This style of humor is seen as a way to "ingratiate oneself or gain approval of others at one's own expense."

Using this framework to compare the use of humor by Lebanese, Canadians, and Belgians, Kazarian & Martin (cited in Jiang et al., 2019) found that individuals from cultures that emphasize harmony and group cohesion are more likely to use affiliative humor, whereas individuals from cultures that value self-sacrifice for the sake of the group are more likely to employ self-defeating humor. Furthermore, individuals from more individualist cultures that embrace competitiveness are more likely to use aggressive humor "to enhance their hierarchical status."

Kazarian & Martin (2004) stress that while Canadians may seem "to joke and laugh in a friendly manner with their friends," they also "have the tendency to engage in aggressive teasing and sarcasm." These forms of humor seemed less visible in Lebanese and Belgians. However, the Lebanese male respondents seemed to use more self-enhancing and self-defeating humor, compared to Canadian males (Belgians wound up to be more in the middle). Hence, the study shows that the Lebanese subjects who used humor to cope with stress and negative emotions tended to use humor "in a self-disparaging or ingratiating way, making fun of themselves to maintain group cohesiveness." This self-disparaging humor may be considered funny in a country like Lebanon, but in the Netherlands or the US someone using such humor may come across as weak or insecure.

This illustrates how easily one's sense of humor can be misinterpreted, especially when gossiping, which is sensitive enough without adding other cultural misunderstandings on top.

Giving nicknames

Amy (19), my student from Hong Kong, told me that she had a part-time job at a French bakery. She found it quite funny to see how her French co-workers often gave nicknames to their customers. "We'd always be talking about the 'hot guy': 'Oh, the hot guy is here!' Or the 'dry cappuccino lady.' We had specific names for specific customers."

James (30), who works in a large electronics and appliances store in Norway, also admits to giving nicknames to annoying customers. "We have this notorious old dude at our store that got the nickname '*rulator mann*' (which means 'walker man'). He is so old and does not know how technology works at all. He usually comes during the daytime and has loads of time on his hands. LOADS. Like, he never leaves. He never buys anything, but spends his time complaining that we give bad service. When he comes by, most of my colleagues just scatter. I remember one time, I thought I would be nice and go and say hello. It could not be that bad. The old man asked if a smart watch could take his pulse if it was not on his wrist. After wasting my time for two hours, he left without buying anything. I went to the canteen area and found the first colleague and ranted out my frustration about *rulator mann*."

In the film *Bridget Jones's Diary* (2001), Bridget (Renée Zellweger), a thirty-something singleton who writes about her love life, calls her boss at a publishing company, Mr. Fitzherbert, "Mr. Tits Pervert" as he has the tendency to stare at her breasts when he is talking to her. In the book by the same title, Bridget Jones also gives nicknames to her friends' evil boyfriends: Vile Richard and Pretentious Jerome.

Eleonora (49) used to work for a large transportation company in Estonia. "We had this colleague who wasn't particularly nice," she recalls. "Years after he left the company, he joined one of the worst political parties in Estonia and made quite a name for himself, not because of his achievements, but rather because he was quite vile. In fact, he was so vile, that behind his back, the entire office called him Karmic Debt."

Some people get nicer nicknames though. In another large, international organization she used to work for, Eleonora says: "I had another colleague who worked in customer support, which meant sometimes dealing with many customers in one day. It's an annoying job to have and customers can call in with all sorts of stupid questions, but this guy never lost his temper or never got annoyed. He loved interacting with people so much, we started calling him 'Canada' because he was always too nice to customers."

While giving nicknames to colleagues or customers happens fairly regularly in many countries, such as France, the UK, and some Latin countries, giving nicknames in the Netherlands is less common. Once, over coffee with a colleague, I vented my frustration about a management assistant, who rolled out all kinds of red tape, blocking me from getting my work done. "She's such a bull dog," I fumed. My colleague was shocked. "How can you say such a thing? That's really rude. She's a nice woman." I quickly learned that commenting on someone's physical appearance or giving nicknames (especially if it could refer to someone's appearance) quickly leads to a faux pas in the Netherlands.

Gender matters

As culture plays a huge role in male-female relationships, in some countries the codes surrounding gossip change drastically depending on the gender of the gossiper.

Tina (26), an Indonesian employee at a five-star hotel in Bali, explains: "A woman usually uses her emotions more than a man does, so it is much nicer to share thoughts with a woman than with a man."

Expectations of how men and women should behave varies greatly across cultures. Anita (29) is Polish and works for a Dutch construction company. When she traveled to Costa Rica for work, she judged one of her philandering colleagues quite harshly. "On the same project, there was a Columbian finance lady,

Figure 9   Mural in Lisbon
Photo by Fer van den Boomen

and she was a lot less disturbed by the story. She said that in her culture, it is typical that men cheat on women. So, for her, it was less shocking. I couldn't accept it. For me, it was disgusting. But for her, it was like a part of the deal—that's what men do." Not that the Columbian woman condoned the cheating, but she was not surprised by it. Needless to say, the way these two women gossiped about the philandering colleague differed considerably, as did their expectations of how men and women behave.

We can also learn a lot about the hidden codes as to how women are expected to behave and how they are talked about. In her thriller *The Boy at the Door* (2018), Norwegian-American author Alex Dahl describes how women in Norway are gossiped about: "Is it every woman's misfortune to feel so judged by other women? In Norway, we have so much freedom, it's almost restrictive. You can have it all; you can work, you can have children, you can be equal to your partner, but you'd better make sure you're doing all of those things—and doing them perfectly—or you're not good enough. Just don't be too completely perfect, because then we'll take you down.... You can be anything you want to be, as long as you want to be just like us." Other women are quick to look at you and say: "Not so flawless after all, apparently, ha ha ha ha."

Yordana (47), a manager at a construction company in Bulgaria, also claims that the styles in which men and women gossip differ significantly. "In Bulgaria we say there are men who are 'female gossipers' (Женска клюкарка). They tend to gossip in a rough way and can be quite offensive. Us, women, we describe things in a different way, we gossip more secretly. We try to act as if we weren't doing it on purpose. For example, a woman would say something like 'I didn't want to tell but...,' or 'I told you because....' Women will give more explanations and justify themselves to avoid coming across as impolite. Men, on the other hand, will tend 'to salt' someone pretty quickly. In Bulgarian, we say that 'we salt someone' (да насоля някого) when we start to talk about them negatively, in a pretty offensive way. When talking about a neighbor, a man would say something like: 'Pfff, what's up with that woman? She isn't cleaning, she isn't cooking, she doesn't go out. What is she even doing?? She is so clumsy, she is incapable.' Those are typical male comments."

Culture also plays a huge role in determining *where* women should or should not gossip. One study (Gilmore, 1978) shows that in a rural Spanish community women have a tendency to gossip in public spaces such as marketplaces and street corners, whereas men tend to do it in more private spaces like barbershops and taverns. Therefore, the difference also lies in the amount of visibility and the location where the gossip activities take place. Doing it in the wrong places would certainly raise eyebrows.

Diyora (30), an academic in Uzbekistan, explains that in her country, gossiping on the street is absolutely not done. "It's really frowned upon when women are standing on the street talking to neighbors. The men look at it like, 'What are you doing on the street wasting time? You should be at home taking care of the house or the kids.' Husbands really don't want their wives to be seen as gossipers. But, if a neighbor knocks on your door and you invite her in for coffee, that's okay, because it's inside the house. At least you are not in public. I think this comes from the fact that in Uzbekistan about 80% of the marriages are arranged. Many families hire a matchmaker, and these often go around the neighborhood to do some research about their client's potential partner. The neighbors the matchmakers come across can be quite nasty and are quick to badmouth others—so this information can diminish their clients' and their love interest's chances of finding a suitable match. I think that's why women who are hanging out on the street have a particularly bad reputation."

It's interesting to note here that women are the ones who are expected to gossip and, also, in a very nasty and destructive way.

Finding the *sweet spot of gossip*

Culture greatly influences the way we gossip. But what is particularly tricky is that most people are not that aware that they follow certain rules and codes that are different from those that apply to others. As Erin Meyer notes in *The Culture Map* (2014), many people are like fish, who are not conscious that they breathe differently as they are immersed in water and take it for granted. They have the impression that everybody else breathes in the same way.

We have seen that many people tend to feel uncomfortable around colleagues from other cultures and avoid contact altogether. This is a pity. Tom (48), a consultant in policy development in the Netherlands, has a better approach. "If the person is from another country or ethnicity, especially in the beginning, I tend to be cautious when I communicate with them. I ask myself if the way I communicate is appropriate. So, because of that, the conversation may be less natural or relaxed. It's like I'm testing them. But I think that there's nothing wrong for me to explore a bit."

Indeed, there is absolutely no harm in treading carefully. Trust takes a long time to build, but it is easily destroyed. So, being aware of some of the cultural differences may be a good way to avoid crucial pitfalls.

Tips for managers and employees

When communicating with colleagues or subordinates from different cultures, it is wise to collect some information about their culture first. At the website Geerthofstede.com you can find online tools to compare two countries. How individualist or collectivist are they? How do they compare in terms of power

distance? Uncertainty avoidance? Are they from cultures that score high on masculinity or femininity? Typically, collectivist cultures tend to be high-context rather than individualistic cultures, which tend to be low-context.

While these categorizations may seem like sweeping generalizations that, very often, can be challenged (and by no means should be accepted at face value), this type of comparison may be a good place to start. As you become more familiar with your colleague or manager, you will adapt your communication (and gossiping) style accordingly. But to start with, you may ask yourself a number of questions, such as where you stand as a gossiper, compared to your listener, on a variety of cross-cultural factors.

1. Are you high-context or low-context?

If you come from a low-context culture, you may find it natural to discuss things explicitly. However, keep in mind that you may be considered as rude by colleagues coming from a high-context culture, where raising an eyebrow or giving a subtle hint would be more than enough. It is also good to be aware that your high-context colleagues may wonder whether there is a deeper meaning to what you are saying. You may be gossiping about Tom's poor performance at work, but your Asian colleague may think you are giving her a message about her own performance. Consider that they will be 'reading the air' even though there is probably nothing there. By wanting to spell everything out, you may also come across as rather flat-footed and unsubtle. Try to pick up cues from body language and learn to get hints.

If you come from a high-context culture, you can safely assume that your colleague coming from a low-context culture will probably miss your subtle hints and insinuations. Best to spell things out more clearly when gossiping in order to avoid misunderstandings. Also, avoid reading too much into things as, most likely, there is no extra meaning or layer to what is being said.

It would be wise to also consider how you and your listener give and receive feedback. Whether someone is from a high- or low-context culture and whether they are used to getting direct or indirect feedback will greatly influence their expectations of gossipers and, also, how they should gossip about the absent third party.

2.   Are you and your listener individualist or collectivist?
Whether your listener comes from a collectivist or individualist culture could affect how quickly you cross the line when gossiping. If you come from an individualist culture and gossip about your colleague's poor performance, you may ask yourself what kind of ties your listener may have with this colleague. Knowing the informal ties (and eventual friendship and family ties) between colleagues is even more essential when working with people from collectivist cultures.

If you come from a collectivist culture, you may offend your individualistic listener if you overtly defend members from your in-group and attack other colleagues.

Furthermore, it is important to keep in mind that people coming from collectivist cultures will have quite a different attitude to friendship than people coming from individualist cultures. Fons Trompenaars, a Dutch interculturalist, notes that, often, people from collectivist cultures tend to be more particularist, that is, they would more likely break rules to protect a friend or family member if need be, than would someone from a universalist and individualist culture. Here, people place rules before relationships, so they would not lie or cheat to protect a friend. This is very much reflected in attitudes towards gossip.

Bogdan (21) works for an international financial organization in Bulgaria. "In general, I don't mind gossip too much," he says, "unless the person who is being gossiped about is my friend. Then, even if the gossip is true, I will still stand behind him. Only when the information is true and the person is not my friend do I accept the gossip. But if the information is not true or the person is my friend, then I really don't accept it."

3. Where do you and your listener stand on the power distance scale?

We have seen that power distance greatly influences the expectations we have of our managers and the way we gossip about them. People coming from a high-power distance culture will most likely be wary of sharing negative gossip about their managers as they may fear the repercussions of getting caught. Moreover, as they expect their managers to make firm decisions and give them clear directions, a manager failing to do this will quickly come across as inadequate and, of course, generate a lot of gossip.

People from low-power distance cultures will most likely have opposite experiences with their managers. When there is a problem they will be less hesitant to approach the manager directly. Also, if a boss is too autocratic and makes decisions without consulting anybody, gossip will probably be about how dictatorial they are.

Therefore, by adapting their styles, managers can reduce the amount of gossip depending on whether they are working with high- or low-power distance colleagues.

4.   Is your listener from a masculine or feminine culture?

If you are from a masculine culture, you may think that by showing that you are privy to a lot of privileged information because of your rank and your relationship with the manager, you will impress your listeners. If they are from a feminine culture this will be far from the truth! You will quickly become the object of gossip yourself as you will come across as a show-off.

If you come from a feminine culture and are quick to bring down a colleague who just got promoted, people from masculine cultures will likely think you are jealous and petty.

As a manager from a masculine culture, you may think that gossiping positively about a colleague will put them in the limelight and inspire others to do better. But this could backfire in a feminine culture, where people are expected to 'act normal' (as the Dutch would say). Contrarily, managers from feminine cultures may seem to downplay the achievements of their high-flying employees by not recognizing them enough, which in turn, could feel demotivating to them.

5.   How do you and your listener score on the uncertainty avoidance scale?

By being aware of one's colleagues' or subordinates' attitudes towards uncertainty, you can better understand their gossiping styles. Colleagues coming from high uncertainty avoidance cultures (like Germany, Greece, Japan, and Mexico) will quickly gossip about unclear instructions at work. Managers working with such employees would be well advised to take this into consideration and communicate with them clearly and regularly. On the other hand, employees coming from low uncertainty avoidance cultures (Canada and the US, for instance) may gossip more readily about rigid rules and instructions. By understanding the various needs of their employees, managers can reduce harmful gossip.

6.   Is your listener from an honor, dignity, or face culture?

Gossiping negatively about someone can quickly take on various meanings depending on whether you come from an honor, dignity, or face culture. For an American coming from a dignity culture, listening to gossip about Joe's incompetence would not have as bad a ring as to someone coming from an honor culture (like Pakistan), who could interpret this as a serious insult or attack on the third party. For a listener coming from a face culture, they may feel humiliated or embarrassed for Joe. So, in such cases, it is wise to tread lightly. Moreover, people from honor and face cultures should be aware that the gossiper does not necessarily have the intent to seriously insult or harm Joe.

7. Be careful as to how you try to gain a colleague's trust and friendship.

You may think that you are making a gesture in order to get closer to a colleague by revealing your bitchy thoughts about Mary. By showing her that you are confiding in her, you hope to bond with her and gain her trust. But your colleague might not see it that way. "If she talks about Mary in this way to me, how is she talking about me behind my back?" During the course of our interviews, we have heard this many times, especially from our subjects from the Netherlands. People from various cultures have very different attitudes to trust and friendship, so it is wise to keep this in mind before confiding too quickly, or in judging someone who spills the beans quickly, too harshly.

8. Know when you have crossed the line. Be careful when using humor!

Understanding cultural differences and codes will be an important first step to avoid crossing the line when you are the gossiper. Be wary when using humor when gossiping, as many cultures may easily take it the wrong way.

From my experiences gossiping in the Netherlands, when my listener starts to contradict me, I can quickly tell that I have crossed the line. On the other hand, I would advise my Dutch listeners to try to understand gossipers from different cultures before dismissing them. They may have a different sense of humor and gossiping style, and follow different codes of conduct. It does not mean they are less trustworthy.

9.   Tread carefully when trying to adapt to another culture. When I was relatively new to my job, I was gossiping with a Dutch colleague, complaining that my manager was giving me way too much work. She told me I should be direct like the Dutch are—that the manager would value honesty and openness. So, when he came to ask me whether I could teach an extra course, I flatly said, "No, I won't do that. Sorry!" I still remember the manager's face. He was shocked, and probably a lot more so than if this reply had come from a Dutch colleague. He just didn't expect me as a Canadian to be so direct. Also, think twice before adopting another culture's humor and gossiping styles.

6.   Place Matters

Another extremely important factor to consider in order to gossip well is *where* to gossip. Certain places seem to lend themselves well to spilling the tea, whereas others must be avoided at all costs. We will examine how gossip flows in traditional office settings, and with the Covid pandemic having forced everyone to work from home, how online work has affected our gossiping behavior. As many employees revert to a more hybrid way of working, flex offices seem to be gaining even more popularity than before. But this is also having a dramatic effect on office gossip.

The traditional office

In the detective novel *Liar Liar* (2020) by Mel Sherratt, Detective Sergeant Grace Allendale certainly has her preferences in terms of office space when it comes to gossip. "They were on the first floor of Bethesda Police Station, a large open office with several partitioned box offices in a row in front of her. It was much better to be in the same building again. [...] It was good to be in close proximity to everyone. Besides, sitting in the main office meant she was a part of the banter or could catch up on the gossip circuit." Indeed, a conducive office setting can really make or break the grapevine.

For some reason, certain places, like the watercooler, are magnets for gossip. But the hallway has a bad rap. I once tried sharing some dirt about a manager with a colleague in the hallway. "Watch out! The walls may have ears," the colleague cried out, pulling me into her office, slamming the door. Only once we were out of anybody's earshot, did she give me her undivided attention.

This reaction is understandable. But are the watercooler and coffee machine so much safer than the hallway?

John Berger, the author of *Contagious* (2013), has an explanation for this. Certain places contain powerful triggers and associations, and these have the ability to greatly influence our behavior. For example, the place where we vote has an influence on our voting choices. The author found that more people voted for a school-funding initiative when the polling took place at a school. Hence, voting in courthouses, churches, firehouses, or schools will create an unconscious bias for many people. I suspect the same is true for gossip. We may be triggered to talk when standing in front of a watercooler or coffee machine, as these seem to go hand in hand with gossip. The same could also be said about other places, such as the smoking area.

The smoking area

I once worked for a television station as a reporter for the evening news. I soon noticed that a group of colleagues were taking regular cigarette breaks. Once, I was discussing business with one of these colleagues. "I really need a cigarette," he said, "do you mind if we continue our meeting outside?" The meeting outside turned out to be a wealth of juicy information. Gossip flowed freely. The smokers standing there openly shared their negative experiences with the executive producer and various colleagues. Soon, like Rachel in *Friends*, I practically took up smoking just to be a part of this group and to be privy to their discussions. Even though I was not a smoker, I started taking regular cigarette breaks.

Jan (23), a worker at a large textile company in the Netherlands, admits: "I happen to be a smoker and, of course, we gossip a lot during our cigarette breaks. We smokers also tend to gossip a lot about the colleagues who don't smoke and talk a lot about what else is wrong with them."

According to the Trimbos Institute (an independent, scientific institute for mental health, alcohol, tobacco, and drugs in the Netherlands), many non-smokers have claimed to be irritated by the time wasted by their smoking colleagues. Apparently, an employee who takes a cigarette break four times a day, for 10 minutes, spends 3 hours and 20 minutes a week smoking, which comes to about 150 hours per year. As most organizations have fewer and fewer smoking areas, employees often waste time walking back and forth to their smoking spot—often with other colleagues also in need of a cigarette break. The study shows that many organizations in the Netherlands are trying to figure out how to make smokers compensate the employer for these lost hours. But are these hours really lost? Or are employees (and especially managers) threatened by the smokers' gossip? One wonders whether the urge to get rid of smoking areas has a more profound reason than health reasons and loss of productivity only.

Working from home

When the Covid-19 pandemic broke out in March 2020, it revolutionized the way we worked and, of course, the way we gossiped. Initially, as we all started working from home, there was the feeling that gossip was simply eradicated from our online universe. There was simply less to talk about (other than the coronavirus and its consequences). All the traditional gossip hot spots like the watercooler, the cafeteria, the colleagues' offices, and the after-work drinks, were suddenly gone.

As we gradually eased into our new home offices, we also gained access to a new window into our colleagues' lives. Some of us gossiped about Mary's kitschy interior decoration or how Thomas's home office can be so messy when he's such a control freak at work. (At least, this was the case before we figured out how to blur or change our backgrounds.) I was quite sure that my younger, more tech-savvy colleagues gossiped about me when my mic went dead for the umpteenth time, or when my camera zoomed in and out uncontrollably, highlighting every wrinkle and pimple along the way.

As we grappled with the technology, especially at the beginning of the lockdown, I witnessed a few noteworthy blunders.

Someone accidentally posted a bitchy comment about their manager on the Teams chat of a large meeting for all to see (thinking that he was on his personal WhatsApp chat). I have seen several co-workers pull exasperated faces and make rude gestures during a meeting, forgetting that their cameras were actually turned on.

Even professionals made mistakes. An American journalist appeared live from his home office on *Good Morning America* in his underpants. He blamed his mishap on a "badly framed camera shot." The audience was only supposed to see his shirt and suit jacket.

In an article in *The Guardian* in 2020, Australian author Alexandra Carlton noticed that once people settled into their routines and talking about the corona virus started to grow old, there was "enormous screenshotting going on." People were sending screenshots around with comments like "Can you fucking believe what he just said?" or DMs and Instagram posts with messages like "Check out this person, I think they're smoking something." The fact that the American journalist in his underpants went viral on Twitter was proof that our appetite for gossip had not diminished.

While it may have seemed like gossip had initially disappeared from our home offices, many studies showed that gossip hadn't gone away. It just migrated to screens. And for some, working online was even more conducive to gossip.

Kristel (29), an account manager for a multinational software company in Germany, recalls: "Before corona, in the office, I think there was less gossip than now. Because, at the moment, we are talking every day. On Skype, BlueJeans, Zoom, Microsoft Teams—you are just talking and talking and talking. That's the only way you communicate with your colleagues. So, the groups start talking about each other now. Like, 'Why isn't she talking to me anymore?' or 'What is wrong with her?' Our talk is certainly different now because there is more freedom about what you can say and because you do not need to whisper about people. You tend to say more because you feel more comfortable and you don't really think of yourself as gossiping if you are on the phone with someone."

Yordona (47), a manager at a construction company in Bulgaria, had no trouble adapting to online gossip, although she admits that it did change her style. "Currently, I gossip via text messages, so I have to be much more straightforward than before. Emojis also help me with this!," she laughs. "So, I personally find gossiping much easier now, and I gossip more now than I did before. When someone has the desire to gossip, he will always find a way. When people are at work they usually work [physically], they don't have that much time for gossiping. Nowadays, being at home without the control of your boss, it's easier to spend time chatting with colleagues. I'm constantly in touch with my colleagues!"

For some, like Han (55), a lecturer at a university in the Netherlands, gossip became a lot more intense once he and his colleagues started working online. "If there was already friction between people at the office, this became more evident online. The failures of management became even more visible. So, I noticed that we're turning more to our direct colleagues for support than we would normally have done. We're giving each other advice and coaching each other. I've had a lot more conversations with tears and complaints than I did before. In times of crisis like this, we feel more sensitive and vulnerable. So, when things don't go so well, it feels a lot worse than normal. At least to me. So, I would say gossip is even more important during corona times than before!"

For some, though, working in such an online environment greatly hampered their desire to gossip. The fear of getting caught and of leaving traces in writing can be a huge deterrent.

Ton (45), a consultant in the Netherlands, explains: "I knew someone who was good friends with one of his colleagues. They were happily gossiping over WhatsApp. But at a certain point, they got into a fight, and were no longer friends. The colleague made a screenshot of the conversation they had and sent it around."

Marleen (56), a pedicurist in the Netherlands, admits that she was always wary of online gossip, even before the pandemic hit. "We have a Facebook group that is open to pedicurists only. It's a members only platform and, I can tell you, there's a lot of gossip going on there! One of the favorite topics is complaining about difficult clients." Even though Marleen finds it tempting to vent on such a platform, there certainly are risks involved. "Once there was a client who was admitted to the group by accident," she recalls. "She saw that her pedicurist complained about a client and thought she recognized herself. Well, lots of clients would recognize themselves, as many of the complaints that come up are similar, but this client made a big issue out of it, and it turned into a full-blown conflict. I'm a lot more careful about venting on this type of platform. I'd much rather go out for coffee with a colleague and discuss my problems face to face."

Hubert (52), an advisor at a Dutch governmental organization, also thinks twice when gossiping online. "During our large Teams meetings, we often do communicate via WhatsApp in smaller groups. And, of course, we send each other some critical comments," he admits. "But, I must say, I am a lot more guarded on WhatsApp than I would be if I were talking to these colleagues face to face. When you put things down in writing, you never know where they end up. Maybe one of the colleagues in the group has a hidden agenda or wants to prove his point to the management team. When you say something verbally, you can always deny it. But you can't if it's in writing."

New problems emerged with the 'e-grapevine.' For one, gossip and rumors spread a lot faster. Certain companies in the US had already sued employees for spreading false information or for provoking emotional distress to colleagues.

During a discussion I had with my students (online), several observed that when it came to online gossip, people were much more likely to roast someone or be rude on social media. For one, people can be anonymous. "They don't see the face of the person they're talking about, so there is less of a guilt feeling," one said. "You would certainly be more diplomatic during a face-to-face conversation," another pointed out.

Onstage, offstage

In a reflective essay about the digital corona organization, Thijs Homan (2020), a professor of change management at the Open University in the Netherlands, notes that two forms of communication had cropped up during the time we were in lockdown. On the one hand, our digital meetings on Zoom and Teams seemed to have become more focused and effective than traditional face-to-face meetings. While we tended to start off these meetings with personal questions, such as how everyone is doing, we fairly quickly moved on to business. Participants tended to be "more careful and more diplomatic," as they couldn't really tell how others were reacting to what they were saying. However, parallel to such *onstage* meetings, another communication channel developed on the side, Homan observes. Because most of the times, during these Zoom meetings, our cameras and microphones were turned off (or our faces did not appear on the main screens), we had the leisure to do something else at the same time. So, other types of informal conversations, or *offstage* meetings, took place via WhatsApp or by phone (if your mic was on mute). In such platforms, we shared with smaller groups what we really thought. "The chair has no clue what he's talking about," or all the other things that we would never say in a formal meeting. These offstage meetings were actually the places where we could gossip and where alliances were formed. In-groups were created via WhatsApp, where others were excluded.

Homan claims that such a setup made people feel quite insecure. Even if you cannot put your finger on it, you can sometimes feel that such gossip is taking place *offstage*. 'Are people talking about me?,' you may have wondered more than once.

Besides this, a new variety of emotions came into being that were not there before the corona crisis. For instance: 'I can't log in to the meeting' shame, 'Can you hear me?' doubt (as no one is responding to what you have just said), 'Should I tell the manager that she is not understandable because her connection is poor?' anxiety, not to mention the lingering feeling of 'How come I'm struggling so much with the technology when others seem to get the hang of it so easily?' inadequacy. Maybe the most nagging insecurity employees have is 'Am I being excluded?'

Generally, the codes of conduct have changed dramatically in this new environment. Gossiping online has become a fine art as the context (or lack thereof has changed enormously).

Homan describes the layers of interactions we have with various colleagues. He calls these 'local somethings,' which are very specific things that develop between people. For example, a local something can be an experience we share with someone "that is at once very stable and that changes constantly." Knowing how to behave with each other, what we can share or not share, what codes to follow. The local somethings are embodied experiences. You pick up signals from body language and intuition about whom to trust. You distinguish between the colleagues whom you greet with a reserved 'hi' and those for whom you would stop in the hallway to ask them how they are. These local somethings, after a while, develop into moral compasses and instructions as to how to interact with various people. We can easily read into a small frown when we say the wrong thing. Or that we are boring a colleague when she takes a quick glance at her watch. This type of context is sorely missing when we are gossiping on WhatsApp. As we don't see the faces of our listeners, we don't receive instant feedback to show when we're crossing the line.

Indeed, online gossip can easily lead to wild misinterpretation.

According to the article by Dhawan & Chamorro-Premuzic, 'How to collaborate effectively if your team is remote' (2020), the biggest problem is that body language is absent from our texts, emails, and conference calls. "The tone of a text or the formality of an email is left wide open to interpretation, to the point that even our closest friends get confused."

Codes of conduct for online gossip

Even with the absence of body language, we can still easily give away more information than we intend to. "There's still a great deal of meta-communication and virtual leakage that happens in digital environments, and it only takes paying attention to read between the lines. For example, the use of exclamation marks or a negative emoji [...] is as powerful a marker of disapproval as a disgusted face," according to Dhawan & Chamorro-Premuzic (2020).

Homan also believes that we are developing new local some-things within our WhatsApp chat groups, even if these are "a lot lesser and scaled down compared to the richness of the local somethings we experience during face-to-face contacts."

However, certain signals and codes of conduct that emerged online are certainly as rich as face-to-face contacts. I once sent a WhatsApp message to a colleague, venting some frustration about a project I was working on. After a few minutes, I saw the two blue arrows next to my message indicating that she had read it. But no response. I hoped that my colleague would reply and commiserate with me, but nothing. Radio silence. Maybe she was busy when she read my message and just forgot to reply?

The speed with which someone responds to you may definitely lead to interpretation. Forgetting to reply or being left unread, also speaks volumes. Such codes are just as telling as ones coming from a facial expression!

At the beginning of the corona crisis, when everyone was getting used to the technology and online work, many blunders and faux pas seemed to be excused. After a while, employees were expected to have a better grasp of the technology and the new codes of conduct. People started to pay more attention to their backgrounds by cleaning them, blurring them, or choosing one of the templates from Microsoft, like a sunny beach resort, to cover up the mess in their home offices. The technology also evolved so more attendees could be seen on screen than the initial four. We could raise a little hand when we had something to say so we didn't speak on top of each other anymore. We became better at making eye contact.

During an online focus group I organized with a few research-ers and lecturers, we discussed how gossip changed in this new digital setting. Were there new codes of conduct in this environment?

When we split up into smaller groups on the Teams chat, one of the researchers, Tony (45), started to gossip about the online behavior of one of his co-workers, another researcher also taking part in the focus group: "Cindy is really interesting when it comes to online behavior. She seems to make good use of the fact that she's being watched as she chooses to leave her camera on. Even when she's doing other things, like grabbing a book during a meeting. It's as if she wants to say, 'Look, I'm getting bored here.' I also see her on her phone quite a bit, and suddenly she and a couple of people in the meeting start to laugh. Cindy could, after all, send messages on WhatsApp discretely under the table, outside of the camera shot. But I suspect Cindy is doing this as a performance or as a sort of provocation. Also, if someone is moving around a lot in front of their camera, everyone's eyes will be on them. Some people can play with this to get more attention."

"Maybe Cindy is still a bit clumsy with the technology and simply forgot to turn off her camera?," I suggest. But Tony thinks that since we've passed this initial phase of getting used to the technology, it must surely be provocation.

When we came back to the larger meeting with all participants present, Tony raised the question about Cindy's online behavior and confronted her in front of the group. "Some people choose to have neutral or artificial backgrounds, but Cindy chooses to keep her hands visible, within the frame. You can really see it when she grabs her phone or reads a book when someone else is talking. So, I wonder, is she simply naive or is she doing this with intent?"

Cindy seemed a little surprised by Tony's comments. "I don't work in an organization so I follow other rules. I always use my phone if I am visiting a company or if I am in a lecture. If my daughter calls me, I always answer the phone. People think that's impolite, but I think it's really okay to answer to my daughter. I do notice that people find this weird, but I do also look at a book or at an app message during a lecture. I find that this is normal behavior. I don't have much to hide, after all."

Whereas certain people would also be offended by Cindy using her phone during a live meeting, this type of behavior may be even more amplified in an online setting.

Daan (32), another participant, observed that Cindy's performance may have come across as a provocation, because in the real world people can't change their camera angle. What you see is what you get. A colleague in a physical meeting can't hide that he is on his phone. But in the virtual world, people have control over what they choose to show. "I can't change the way I see you. Only you can change that. You have control over my eye, basically," Daan explained.

Shrinking networks

As time went by, and we were well into the pandemic, we noticed that people seemed to be gossiping less and with fewer people.

During a workshop in one of my classes, several first-year ICM (International Communication Management) students discussed how the current online environment affected their gossiping behavior. Interestingly, these students never had the opportunity to meet in person, and quite a few were attending classes from their home countries. "We don't gossip much because we're not well bonded. But we're not well bonded because we can't gossip," one of them observed.

Around this time, I also gave a lecture about gossip to 90 Parisian students as a part of their university's online International Days. It was very efficient: in one click, I was in Paris. But it felt like I was suddenly parachuted in front of a crowded lecture hall with a blindfold on. No welcome ceremony, no coffee, no petits fours, no informal drinks to help me ease into it. I asked the bubbles on my computer: "Do you gossip differently now that everything is online?"

After a long silence, one icon started to flash on my screen: "Well, we gossip a lot less now, as nothing much is going on, and we have a lot less to talk about. There are no parties, very few social gatherings, and no physical lectures, so not much is happening." Life is pretty boring these days, the students agreed.

Ask people working in a variety of organizations now, and their answers will have a similar ring. Jamie (55) is British and works in financial services at a large, international bank. "Now that I work remotely, the chances of me talking to other individuals is quite rare. In the past, when I was working in banks, then yes, there was quite a bit of gossip."

Daniel (45), an IT architect at a bank in Hungary, also observes that in the past colleagues who were fairly close to each other would meet regularly for coffee or drinks after work. "Because of the virus, we transformed this into a virtual coffee taking place at our home office. Instead of gossiping daily, though, people now tend to do it weekly or monthly. In any case, gossip sure has decreased!" Daniel claims that he and his colleagues have been working from home for about 80-90% of the time since March 2020. "People did not meet physically since. In this past year, I think I've met about 8 people out of 80 in person."

For some, this feels like a positive trend. In an article called 'Will the world ever be the same after Covid-19? Two lessons from the first global crisis of a digital age,' Fenwick et al. (2021) note how remote work allows us to collaborate better and faster with colleagues. "There is no need to make appointments. We don't have to be stuck in traffic and think about what to wear. Authenticity rules." Maybe. But what happened to networking? Meeting colleagues from other departments? What happened to the really good gossip?

"The office was never that great anyway," the authors continue. "The gossip and back-biting, the nay-sayers and free riders. [...] Ironically, social distancing has brought us closer together and created a better environment for serendipity than the open spaces or bathrooms of the modern office."

I totally disagree! For one, the number of people we could speak to had greatly diminished. I may call a colleague I know well, once in a while to let out steam, but I wouldn't call the other, less direct colleagues that I used to enjoy chatting with in front of the coffee machine at work. It felt like my broader network was fading away.

King & Kovács (2021) claim in their article 'Research: We're losing touch with our networks,' that during the pandemic, our personal networks have shrunk considerably. Before the pandemic, an average person at work would interact with eleven to sixteen people a day that they didn't know very well (between watercooler chats and random meetings in the hallway).

Since we spent a lot less time talking to strangers and distant colleagues during the pandemic, we tended to focus a lot more on family, friends, and close colleagues. Often, the person closest to you is your partner. Ted (55), a lecturer at a large educational institution in the Netherlands, observes: "Now I tend to gossip with my wife because she's sitting in a room nearby. If I have a bad experience with a colleague, I'll turn to her and really let go."

Naturally, this can be an important source of comfort. However, losing touch with our distant acquaintances has serious consequences. "For companies, it can lead to less creativity and more groupthink. People with fewer connections at work are less likely to identify with the organization," King & Kovács note.

Chats in front of the coffee machine are certainly not a waste of time, as they lead to increased happiness and give employees a stronger sense of belonging to the organization.

Countless studies show how the lack of social contact during lockdown had an impact on our mental health and performance at work. And it wasn't just about the amount of social contacts, but the variety. In the article, 'The social biome: How to build nourishing friendships—and banish loneliness,' communication professor Jeffrey Hall (cited in Sarner, 2021) compares the social contacts in our lives to our food intake.

"Social interactions, like food, have 'calories' that can make you feel socially nourished," he explains. "And just as with what you eat, it is not just quantity that matters to health, but variety. Just as you need a mix of food groups on your plate, so you need a mix of modes of communication and types of relationships in your social diet."

Flex offices

When the measures eased and people slowly returned to work, many workplaces felt the need to become more flexible and adapt to a more hybrid way of working. Flex offices suddenly seemed to gain popularity. This was certainly the case at my university. Offices were being transformed to flex offices, even before the pandemic hit. One by one, various departments were being rebuilt: no more walls—just one large space with 30 or so work stations. In this way, rather than hiding in our small office rooms, we would be forced to talk to all of our colleagues and share ideas and experiences. The thinking was that this type of setting would lead to innovative projects and state-of-the-art pedagogy. But I wondered how such a flex space would influence the way we gossip. Will being in contact with more colleagues in one space lead to more interesting conversations?

Bernadette Nooij, from Facility Management at The Hague University of Applied Sciences, did research on the effects such flex spaces have on employees. "These types of offices tend to kill gossip altogether," she told me. "Paradoxically, even though we see our colleagues more often, we have less opportunity to gossip. In the past, we used to visit each other in our offices and talk freely. Now that we have this new open space, colleagues are always looking over their shoulders before sharing something." And if there are too many people around (which tends to be the case), employees just refrain from talking altogether. "Not having walls anymore," Nooij explained, "means that the work space is not safe—rather, it's a space where you need to be constantly on your guard."

Most of the employees we interviewed were also very much in favor of the traditional office.

Jean-Paul (24), a veterinary doctor in Brittany, France, reveals: "In my clinic, I tend to go from room to room. I'm always moving around and facing different people. So, of course, there's always a moment where you start talking about others. That wouldn't happen if we were in an open space."

"I used to work in a flex office," says Gert (59), who is employed at an energy company in the Netherlands. "This is one of the worst inventions ever. You can't concentrate because people are constantly talking about all sorts of things such as football and cars—but rarely about work." And rarely about anything really juicy either that makes wasting time worthwhile.

Janet (62) works for a large educational institution in the Netherlands. "We used to have a strong family culture in our department," she says. "But now that we went to a flex office space, people tend to work more from home. There's a lot of absence: the colleagues come in to do their thing, and then they're gone. So, the connection we once had [when we had small offices], dissolved over time. We have a totally different type of work culture now."

Even though there are small rooms in Janet's department that are designed for employees to conduct private meetings, they are rarely used to share gossip. "Gossip doesn't work that way. It needs to happen spontaneously. You don't book a room to gossip with a colleague!"

Van Meel (2011) claims that even though we are working in a more and more "digital, loose, informal, flexible, and mobile" environment, the conventional office space still remains the most popular. The majority of employees like flexibility and enjoy working from home occasionally. But they have a strong need to stay connected to their colleagues in order "to share gossip and exchange tacit knowledge."

As the pandemic brought on hybrid work, office setups like hot-desking or hoteling, where employees book a random desk every time they come to work, gained in popularity with many employers. Even though such concepts existed since the late 1980s, *The Globe and Mail* (Subramaniam, 2022) claims that hot-desking has become one of the most popular hybrid-work-related changes since the beginning of the pandemic. "It's a saving tool. Why have a hundred desks for a hundred employees when many of them only come in fewer than three times a week?" Yet, more and more studies show that such office spaces increase employee dissatisfaction. Rather than feeling more connected to their colleagues, they suffer from a lack of privacy and tend to want to work from home even more. And their connection with the office becomes even weaker.

Moreover, according to a *Harvard Business Review* study by Bernstein & Waber (2019), firms that switched to open offices saw their employees' face-to-face interactions fall by 70%. People sitting in such offices were quick to build an invisible wall around themselves, which eighteenth-century French philosopher Denis Diderot called the 'fourth wall.' "It prevents actors from being distracted by the audience and allows them to divorce themselves from what they cannot control (the audience) and focus only on what they can (the scene)." The authors claim that in open offices, fourth wall norms spread quickly. "If someone is working intently, people don't interrupt her. If someone starts a conversation and a colleague shoots him a look of annoyance, he won't do it again." However, fourth walls are not strong enough to invite gossip.

So why do firms insist on creating such office spaces, when evidence shows that they impede collaboration and team building? Cutting costs is the obvious answer. But what if there was a deeper reason?

Research (Clegg & Van Iterson, 2009; Ellwardt et al., 2012b) shows that managers tend to feel threatened by their employees gossiping, and most will do anything they can to get rid of it. Could that be an incentive for management to break down the walls and create an open office space (other than solely for budgetary considerations)? This question definitely warrants further research!

If I look at my own department, the traditional gossip hot spots have all come under siege over time: students were recently given access to the staff-only washroom. The teachers' room was stripped of its coffee machine and kitchen. And as we have seen, smokers are pushed further and further away and come under fire for wasting time.

Impact of culture on place

Culture also plays a huge role towards *where* gossiping is considered acceptable. Some places like the coffee machine and the watercooler have acquired a solid reputation as the 'place to be.' In Finland, it's the sauna. Evelien (40), a Dutch lecturer, was invited to give a workshop in a Finnish university: "At the beginning, I found that the participants were rather shy and quite reserved. They did warm up and open up as the workshop progressed, but I was really surprised when a few of my colleagues invited me to join them in the sauna at the end of the day. They suddenly opened up a lot and gossiped freely about all kinds of things. 'You'd be surprised about the topics that come up in the sauna,' they told me."

One of my Swedish students told me that most gossiping takes place during *fika*—which she explained was a special type of coffee break. "It's about having coffee and spending quality time with somebody else." And, of course, gossiping.

Chien (21), who works at a radio studio in Vietnam, says that at his workplace, gossip flows freely during *bàn nhậu* (drunk gatherings) where people readily "talk about someone else's success or failure."

In Delhi, it is the *tapris* (tea stalls) lining the streets outside offices, that are the gossip hot spots. In a BBC article, Bhateja (2020) writes: "Stepping out into the street with colleagues to share a milky tea with a hint of spices such as ginger or cardamom is an Indian office ritual. These stalls, carts, and shops are vital hang-outs of office-goers who come to take a break, gossip about their bosses or discuss personal lives."

Arul Kani, a social scientist based in Bengaluru, told the BBC that Indians "have a very different concept of public spaces compared to Americans or Europeans." There is a culture of chatting over food in communal areas. "Public spaces work as equalizers. Most people have unrestricted access to these. Everyday relationships are formed at these tea shops, whether it is colleagues who are sharing tea and samosas or university students debating politics." Because India is a country that scores high on power distance, and has a very hierarchical management model, employees do not feel safe gossiping in the office, Kani explains. So, many escape to a *tapri* to do this.

Culture and remote work

Looking at the attitude towards space and gossip across various cultures, we can easily guess how the pandemic and the change to remote work (and gossip) has affected people differently.

In the midst of the pandemic, an opinion piece by Hannah Jane Parkinson (2021) in *The Guardian*, 'From gossip at the tea point to watercooler chat, I miss the office,' seemed to be a cry from the heart. "I really miss the office," the author wrote. "By which I mean I miss my colleagues, and I miss the friends with whom I happen to work. [...] 'Watercooler chat' has become an anachronistic term, but the spirit endures. The thrill of working in a big organization is bumping into people constantly. A trip to the loo can yield multiple encounters with pals, be it brief waves of hello, or gossipy asides leaning on the tea point, or gales of laughter in the swapping of anecdotes. It almost makes me tearful with nostalgic longing as I write this."

Interestingly enough, while much of the research showed that employees working from home suffered from greater isolation and shrinking networks, other studies came to the opposite conclusion. The Dutch newspaper *de Volkskrant* (De Ruiter, 2021) claimed that 22% of working employees hadn't seen a colleague in person for over a year. According to a survey, 70% of employees working from home spoke to no more than one person a day. But this didn't make them particularly unhappy. Employees felt just as satisfied and connected to their organization as before the Covid crisis started. Even burn-out symptoms were lower (except in the fields of education and health care). The researchers believed that people could work undisturbed at home, and didn't have to suffer from certain colleagues' "annoying behavior." Employees seemed quite satisfied to meet certain closer colleagues online.

Cultural differences certainly explain such findings. As the Dutch score quite high on individualism, they tend to be happy to spend more time with their close, nuclear families, and have weaker ties with larger networks, more distant relatives, and their communities.

Similar studies from countries that score higher on collectivism, like India and Malta, show that people in similar work situations suffer a lot more from mental health issues because of the isolation and reduced networks.

In their article 'Covid 19 in Malta: The mental health impact,' Paulann & Reuben Grech (2020) note that Maltese people have close social contacts with each other and "tend to gossip and observe each other's actions closely." The pandemic "led many to resort to heavy use of social media," which led to mental health challenges such as "information overload" and "mental exhaustion." Physical distancing was also particularly painful, as Maltese people "normally have a strong tactile communication." The breakdown of such communication channels certainly affected their gossiping styles and, therefore, their ways of connecting with their social networks, colleagues, and organizations.

Not only did many *tapris* go bust in India, but many workers suffered from their absence, as these *tapris* provided remedies against long hours, demanding workloads, and, in many cases, toxic work cultures. Pallavi Joshi, a clinical psychologist at the Sri Balaji Action Medical Institute in New Delhi, recognized that a lack of such platforms indeed caused serious mental health issues (Indo Asian News Service, 2020).

Finding the *sweet spot of gossip*

In my article 'An intercultural analysis of gossip' (Darmon, 2019), I presented a scenario to German, Dutch, and Chinese students in which the secretary at work warns a colleague during the office party that her date, Jack, has been sleeping

around and that she is not the first. My German students were quick to point out that while the secretary might have a good reason to warn the poor woman, to choose the office party to do so was a poor decision. She should have met up with her in a quiet spot to break the news to her. Or gone out with her for coffee in a quiet spot. Gossiping in the wrong place can make people doubt your intentions. By choosing the Christmas party to warn a colleague, the secretary was perceived as bitchy, and my interviewees even wondered whether she was trying to get even with the sleazebag. If she had warned her in a different place, she would have been seen as trying to warn and protect the colleague.

So, place matters greatly. Certain types of office settings will be conducive to gossip, whereas others are best avoided. People from different cultures have different attitudes towards public and private space and will make use of them differently when gossiping. One of the most important challenges for office gossip is the shift towards remote working. Although it seemed seriously threatened for a while, we saw that it moved to screens and, with that, new rules and codes of conduct emerged.

Tips for employees

1. Be mindful of where you are gossiping.
Realize that by gossiping in the wrong place, you may come across as indiscreet or untactful. Take culture into account! If you are working with colleagues from different cultures, learn where their gossip hot spots are and be sure to join them (and avoid the other places).

2. When working from home, try to engage with more colleagues.
It's important to cultivate our more distant acquaintances and colleagues at work. So, try to find alternate ways of engaging in small talk with people. Participating in group chats on Whats-App, for example, is a good first step, according to Hall (cited in Sarner, 2021). And even if we are struggling with Zoom fatigue, it is worthwhile to show up to virtual drinks at work. In this way, we'll find out what is going on in the lives of our colleagues and we'll have more to talk about. This will create fertile ground for more meaningful relationships, which, in turn, will bring about some juicy gossip.

3. Try to stay behind after the end of an online meeting.
Thijs Homan advises people to linger around at the end of an *onstage* Teams or Zoom meeting. Don't log out immediately. You'll see who is still there, and that may be the opportunity to see who stays behind and join the *offstage* discussion.

4. Adapt your gossiping style when working remotely and online.
Gossiping online and via groups like WhatsApp can be tricky as we lack the feedback provided by non-verbal cues such as body language and facial expressions. So, tread carefully! Learn to read between the lines by seeing how quickly and enthusiastically a fellow gossiper responds. In a face-to-face conversation, you would receive feedback from your listener's expression and body language and can quickly backpedal if need be, but this option

is not there on WhatsApp. So, spill the beans gradually. Wait for your colleague to incriminate himself as well, before going any further. Keep in mind that everything you write is there to stay and could eventually be used against you.

5.   Be careful of what you show onscreen.
Since people are more in control over what they choose to show in an online setting, the rules and codes seem to have become stricter. Because you have the possibility of doing something unrelated to the meeting without being seen, but choose to do it in front of your camera anyway, you can be certain that this will lead to gossip on the part of your co-workers.

Tips for managers

1.   Provide platforms and places where your employees can talk freely.
Especially if you work in flex offices, keep in mind that your employees need a safe place to meet and talk. Make sure there is a kitchen, a coffee machine, a smoking area! These will not lead to a loss of productivity, but will be a sure way to increase team building and employee well-being. If you work online, organize after-work drinks or events on platforms like Teams or Zoom.

Conclusion: The Sweet Spot of Gossip

Regularly, I see articles appear on social media, condemning gossip in organizations and showing managers how to eradicate it from their offices and urging employees to abstain from it completely. Yes, it would be wonderful to have a workplace so transparent and open, where all employees get along perfectly, and have no trouble addressing all kinds of issues with each other. In such a case, there probably would be hardly a need to gossip. But this is utopic! Gossip has been a part of human nature for centuries and will always continue to be.

Not only is gossip unavoidable, but it actually serves an important function in the workplace if harnessed properly. Rather than trying to eliminate it, a better strategy for managers is to accept it and work with it. My *sweet spot of gossip* approach provides a good tool to help you understand the workings of gossip and to reflect on your behavior so that you can navigate office life and politics more effectively.

In order to gossip successfully, we must consider several factors before loosening our tongues. To begin with, the amount of time we spend gossiping influences how we are perceived. People who either gossip too much or too little tend to be perceived negatively. As this book shows, moderate gossipers have more close friends and better relationships at work than low and high gossipers. So, it is important to spend enough time at the watercooler, but not too much.

However, it is not just the amount that determines whether one gossips successfully. We must also take other important factors into account, such as reasons, credibility, mechanisms, whom to gossip with, culture, and place, as these play an equally crucial role in learning how to gossip well.

Reasons for gossiping

We usually gossip in order to be liked, to gather information, to maintain group norms, to learn about the corporate culture, to bond, to let out steam, to confirm our views, to make sense of confusing situations, to entertain, to compete, or to influence. Yet, while we may gossip for any of these reasons, we have seen that some are more noble than others. People who gossip to help others, protect the corporate culture, or to warn others about freeloaders, tend to be perceived positively, whereas people who gossip to influence, to compete, or to push forward a hidden agenda are usually perceived negatively.

So, not only do *you* want to gossip for the right reasons, you also want your *listener* to know that you are gossiping for the right reasons.

Credibility

Remember that one of the most important qualities to have as a professional and as a talented gossiper is credibility. Whereas

I strongly advise you to gossip at work, staying clear of rumors is certainly wise.

As we have discussed, rumors tend to be speculative and unsubstantiated talk. Gossip, on the other hand, is considered to be more accurate. Gossipers usually give a lot of firsthand testimony: what happened to them, what they saw, what they heard. No firsthand account of an event is ever a rumor, although it may later turn into one.

One of the key differences between rumors and gossip is authorship. When people spread rumors, they often hide behind phrases like "I heard that..." or "According to sources...." When no author can be held accountable, the stories tend to become a lot more exaggerated and nasty. On the other hand, if gossipers were to spread false information, they could potentially be punished by being excluded, ostracized, or, at the very least, perceived in a negative way.

Therefore, when gossiping at work, you need to convince your listener(s) that what you are saying is true and that you are accountable for what you are saying. Before sharing the juicy story you heard at the watercooler about Jane, find out who the author is. If the author is unknown, best to keep your mouth shut.

Mechanisms

Science shows that when we are just about to share a good bit of gossip, our brains receive a hit of dopamine, a substance that gives us a high and makes us feel good. Dopamine is also extremely addictive. This may explain why we love to gossip and can't help ourselves from talking. Gossiping is also a part of our evolution. In the past, if we didn't gossip about which tribes were hostile and which we could trust, we would not survive.

Understanding the mechanisms of gossip, knowing which topics are good to discuss and which aren't, knowing which circumstances can loosen our tongues (such as feeling strong emotions or feeling the need to reciprocate) can help us gain more control over our lips. Besides, when managers understand

and accept that their employees will undeniably gossip about them, they will make fewer efforts to eliminate gossip from the work floor altogether, but try to manage it (and especially nip harmful rumors in the bud), by being more open and transparent. Managers can even use gossip to test important decisions ahead of time.

The who

We have seen that certain professions have the reputation to be bigger gossips, especially professions that are dominated by women. While women tend to be more quickly seen as gossips and suffer from harsher stereotypes, many studies show that men gossip just as much as women. Many studies claim that the difference especially lies in how women are perceived. Women are quickly seen to engage in "idle talk," "tattle," and "run about," whereas men "shoot the breeze" and "talk shop."

It is important for a woman to be aware of such biases before engaging in gossip with colleagues she does not know well. Hence, women are advised to tread a lot more carefully before gossiping, especially at the start of a new relationship. Also, making colleagues aware of such biases and prejudices can be a good start to breaking them.

The prejudice can also work in the opposite direction. We may trust a woman more as we assume that she would naturally indulge in gossip. Especially if she is a hairdresser or manicurist! Learning whom to trust and understanding the types of alliances that are formed on the work floor is of paramount importance.

Culture

Many of the people we spoke to admitted that they didn't adapt their style at all when gossiping with people from different cultures. This is problematic! People from various cultures often have a different sense of humor and different ways of expressing themselves. Someone from a low-context culture, where communication is very direct and explicit, may dig for dirt in a very pressing way. This may offend someone from a high-context culture, who relies more on subtle hints and non-verbal codes when gossiping.

We have seen how various intercultural theories, such as power distance, masculinity versus femininity, uncertainty avoidance, or universalist versus particularistic cultures are applied to gossiping. This illustrates how different the hidden codes are from one culture to the next.

By being aware of these differences, you can adapt your gossiping style. Tread carefully in the beginning when gossiping with colleagues from different cultures. Pay attention to what types of topics are discussed, the vocabulary used, and how friendships are built, to name a few.

Place

The coffee machine and watercooler always seem to go hand in hand with gossip. So is the smoking area and the local bar. In India, the numerous *tapris* (tea stalls) on the streets, lining up in front of office buildings, are also hotbeds for gossip. As are saunas in Nordic countries. Nevertheless, other places, such as hallways, tend to have a bad rap as they are seen as less private (which is not very logical as the watercooler and coffee machine are often located in the hallway).

We have also seen how the design of an office or workspace can influence the amount and flow of gossip. Studies showed that flex offices (and similar setups like hot-desking and hoteling) make it difficult for employees to gossip, as no one feels safe enough to speak freely. While some managers see this as an advantage, research shows that eradicating gossip greatly affects the corporate culture and employee well-being.

When we turned to remote working during corona times, we saw how this affected office gossip in a dramatic way. Although many feared this era would mark the end of office gossip, it didn't. Gossip just migrated to screens, but by doing so it bought dramatic changes to our gossiping styles. New codes emerged as we switched to phones and computers.

***

Many of the characteristics we described for various office places (whether online, hybrid, or in a traditional office) will continue to apply long into the future.

I am confident that gossip will always find its way into different work environments and flourish regardless of the office or platforms used. Gossip will take hold of whatever platforms we choose to use and will shape them according to its needs. For instance, Tim Kildaze (2022), a journalist for Canadian paper *The Globe and Mail*, observes how gossip has already done this to LinkedIn, morphing it into "one of the wildest places on the internet" since the beginning of the pandemic. In the past, LinkedIn used to be a discreet, purely professional, networking platform, but it has now become a place where users post "stuff they used to brag or vent about in person" to smaller groups of colleagues. "Food courts used to be lovely hotbeds of gossip," the author writes. "But that's been taken away, so now people post for the world to see."

What are the consequences of such changes? How can one remain professional on such platforms and gossip effectively?

Looking at how quickly gossip research has grown over the last couple of decades, I am certain that gossip will continue to be a topic that employers and managers will have to contend with and that it will continue to be the topic of future research as it spreads to novel online platforms in hybrid workplaces.

In the meantime, I hope that you will now be well equipped to gossip successfully, forge new alliances at work, solidify existing ones, and gain the trust of colleagues from different cultural backgrounds.

About the author

Dominique Darmon has been a senior lecturer at The Hague University of Applied Sciences since 2012. She teaches journalism and media, intercultural communication, communication and behavior, and ethical communication. As a member of the Lectoraat Change Management (Change Management Research Group), she is exploring the role of gossip in organizations. Dominique has more than fifteen years of experience as a television producer for Canadian broadcasters. She also worked for SNV Netherlands Development Organisation as its international campaign manager. Her work has taken her around the world.

Photo by Solography Studios, Montreal.

Acknowledgements

I really had fun writing this book and am very grateful to have had the opportunity to embark on such a project! I could not have done it without The Hague University of Applied Sciences, and especially not without my students. So, I would like to thank them, first and foremost.

The idea to even begin researching gossip came after an animated discussion in a corporate communications class I gave several years ago. My group's enthusiasm gave me the idea to pursue the topic further. Since then, my students have constantly been involved in my research.

My International Communication Management (ICM) students listened to me lecture about gossip throughout the years, and the comments and experiences they shared were a great source of inspiration. Some even volunteered in their free time to work with me, interviewing and participating in focus groups. Thank you! I am grateful to my Journalism and Media minor students, as they have conducted many of the interviews in the book.

I would like to name each of my students—there are hundreds—but many have urged me to keep their interviewees anonymous at all costs. I did not want to risk jeopardizing their anonymity, not even by a little.

I am also indebted to my student assistants: Fernanda Gomes, Zunaica Phillips, and Danina Gospodinova.

A big thank you to Jacco van Uden, of the Change Management Research Group at The Hague University of Applied Sciences, for all of his guidance, encouragement, and support from the very beginning. I also thank my colleagues in the research group and in the BA program in International Communication Management/Communication (ICM/COM) for listening to me and giving me advice along the way.

I am also extremely grateful to my agent, editor, and translator, Laurens Molegraaf, for all of his hard work and dedication. And thanks to Inge van der Bijl and everyone at Amsterdam University Press for believing in the project and bringing it to life.

Last, but not least, I want to thank my daughter, Julie, for having made the first graphic designs of some of my diagrams, and husband, Eric, for his incredible support. His optimism was contagious, and he never ceased to believe in me, even when things were tough.

Sources

Books and articles

Alvesson, M. (2003). Methodology for close up studies: Struggling with closeness and closure. *Higher Education, 46*, 167-193.

Ayim, M. (1994). Knowledge through the grapevine: Gossip as inquiry. In R. F. Goodman & A. Ben-Ze'ev (Eds.), *Good gossip* (pp. 85-99). University Press of Kansas.

Baumeister, R., Vohs, K., & Zhang, L. (2004). Gossip as cultural learning. *Review of General Psychology, 8*(2), 111-121.

Beersma, B., & Van Kleef, G. (2008). Why people gossip: Social functions, antecedents, and consequences. Paper presented at EGOS, Amsterdam.

Beersma, B., & Van Kleef, G. (2012). Why people gossip: An empirical analysis of social motives, antecedents, and consequences. *Journal of Applied Social Psychology, 42*(11), 2640-2670.

Berger, J. (2013). *Contagious: Why things catch on.* Simon & Schuster.

Berger, J. (2014). Word of mouth and interpersonal communication: A review and direction for further research. *Journal of Consumer Psychology, 24*(4), 586-607.

Bernstein, E., & Waber, B. (2019, November-December). The truth about open offices. *Harvard Business Review.* https://hbr.org/2019/11/the-truth-about-open-offices

Bochner, A. (2012). On first-person narrative scholarship: Autoethnography as acts of meaning, *Narrative Inquiry, 22*(1), 155-164.

Bordia, P., Hobman, E., Jones, E., Gallois, C., & Callan, V. J. (2004). Uncertainty during organizational change: Types, consequences, and management strategies. *Journal of Business and Psychology, 18*(4), 507-532.

Boyes, A. (2021, January 6). Are they mad at me... or are they just blunt? *Harvard Business Review.* https://hbr.org/2021/01/are-they-mad-at-me-or-are-they-just-blunt

Braun, D., & Kramer, J. (2015). *De corporate tribe.* Vakmedianet. English edition: (2018). *The corporate tribe.* Taylor & Francis.

Bregman, P. (2018, May 17). The next time you want to complain at work, do this instead. *Harvard Business Review.* https://hbr.org/2018/05/the-next-time-you-want-to-complain-at-work-do-this-instead

Brown, T. (2014). The calm before the storm: An autoethnographic self-study of a physical education teacher educator. In A. Ovens & T. Fletcher (Eds.), *Self-study in physical education* (pp. 141-150). Springer.

Burke, L., & Morris Wise, J. (2003). The effective care, handling, and pruning of the office grapevine. *Business Horizons.* https://www.sciencedirect.com/science/article/pii/S0007681303000314

Canen, A. G., & Canen, A. (2012). Challenging envy in organizations: Multicultural approaches and possibilities. *Business Strategy Series, 13*(5), 199-207.

Capps, D. (2012). Gossip, humor, and the art of becoming and intimate of Jesus. *Journal of Religious Health, 51*, 99-117.

Chang, K., & Kuo, C. C. (2020). Can subordinates benefit from manager's gossip? *European Management Journal, 39*(4), 497-507. https://doi.org/10.1016/j.emj.2020.09.009

Clegg, S. R., & Van Iterson, A. (2009). Dishing the dirt: Gossiping in organizations. *Culture and Organization, 15*, 257-289.

Cole, J., & Scrivener, H. (2013). Short term effects of gossip behavior on self-esteem. *Current Psychology, 32*(3), 252-260.

Costas, J., & Grey, C. (2014). Bringing secrecy into the open: Towards a theorization of the social processes of organizational secrecy. *Organization Studies, 35*(10), 1423-1447.

Darmon, D. J. (2018). Researching the mechanisms of gossip in organizations: From fly on the wall to fly in the soup. *The Qualitative Report, 23*(7), 1736-1751.

Darmon, D. J. (2019). An intercultural analysis of gossip. *Intercultural Communication Studies, 28*(1), 66-85.

Daumit, R. Q. (2009). *Confessions of a hairdresser: Gossip, gossip, and more gossip.* CreateSpace Independent Publishing Platform.

De Backer, C. J. S., Larson, C., Fisher, M. L. McAndrew, F. T., & Rudnicki, K. (2016). When strangers start to gossip: Investigating the effect of gossip on cooperation in a prisoner's dilemma game. *Evolutionary Psychological Science, 2*, 268-277. https://doi.org/10.1007/s40806-016-0063-7

De Gouveia, C. M., Van Vuuren, L. J., & Crafford, A. (2005). Towards a typology of gossip in the workplace. *South African Journal of Human Resources, 3*(2), 56-68.

De Knecht, S. (2017, December 12). Integriteit bewaken bij praktijkgerichtonderzoek. *Science Guide.* https://www.scienceguide.nl/2017/12/integriteit-bewaken-praktijkgericht-onderzoek/

Dhawan, E., & Chamorro-Premuzic, Y. (2020, February 27). How to collaborate effectively if your team is remote. *Harvard Business Review.* https://hbr.org/2018/02/how-to-collaborate-effectively-if-your-team-is-remote

DiFonzo, N. (2011, October 10). Gossip part 2: The bad, the good, and the ugly. *Psychology Today.* https://www.psychologytoday.com/ca/blog/around-the-watercooler/201110/gossip-part-2-the-bad-the-good-and-the-ugly

DiFonzo, N., & Bordia, P. (2007). Rumor, gossip and urban legends. *Diogenes, 54*(1), 19-35.

Dijkstra, M., Beersma, B., & Van Leeuwen, J. (2014). Gossiping as a response to conflict with the boss: Alternative conflict management behavior? *International Journal of Conflict Management, 25*(4), 431-454.

Dreby, J. (2009). Gender and transnational gossip. *Qualitative Sociology, 32*, 33-52.

Dunbar, R. (2004). Gossip in evolutionary perspective. *Review of General Psychology, 8*(2), 100-110.

Ellis, C., Adams, T., & Bochner, A. (2011). Autoethnography: An overview. *Forum: Qualitative Social Research, 12*(1), 1-12.

Ellwardt, L., Steglich, C., & Wittek, R. (2012a). The co-evolution of gossip and friendship in workplace social networks. *Social Networks, 34*(2), 623-633.

Ellwardt, L., Wittek, R., & Wielers, R. (2012b). Talking about the boss: Effects of generalized and interpersonal trust on workplace gossip. *Group & Organization Management, 20*(10), 1-29.

Elmer, N. (1994). Gossip, reputation, and social adaptation. In R. F. Goodman & A. Ben-Ze'ev (Eds.), *Good gossip* (pp. 117-138). University Press of Kansas.

Epstein, J. (2011). *Gossip*. Mariner Books.

Evans, J., Slaughter, J., Ellis, A., & Rivin, J. (2019, March 11). Making jokes during a presentation helps men but hurts women. *Harvard Business Review.* https://hbr.org/2019/03/making-jokes-during-a-presentation-helps-men-but-hurts-women

Farley, S. (2011). Is gossip power? The inverse relationship between gossip, power, and likability. *European Journal of Social Psychology, 41,* 574-579.

Farley, S., Timme, D., & Hart, J. (2010). On coffee talk and break-room chatter: Perceptions of women who gossip in the workplace. *Journal of Social Psychology, 150*(4), 361-368.

Fedewa, N., Krause, E., & Sisson, A. (2013). Spread of a rumor. *SIORU, 16,* 94-109. http://evoqeval.siam.org/Portals/0/Publications/SIURO/Vol6/Spread_of_A_Rumor.pdf?ver=2018-04-06-151847-513

Fenwick, M., McCahery, J. A., & Vermeulen, E. P. M. (2021). Will the world ever be the same after Covid-19? Two lessons from the first global crisis of a digital age. *European Business Organization Law Review, 22,* 125-145. https://link.springer.com/article/10.1007/s40804-020-00194-9

Ferrari, F. (2014). Eavesdropping and violating privacy: Positive applications of gossip in the workplace. Paper presented at IBIMA Conference, Milan. https://ibima.org/accepted-paper/eavesdropping-violating-privacy-positive-applications-gossip-workplace/

Forber-Pratt, A. J. (2015). "You're going to do what?" Challenges of autoethnography in the academy. *Qualitative Inquiry, 21*(9), 821-835.

Foster, E. (2004). Research on gossip: Taxonomy, methods, and future directions. *Review of General Psychology, 8*(2), 78-99.

Frankel, L. (2014). *Nice Girls Still Don't Get the Corner Office: Unconscious Mistakes Women Make That Sabotage Their Careers.* Business Plus.

Giardini, F. (2012). Deterrence and transmission as mechanisms ensuring reliability of gossip. *Cognitive Processing, 13*(Suppl.2), 465-475.

Giardini, F., & Wittek, R. (2019a). Gossip, reputation, and sustainable cooperation: Sociological foundations. *The Oxford handbook of gossip and reputation* (pp. 23-46). Oxford University Press.

Giardini, F., & Wittek, R. P. M. (2019b). Silence is golden: Six reasons for inhibiting the spread of third-party gossip. *Frontiers in Psychology, 10.* DOI: 10.3389/fpsyg.2019.01120

Gilmore, D. (1978). Varieties of gossip in a Spanish rural community. *Ethnology, 17,* 89-99.

Glaser, J. (2013, February 28). Your brain is hooked on being right. *Harvard Business Review.* https://hbr.org/2013/02/break-your-addiction-to-being

Gorden, H. (2007, September 27). Office gossip: Management creates or prevents. https://ezinearticles.com/?Office-Gossip---Management-Creates-or-Prevents&id=754073

Grech, P., & Grech, R. (2020). Covid 19 in Malta: The mental health impact. *American Psychological Association, 12*(5), 534-535.

Green, A. (2014, January 16). Managing: How to stop employees from gossiping. *The Business Journals*. http://www.bizjournals.com/bizjournals/how-to/human-resources/2014/01/managing-stopping-gossip.html

Grosser, T., Lopez-Kidwell, V., & Labianca, G. (2010). A social network analysis of positive and negative gossip in organisational life. *Group and Organization Management, 35*(2), 177-212.

Hall, E. (1976). *Beyond culture*. Anchor Press.

Harari, Y. (2014). *Sapiens: A brief history of humankind*. Anchor Press.

Heath, S. (2007). Secret agonies in analytic communities: Gossip, envy, secrecy and belonging. *Journal of Jungian Theory and Practice, 9*(1), 5-10.

Hofstede, G., Hofstede, G. J., & Minkov, M. (2010). *Cultures and organizations: Software of the mind* (3rd ed.). McGraw-Hill.

Hofstede, G. J. Country comparison graphs. https://geerthofstede.com/country-comparison-graphs And Hofstede's Globe. https://geerthofstede.com/hofstedes-globe

Ivancevich, J., Konopaske, R., & Matteson, M. (2008). *Organizational behaviour and management* (8th ed.). McGraw-Hill.

Jemielniak, D., Przegalinska, A., & Stasik, A. (2018). Anecdotal evidence: Understanding organizational reality through organizational humorous tales. *Humor 2018, 31*(3), 539-561.

Jiang, T., Li, H., & Hou, Y. (2019). Cultural differences in humor perception, usage and implications. *Frontiers in Psychology, 10*(123), 1-8.

Kazarian, S. S., & Martin, R. A. (2004). Humour styles, personality, and well-being among Lebanese university students. *European Journal of Personality, 18*, 209-219.

King, M., & Kovács, B. (2021, February 12). Research: We're losing touch with our networks. *Harvard Business Review*. https://hbr.org/2021/02/research-were-losing-touch-with-our-networks

Klarrech, E. (2018, September 20). Titans of mathematics clash over epic proof of ABC conjecture. *Quanta Magazine*. https://www.quantamagazine.org/titans-of-mathematics-clash-over-epic-proof-of-abc-conjecture-20180920/

Kurland, N., & Pelled, L. (2000). Passing the word: Toward a model of gossip and power in the workplace. *The Academy of Management Review, 25*(2), 428-438.

Luna, A., & Chou, S. (2013). Drivers for workplace gossip: An application of the theory of planned behavior. *Journal of Organizational Culture, Communications and Conflict, 17*(1), 115-129.

Luyben, L., & Posthouwer, I. (2019). *Small talk survival: Praktische gids voor de gesprekken tussendoor*. Ambo|Anthos.

Manaf, M., Ghani, E., & Jais, I. (2013). Gossip has it! An in-depth investigation of Malaysian employees on gossip activities at the workplace. *Canadian Social Science, 9*(4), 34-44.

Martinescu, E., Janssen, O., & Nijstad, B. (2014). Tell me the gossip: The self-evaluative function of receiving gossip about others. *Personality and Social Psychology Bulletin, 40*(12), 1668-1680.

Martinescu, E., Janssen, O., & Nijstad, B. (2019). Gossip as a resource: How and why power relationships shape gossip behavior. *Organizational Behavior and Human Decision Processes, 153,* 89-102.

McAndrew, F. (2014). How "the gossip" became a woman and how "gossip" became her weapon of choice. In M. L. Fisher (Ed.), *The Oxford handbook of women and competition* (pp. 1-18). http://www.oxfordhandbooks.com/view/10.1093/oxfordhb/9780199376377.001.0001/oxfordhb-9780199376377-e-13

Meyer, E. (2014). *The culture map: Decoding how people think, lead, and get things done across cultures.* Public Affairs.

Michelson, G., & Mouly, S. (2000). Rumour and gossip in organisations: A conceptual study. *Management Decision, 38*(5), 339-346.

Mills, C. (2010). Experiencing gossip: The foundations for a theory of embedded organizational gossip. *Group & Organization Management, 35*(2), 213-240.

Minkov, M. (2013). *Cross-cultural analysis: The science and art of comparing the world's modern societies and their cultures.* Sage.

Murphy, K. (2019). *You're not listening: What you're missing and why it matters.* Celadon Books.

Noon, M., & Delbridge, R. (1993). News from behind my hand: Gossip in organizations. *Organization Studies, 14*(1), 23-46.

Nunez, C., Nunez Mahdi, R., & Popma, L. (2014). *Intercultural sensitivity: From denial to intercultural competence* (3rd ed.). Royal van Gorcum.

O'Connor, C., & Weatherall, J. (2019). Why we trust lies. *Scientific American, 321*(3), 54-61.

Peters, K., & Kashima, Y. (2015). Bad habit or social good? How perceptions of gossiper morality are related to gossip content. *European Journal of Social Psychology, 45*(6), 784-798.

Popova, D. (2016). Decolonization of the self: Reflection and reflexivity. In G. A. Tilley-Lubbs & S. B. Calva (Eds.). *Re-telling our stories* (pp. 173-185). Sense.

Quast, L. (2013, October 14). New Mangers: 5 ways to stop negative office gossip. *Forbes.* http://www.forbes.com/sites/lisaquast/2013/10/14/new-managers-5-ways-to-stop-negative-office-gossip/

Rabeau, M. (2008). Guess What? Someone saw them having a drink together! Workplace romance as a hot topic for organizational gossip. Paper presented at EGOS, Amsterdam.

Rayner, C., Hoel, H., & Cooper, C. (2002). *Workplace bullying: What we know, who is to blame, and what can we do?* Taylor Francis.

Riegel, D. G. (2018, October 12). Stop complaining about your colleagues behind their backs. *Harvard Business Review.* https://hbr.org/2018/10/stop-complaining-about-your-colleagues-behind-their-backs

Riggio, R. (2010, February 2). Workplace bullying: Applying psychological torture at work. *Psychology Today.* https://www.psychologytoday.com/blog/cutting-edge-leadership/201002/workplace-bullying-applying-psychological-torture-work

Robinson, B. (2016). Character, caricature, and gossip. *The Monist, 99*(2), 198-211.

Rooks, G., Tazelaar, F., & Snijders, C. (2011). Gossip and reputation in business networks. *European Sociological Review, 27*(1), 90-106.

Rosnow, R.L.,& Fine, G.A. (1976). *Rumor and Gossip: The social psychology of hearsay.* Elsevier.

Severance, L., Bui-Wrzosinska, L., Gelfand, M. J., Lyons, S. L., Nowak, A., Borkowski, W., Soomro, N., Soomro, N., Rafaeli, A., Tresiter, D. E., Lin, C.-C., & Yamaguchi, S. (2013). The psychological structure of aggression across cultures. *Journal of Organizational Behavior, 34*(6), 835-865. https://doi.org/10.1002/job.1873

Tucker, J. (1993). Everyday forms of employee resistance. *Sociological Forum, 8*, 24-45.

Turner, M., Mazur, M., Wendel, N., & Winslow, R. (2003). Relational ruin or social glue? The joint effect of relationship type and gossip valence on liking, trust, and expertise. *Communication Monographs, 70*(2), 129-141.

Usunier, J. C., & Lee, J. A. (2005). *Marketing across cultures* (4th ed.). Prentice Hall.

Vaillancourt, T., & Sharma, A. (2011). Intolerance of sexy peers: Intrasexual competition among women. *Aggressive Behavior, 37*, 569-577.

Van Iterson, A., Waddington, K., & Michelson, G. (2011). Breaking the silence: The role of gossip in organizational culture. In N. M. Ashkanazy, C. P. Wilderom, & M. F. Peterson (Eds.). *Handbook of organizational culture and climate* (2nd ed., pp. 375-392). Sage.

Van Meel, J. (2011). The origins of new ways of working. *Facilities, 29*(9/10), 357-367.

Waddington, K. (2012). *Gossip in organizations.* Routledge.

Wardle, C. (2019, September 1). Misinformation has created a new world disorder. *Scientific American.* https://www.scientificamerican.com/article/misinformation-has-created-a-new-world-disorder/

Wardle, C., & Derakhshan, H. (2017, September 27). *Information Disorder: Toward an Interdisciplinary Framework for Research and Policymaking.* Council of Europe report DGI(2017)09. https://rm.coe.int/information-disorder-toward-an-interdisciplinary-framework-for-researc/168076277

Watson, D. C. (2012). Gender differences in gossip and friendship. *Sex Roles, 67*(9-10), 494-502. doi:https://doi.org/10.1007/s11199-012-0160-4

Weick, K. E. (2001). *Making sense of the organization.* Blackwell.

Wilson, D. S., Wilczynski, C., Wells, A., & Weiser, L. (2000). Gossip and other aspects of language as group-level adaptations. In C. Heyes & L. Huber (Eds.), *The evolution of cognition* (pp. 347-365). MIT Press.

Wittek R., & Wielers R. (1998). Gossip in organizations. *Computational & Mathematical Organization Theory, 4*(2), 189-204.

Yanow, D., Ybema, S., & Van Hulst, M. (2012). Practicing organizational ethnography. In G. Symon & C. Cassel (Eds.), *The practice of qualitative organizational research: Core methods and current challenges* (pp. 331-350). Sage.

Yao, B., Scott, G., McAleer, P., O'Donnell, P., & Sereno, S. (2014). Familiarity with interest breeds gossip: Contributions of emotion, expectation, and reputation. *PLOS ONE, 9*(8), 1-6.

News

Althuisius, J. (2014, June 7). Met smaak roddelen. *de Volkskrant.* https://www.volkskrant.nl/nieuws-achtergrond/met-smaak-roddelen~bbedb36d/

Associated Press. (2020, September 6). Pope Francis says gossip is "a plague worse than Covid." *The Guardian.* https://www.theguardian.com/world/2020/sep/06/pope-francis-says-gossip-is-a-plague-worse-than-Covid

Bhateja, A. (2020, June 26). Will coronavirus end India's tapir chai culture? *BBC.* https://www.bbc.com/worklife/article/20200626-will-coronavirus-end-indias-tapri-chai-culture

Burnett, J. (2018, March 28). 3 ways to move forward when you get caught gossiping about a colleague. *The Ladders.* https://www.theladders.com/career-advice/3-ways-to-move-forward-when-you-get-caught-gossiping-about-a-colleague

Carlton, A. (2020, April 23). "There's enormous screenshotting going on": How Covid-19 changed the way we gossip. *The Guardian.* https://www.theguardian.com/lifeandstyle/2020/apr/24/theres-enormous-screenshotting-going-on-how-Covid-19-changed-the-way-we-gossip?CMP=share_btn_link

Carmichael Lester, M. (2022). Tear down the rumor mill: Building a gossip-free workplace to tame office politics. *Monster.* Retrieved from http://career-advice.monster.com/in-the-office/workplace-issues/office-politics-tear-down-rumor-mill/article.aspx

Coronavirus: US news reporter appears on air without trousers in live WFH fail. (2020, April 29). *Sky News.* https://news.sky.com/story/coronavirus-us-news-reporter-appears-on-air-without-trousers-in-live-wfh-fail-11980336

Dash, S. (2020, August 7). No coffee breaks or water cooler gossip: Work from home is hurting office friendship and the team vibe. *Business Insider India.* https://www.businessinsider.in/careers/news/work-from-home-is-hurting-office-friendship-and-the-team-vibe/articleshow/77407573.cms

Davies, W. (2020, July 2). What's wrong with WhatsApp. *The Guardian.* https://www.theguardian.com/technology/2020/jul/02/whatsapp-groups-conspiracy-theories-disinformation-democracy

De Ruiter, M. (2021, April 20). Werkenden hebben minder sociaal contact en knappen daar juist van op. *de Volkskrant.* https://www.volkskrant.nl/nieuws-achtergrond/werkenden-hebben-minder-sociaal-contact-en-knappen-daar-juist-van-op~bc374202/

Dommu, R. (2018, October 13). Natalie Portman speaks about me too and advises women to gossip well. *Out Magazine.* https://www.out.com/popnography/2018/10/13/natalie-portman-speaks-about-metoo-advises-women-gossip-well

Dutch PM Rutte narrowly survives no confidence vote. (2021, April 2). *BBC.* https://www.bbc.com/news/world-europe-56611399

Ellis-Petersen, H. (2019, May 1). Have you heard about the Philippine mayor who banned gossip? *The Guardian.* https://www.theguardian.com/world/2019/may/01/have-you-heard-about-the-philippine-mayor-who-banned-gossip

Galt, V. (2007, May 31). Expert on the consequences of gossiping about your boss. *The Globe and Mail.* https://www.theglobeandmail.com/opinion/expert-on-the-consequences-of-gossiping-about-your-boss/article1077024/

Gossip: Evolutionary necessity? New study suggests yes. (2011, October 19). *Huffington Post.* http://www.huffingtonpost.com/2011/10/19/gossip-evolutionary-necessity_n_1020050.html

Gossip in everyday life is essential for cooperation. (2021, November 4). Vrije Universiteit Amsterdam. https://vu.nl/en/news/2021/gossip-in-everyday-life-is-essential-for-cooperation

Hotse Smit, P. (2014, November 1). Hoe nieuws zich verspreidt: KLM-ontslagen. *de Volkskrant.* https://www.volkskrant.nl/economie/hoe-nieuws-zich-verspreidt-klm-ontslagen~b7a8bf56/

Indo Asian News Service. (2020, March 30).Coronavirus lockdown: Is it gossip you're missing the most while working from home? *Hindustan Times.* https://www.hindustantimes.com/sex-and-relationships/coronavirus-lockdown-is-it-gossip-you-re-missing-the-most-while-working-from-home/story-qMKhWLWHIOOY2kGRfJbrlM.html

Jenkin, T. (2014, December 15). Why your co-workers talk behind your back. LinkedIn. https://www.linkedin.com/pulse/why-your-coworkers-talk-behind-ted

Kaag onder vuur na terugnemen drankroddel over Remkes. (2021, October 5). *RTL Nieuws.* https://www.rtlnieuws.nl/nieuws/video/video/5258540/kaag-onder-vuur-na-terugnemen-drankroddel-over-remkes

Keizer, B. (2021, April 30). Ministers moeten toch ergens zeggen dat ze gek worden van die Heilige Omtzigt? *Trouw.* https://www.trouw.nl/opinie/ministers-moeten-toch-ergens-kunnen-zeggen-dat-ze-gek-worden-van-die-heilige-omtzigt~b13b3439

Kiladze, T. (2022, January 16). The pandemic turned LinkedIn into one of the wildest places on the internet, *The Globe and Mail.* https://www.theglobeandmail.com/business/commentary/article-the-pandemic-turned-linkedin-into-one-of-the-wildest-places-on-the/

Mazur, M. (2013, February 6). How to stop office gossip once and for all. *Communication Rebel.* http://www.drmichellemazur.com/2013/02/how-to-stop-gossip.html

McDonald, S. N. (2013, October 31). Ottawa professor: Women evolved to talk smack about each other. *Washington Post.* https://www.washingtonpost.com/blogs/she-the-people/wp/2013/10/31/ottowa-professor-women-evolved-to-talk-smack-about-each-other/

Nato summit: Trump calls Trudeau two-faced as palace gossip goes viral. (2019, December 4). *BBC.* https://www.bbc.com/news/world-europe-50653597

Parkinson, H. J. (2021, June 18). From gossip at the tea point to watercooler chat, I miss the office. *The Guardian.* https://www.theguardian.com/lifeandstyle/2021/jun/18/gossip-tea-point-watercooler-chat-miss-the-office

Prime minister denies lying but won't reveal who warned him about Omtzigt comment. (2021, April 1). *Dutch News.* https://www.dutchnews.nl/news/2021/04/prime-minister-denies-lying-but-wont-reveal-who-warned-him-about-omtzigt-comment/

Sarner, M. (2021, March 24). The social biome: how to build nourishing friendships—and banish loneliness. *The Guardian*. https://www.theguardian.com/lifeandstyle/2021/mar/24/the-social-biome-how-to-build-nourishing-friendships-and-banish-loneliness

Subramaniam, V. (2022, January 18). The great divide over "hot-desking" pits cost savings for companies against alienation for employees. *The Globe and Mail*. https://www.theglobeandmail.com/business/article-the-great-divide-over-over-hot-desking-while-companies-see-cost/

Van Kalken, N. (2019, January 13). Mijn collegas roken. Ik heb daarom meer werk. Wat kan ik doen? *Algemeen Dagblad*. https://www.ad.nl/ad-werkt/mijn-collega-s-roken-ik-heb-daarom-meer-werk-wat-kan-ik-doen~a353cdfa/

Talks

Dolar, M. (2019, June 10). *Gossip, Rumors and Philosophy*. YouTube. https://www.youtube.com/watch?v=NHZf4V8Bs2c

Galbreath, C. (2012, November 6). *Negative Effects of Office Gossip on the Work Environment: Career Development*. e-How. YouTube. https://www.youtube.com/watch?v=6xKTtGyA-IU

Homan, T. (2020, April 17). On- en off-stage in de digitale corona-organisatie: Een reflectief essay. https://thijs-homan.nl/wp-content/uploads/2020/04/Thijs-Homan-On-en-off-stage-in-de-digitale-corona-organisatie.pdf

Kahneman, D. (2021, July 15). *The Power of Gossip*. DENK Producties. YouTube. https://www.denkproducties.nl/video/the-power-of-gossip

Owen, T., & Dwivedi, T. (2021, October 27). *Alumni Webcast: "Facebook and Us: It's Complicated."* McGill University. YouTube. https://www.youtube.com/watch?v=zSrU6NX58l8

Wismeijer, A. (2020, November 28). *Waarom roddelen wij over BN'ers?* Universiteit van Nederland. YouTube. https://www.universiteitvannederland.nl/college/waarom-roddelen-we-over-bners

Popular culture (literature)

Atwood, M. (1985). *The Handmaid's Tale*. Penguin Random House.

Child, L. (2016). *Night School*. Bantam Press.

Clark, J. (2020). *The Last Flight*. Sourcebooks Landmark.

Dahl, A. (2018). *The Boy at the Door*. Head of Zeus.

Ferrante, E. (2012). *The Story of a New Name*. Europa Editions.

Ferrante, E. (2014). *Those Who Leave and Those Who Stay*. Europa Editions.

Fielding, H. (1996). *Bridget Jones's Diary*. Picador.

Jewell, L. (2019). *The Family Upstairs*. Arrow Books.

Kafka, F. (1925). *The Trial*. Tribeca Books.

Lagercrantz, D. (2017). *The Girl Who Takes an Eye For an Eye*. MacLehose Press.

Larsson, S. (2008). *The Girl With the Dragon Tattoo*. MacLehose Press.

Lewis, C. S. (1946). *That Hideous Strength: A Modern Fairy-Tale for Grown-Ups*. Collier Books.

Penny, L. (2019). *A Better Man*. St. Martin's.

Sandemose, A. (1933). *En flyktning krysser sitt spor* (*A fugitive crosses his tracks*). Tiden.

Shaw, W. (2016). *The Birdwatcher*. Riverrun.

Sherratt, M. (2020). *Liar Liar*. Harper Collins.

Popular culture (series and films)

"Andy gets a makeover," *The Devil Wears Prada*. (2006). YouTube. https://www.youtube.com/watch?v=HSPYgwP9R84

Brown, S. J., Fey. S., Fuller, J., Collins, L., & Benoliel. R. (Producers). (2020). *Emily in Paris* [television series]. Netflix.

Cretton, D. D. (Dir.). (2019). *Just Mercy* [film]. Endeavor Content, Working Title Films.

Donck, M. (Dir.). (2016). *La Trêve* [television series]. RTBF.

"Elaine mocked in Korean by manicurists," *Seinfeld*. (1994). (Season 6 clip). YouTube. https://www.youtube.com/watch?v=RlthyohSvGw

Gaiman, N., Kieth, S., & Dringenberg, M. (Creators). (2016-2021). *Lucifer* [television series]. Fox/Netflix.

"Gossip in 3 minutes," *The Office US*. (2011). YouTube. https://www.youtube.com/watch?v=OeEphjImzsA

Guggenheim, D. (Creator). (2016a). *Designated Survivor*, Season 2, Episode 3 [television series]. Netflix/American Broadcasting Company.

Guggenheim, D. (Creator). (2016b). *Designated Survivor*, Season 3, Episode 5 [television series]. Netflix/American Broadcasting Company.

Howitt, P. (Dir.). (2003). *Johnny English* [film]. Studio Canal, Working Title Films.

Hughes, A., & Vayntrub, M. (2020). "The secret joy of having a mutual enemy: Making fun with Akilah Hughes and Milana Vayntrub." (2020). YouTube. https://www.youtube.com/watch?v=E8NuagMoTUQ

Kay, G. (Creator). (2021). *Lupin* [television series]. Gaumont Television.

Luketic, R. (Dir.). (2001). *Legally Blonde* [film]. Metro Goldwyn Mayer.

Maguire, S. (Dir.). (2001). *Bridget Jones's Diary* [film]. Universal Pictures.

Meriwether, E. (Creator). (2011-2018). *New Girl* [television series]. Fox.

Opening Intro. *Gossip Girl*. (2008). YouTube. https://www.youtube.com/watch?v=P3Nmt3Ttcic

Peet, A., & Wyman, A. J. (Creators). (2021). *The Chair* [television series]. Netflix.

"Pillow talk," *La Casa de Papel*. (2017). (Part 5, Episode 9). ANTENA3.

"Rachel gets peer pressured into smoking," *Friends*. (1998-1999). (Season 5 clip). YouTube. https://www.youtube.com/watch?v=nzDJdZLPeGE

"Rachel works on her gossiping problem," *Friends*. (1998-1999). (Season 5 clip). YouTube. https://www.youtube.com/watch?v=XbywiblA1eQ

Shanley, J.P. (Dir.). (2008). *Doubt* [film]. Goodspeed Productions.

Tenney, S. (Creator). (2019-2022). *Virgin River* [television series]. Netflix.

"Was that wrong?" *Seinfeld*. (1991). (Season 3 clip). YouTube. https://www.youtube.com/watch?v=-RvNS7JfcMM

"Who is better: Harvey vs. Louis?" *Suits*. (2011). (Season 1 clip). YouTube. https://www.youtube.com/watch?v=VKfBR5lonnM

Index